Being Silent They Speak

The author David J.B. Smith is a keen amateur Royal Navy researcher with a specific interest in the Royal Navy during World War II. Joining the Senior Service himself as a RADAR Operator at the age of 17 years, he went on to enjoy a full and varied 23-year Royal Navy career. David eventually retired from Service life as a Chief Petty Officer (Seaman). He now lives in a quiet quayside village in sunny South West Devon, England.

This paperback book by David J.B. Smith
is also available as an eBook

Follow the author on Twitter @BeingSilentThey

Being Silent They Speak

The Story of a WWII Submarine Unbeaten

DAVID J.B. SMITH

STAND-EASY

Cover Artwork: By Oliver Marquardt,
Kriegsmarine U-boat Grid Chart covering the Bay of Biscay area

First published in Great Britain 2012
This 1st paperback edition published 2013

Published by Stand-Easy

Plymouth, Devon, England

www.unbeatenblog.weebly.com

ISBN 978-0-9573925-0-2

For my sons Rhys and Oliver

'Always remember the brave men in this book,
for it is to them you owe your freedom'

Dedicated to the late Jack Casemore,
a 'Swashbuckling Sailor'

'The dangers of the sea should always take precedence
over the violence of the enemy'

Rear-Admiral Ben Bryant CB, DSO and two bars, DSC

Contents

Author's Preface

His Majesty's Submarine *Unbeaten* was last heard from via a signal sent to Flag Officer Submarines on 1 November 1942. The signal simply stated: '*Operation Bluestone completed*'. After this date the 58-metre British U-Class submarine inexplicably disappeared. *Unbeaten* was fully operational for just over two years. During her short tenure she successfully returned to war-torn Malta many times, symbolically flying her Jolly Roger. *Being Silent They Speak* endeavours to highlight the varied triumphs, tragedies, events and sacrifices of submarine life during World War II. This meticulously researched true story follows *Unbeaten* through her build at Vickers of Barrow, her war deployment to Malta and back, and then on to the submarine's final departure from Holy Loch.

The crew of *Unbeaten* were the last to see the legendary British submarine *Upholder* before her Commanding Officer Lt. David Wanklyn VC and his indomitable crew also disappeared forever. Several submarines have had books written about them. *Unbeaten's* activities were no less daring than those of *Upholder* or any other submarine taking part in World War II. Exactly 70 years on, this compelling and revealing book encompasses all of

Unbeaten's war patrols and expands on her final clandestine tasking in November 1942. The account of this secret operation, concludes with an extreme twist of fate, which could leave the final chapter open forever and the last crew of *Unbeaten* still on patrol.

It was during a family Christmas in 2009 when I was first told about an extended relative who served on board a Royal Navy submarine during World War II. His name was Leading Telegraphist Albert E. Piper. It was subsequently discovered that Albert and the rest of his shipmates had gone missing in 1942. The Piper family, from Plymouth in Devon, had always thought that Albert's submarine was sunk just off Plymouth Sound. Albert's mother died never knowing the location of her son's final resting place or indeed the circumstances surrounding his death. Tragically, Albert also left behind his wife and an unborn baby daughter. After only minor research it was shockingly revealed that *Unbeaten* had possibly been sunk by 'friendly fire' in the Bay of Biscay on Armistice Day 1942. From this point on, my research continued at a pace and finally unearthed an enthralling story of daring bravery, intrigue and human tenacity.

The two years of research in preparation for this book have taken me all over the world via emails and through correspondence on *Unbeaten's* dedicated website. When conceptualising this book, the assistance received from family members of the late crew, and from surviving crew members who left the submarine before her final deployment, have made this story all the more compelling. Everyone who has contributed towards this book has been absolutely fantastic. Not one person or organisation has declined any requests for information. Thank you all. Individuals are mentioned in the acknowledgement pages, along with the names of distinguished fellow naval researchers who have provided their essential subject matter expertise and time.

I believe this book to be a definitive testament documenting the movements of *Unbeaten* and her intrepid crew between 1939 and

1942. I really hope that my research fills in a few blanks for the families of these brave men. I also hope that naval historians will find the subject matter beneficial for research purposes. The information was out there; it just needed someone to search for it, prove and dismiss false information, then collate all the facts in one central location. I feel very strongly that the story of these brave submariners should be told, and finally, exactly 70 years later, here it is: *Being Silent They Speak*.

David J.B. Smith
Plymouth, November 2012

Foreword

By Admiral Sir James Perowne KBE, President of the Submariners' Association.

David J.B. Smith and I served together on HMS Norfolk, an anti-submarine frigate, in the early 1990's, so it was with some surprise that I was invited to write the foreword to a book about a submarine which served in World War II. Being a submariner myself with both conventional and nuclear submarine commands under my belt, I was delighted to accept. This is a very well researched book about a submarine little knowledge of which was in the public eye. *Unbeaten* had not been commanded by one of the great war aces who won Victoria Crosses like David Wanklyn of *Upholder* or Anthony Miers of *Torbay,* neither had her Commanding Officer, Lieutenant Commander Edward Woodward, written a book of his memoirs like Alastair Mars of *Unbroken.* Even so *Unbeaten* has an exemplary war record having served in the Mediterranean Sea from April 1941 until June 1942, a time when Royal Navy submarines in that theatre were taking losses of over 60%. Despite this *Unbeaten* completed 17 patrols, sank two enemy submarines, one German and one Italian, as well as numerous surface ships supporting the Afrika Corps in Libya. All this has been painstakingly researched by the author who has done a magnificent job in putting her exploits together not only in a readable way but also capturing the highs and lows, the exhilaration and the terror of these dangerous and demanding patrols. Her Commanding Officer was rightly awarded the DSO.

Tragically, having survived in this most difficult theatre at the most dangerous time (submarine losses in the Mediterranean dropped dramatically from 1943 onwards) *Unbeaten* was sunk by an RAF Wellington maritime patrol aircraft on 11 November 1942, while on surface passage in the Bay of Biscay, with the loss of all her officers and ship's company. This is retold in a most moving way in the last two chapters as the author had an extended relative who was lost in this blue on blue engagement. He has corresponded with a number of the relatives of those who were lost and this adds a very personal touch to what would otherwise be a bland wartime statistic.

David J.B. Smith is to be congratulated on such a useful contribution to the history of Royal Navy submarines in the Second World War.

Admiral Sir James Perowne KBE,
November 2012.

Prologue

BAY OF BISCAY, 1942
46-50°N, 06-51°W

It's bloody cold up top tonight. The wind is relentless – it whistles through the jumping wire and plays it like a screeching violin. The middle watch is dragging. Occasionally a squall sweeps through, providing horizontal rain mixed with hail, but it's still a relief to be on watch high on top of the conning tower, leaning on the cowl and breathing in that sweet, fresh air. The lookout is content to be alone with his thoughts and feel the familiar, steady heartbeat of the boat's diesel engines throbbing up through the deck plates and vibrating through his frozen, boot-clad toes. Shifting from one foot to the other, and nursing a warm mug of cocoa, he looks ahead and watches the white horses of infant Atlantic rollers breaking over the bow. His eyes follow them as they gradually dissipate and slide down either side of the dark, sleek submarine casing.

It's only two days' transit to Bishop Rock Lighthouse and the rendezvous. The stokers have rung on some homeward bounders and he's thinking of being anywhere but here. He finds himself quietly transported to a time when he is seated at home in a comfy armchair, next to a warm, glowing fire. His wife passes him a bottle of pale ale and four-year-old Johnny is tuning in the radio so his father can listen to the news before supper. His son was just three when he last saw him. When he gets home life will be so good. Most of the seemingly endless submarine patrols have been melancholy events mixed with pulse-quickening excitement and peppered with short bursts of manic, wide-eyed, heart-stopping terror. Will he ever be the same person again? All he knows for sure is that he would rather be anywhere on Earth than here.

When moving silently through the ocean layers, the submariner's ears have become susceptible and acutely sensitive to hearing hydrophone effect. But tonight, on the surface, he can hear another noise, a noise different from all the others – a low, distant, constant, guttural rumble.

This is not a sound he is used to hearing, yet it is familiar to him. But what is it? Thoughts of home disappear as rapidly as they appeared. Little Johnny's face fades to grey, then black, then it is gone – blank, nothing. In an instant, he feels his face drain of all colour, the hairs on the back of his neck prick up and he feels physically sick from the pit of his stomach. The biting cold is forgotten in a shot as he realises what that noise is and what it means to his life to be caught on the surface. His worst fears are confirmed when the whole world is lit up, illuminated, like someone switching on an extremely bright light in a pitch dark bedroom.

He closes his eyes and instinctively raises a gloved hand in an attempt to reduce the glare. The tin mug is involuntarily discarded, bouncing off the boat's side before entering the water to be committed to the deep, lost forever. As the metallic mug hits the casing, it makes a dull, bell-like ting, a sound barely noticed by the remainder of the crew who are down below, going about their everyday routines – for night is day in the arduous world of a submariner in World War II. The men working under the water line, deep down inside the casing, are totally oblivious to the reality that they only have seconds of calm remaining before entering some kind of hell.

Once the dark silhouette of the bright light that was brutally etched onto his eye-balls recedes, he focuses on the cause of that light. A giant behemoth is heading straight for him, crabbing towards the exposed submarine, at what would be a terrifying speed, but which appears to him in slow motion. From the belly of this fire-breathing, winged dragon, two dustbin-sized shapes cartwheel into view, exiting from beneath. They fall with an innocent silence but display an underlying menace as they glide down towards the boat's stern.

His mouth is dry and it seems like he is frozen in time, but he knows what this is. Adrenaline kicks in and things around him are moving ultra-fast now. This should not be happening, not to him, not in this position. The boat is in a safe zone, for God's sake! The two depth charges straddle the stern, and in the seconds before detonation, which he well knows is coming and unavoidable, he instinctively considers his options. Go below, or jump? The sea temperature is very cold at this time of year; around 2.8°c, a person would last 10-15 minutes in the water before hypothermia set in. By the last fix he saw on the chart, they were approximately 111 nautical miles from land. Options, what options?

1

WHAT A WONDERFUL FEAT OF ARMS

When Germany invaded Poland on 1 September 1939, the lives of almost everyone on Earth would change irrevocably overnight, whether they knew it or not. On the morning of 3 September, Sir Neville Henderson, British Ambassador to Germany, delivered an ultimatum to the presiding German government stating that if hostilities against Poland did not cease by 11:00 of that day, then a state of war would exist between Britain and Germany. So it was that at 11:15 on the first Sunday of that summer month, Britain, Australia, New Zealand and France collectively declared war on Germany. The then British Prime Minister, Neville Chamberlain, broadcast to a pensive nation and announced that the war against Germany had begun. However, 15 minutes earlier, several British submarines, previously deployed in positions at sea, listened intently for call-sign GBR, which represented the Rugby radio transmission facility at Hillmorton. A broadcast was made as follows: 'All ships from Rugby most immediate … Total Germany … repartition … Total Germany'.[1] The time of origin was 11:00 on the nose. This was the moment when British submariners located at sea realised that not only were they the hunters but they would now become the hunted.

A War Cabinet was formed, which included Winston Churchill as First Lord of the Admiralty. This appointment was signalled to all Royal Navy vessels and installations with the message, 'Winston is back'.[2] Shortly after the declaration of war, the Royal Air Force made pre-emptive strikes on the Kriegsmarine, the autonym of the German Navy during the Nazi regime of World War II. On 4 September German warships in the Heligoland Bight were attacked in a daring daylight raid. The pocket battleship *Admiral Scheer* was hit three times but the bombs did not explode. The cruiser *Emden* was damaged by the wreckage of a shot-down Blenheim. Several of the attacking British aircraft were lost.

This era of World War II, after the invasion of Poland but before the Battle of France in May 1940, was named by the Americans as the 'Phoney War', due to there being limited military activity in Europe. Winston Churchill referred to the same period as the 'Twilight War', while the Germans referred to it as 'Sitzkrieg', which translates as 'Sitting War'. During this epoch, the United States proclaimed its neutrality. However, its near neighbour and member of the British Empire, Canada, also declared war on Germany, and with this the Battle of the Atlantic began. By the time it was over, many lives would have been lost and thousands of tons of shipping, including many submarines, would lie at the bottom of the world's second biggest ocean.

Germany had also sent all available U-boats to sea in anticipation of war breaking out. History shows that Konteradmiral Karl Dönitz had ensured that 22 German submarines were in position patrolling the Atlantic on the first day of war. In the wrong place at the wrong time was the Twin Screw Steamship *Athenia* of the Anchor-Donaldson Line, with her 1,418 passengers. She had not long sailed from Glasgow, on 2 September, and was bound for Montreal in Canada. Ironically, over 300 of the passengers were Americans trying to get home before the outbreak of war.

That evening, the *Athenia* was west of Donegal and heading across the Atlantic. Unbeknown to the grand old lady, she was to become the first victim of the Battle of the Atlantic. The German VIIA Type U-boat *U30*, commanded by Oberleutnant Fritz Julius Lemp, had earlier in the day received a broadcast from the German Admiralty ordering that submarines were to 'Commence hostilities against Britain forthwith'.[3] This order was effective immediately. *U30* was patrolling out of normal shipping lanes that night. Sometime around twilight, Oberleutnant Lemp looked through the periscope and saw a darkened vessel zigzagging at a great rate of knots only a short distance away. *U30* closed the vessel and the crew were told to make ready two tubes. At 19:40, *U30* fired two G7 torpedoes towards the vessel. The first torpedo hit amidships, leaving a gaping hole in the bulkhead between the engine room and the boiler room; this stopped the ship dead in her own wake. However, the second torpedo ran wild and missed. Fearing this torpedo would come back and hit them, *U30* went deep. Problems with torpedoes would be a recurring nightmare for German U-boats throughout the early stages of World War II. Once safe, *U30* came back up to periscope depth, where Lemp focused on the vessel, which was the liner *Athenia* - she was listing to port. One further torpedo was fired by *U30* but again went awry, missing its intended target totally.

There is much conjecture about what happened next. Some say that *U30* surfaced and carried out gun action on the *Athenia* before departing. Witnesses also say that more lives could have been saved had it not been for an accident with one of *Athenia's* lifeboats that came in contact with a propeller of the Norwegian vessel MS *Knute Nelson*, which was attempting to rescue survivors. The unfortunate lifeboat capsized. In the lifeboat were 52 female passengers and three crewmen. Sadly, only eight people from that lifeboat survived. *Athenia* managed to stay afloat until 10:00 the next morning and this provided enough time for other vessels to respond to her frantic SOS broadcast and to rescue the majority of passengers and crew. The *Athenia* sank north-west of Ireland; she slipped under the ocean stern-first, taking with her the lives of 112 people. It was later learned that U-boat commanders had previously been ordered not to attack passenger liners and Hitler personally issued an order that no further attacks should be made on passenger liners unless it was obvious that they were travelling within a convoy. *U30* slipped quietly away to the depths from where she came; and propelled her Captain into infamy.

If the *Athenia* tragedy did not bring the war home to Britain's doorstep, then the sinking of one of the nation's biggest battleships, sitting comfortably in the sprawling naval anchorage at Orkney, certainly would. The attack was designed to shock the entire British nation; it transpired that the operation was planned by Dönitz himself. Around 4 a.m. in the morning of Friday 13 October 1939, just off the Orkney Islands, a German U-boat lay quietly, deep down in the dark ocean, patiently sitting on the bottom of the North Atlantic near the windswept Scottish Isle, listening and waiting with terrible intent.

Early in the morning of 14 October, HMS *Royal Oak* was quietly riding her anchor and cable within the safe confines of a far-reaching, virtually landlocked bay called Scapa Flow. This had been the scuttling site of the German Imperial Fleet in 1919, but was now used as it was back in 1914, as a location from which the Royal Navy could sail to attack the German Fleet if they tried to break out into the North Atlantic. On that windy, rainy night, as *Royal Oak* was acting as anti-aircraft cover for Kirkwall and the onshore Netherbutton radio direction-finding station (RDF), the middle watch was passing peacefully. Inexplicably, a dull, muffled explosion was heard that caused only minor alarm among the sleeping crew. However, only a short while later, shockingly and with no inclination, the silence was shattered by a massively powerful explosion.

The 'Mighty Oak' had been felled by two swings of a German axe, torpedoed by the VIIB Type U-boat *U47*, which was under the formidable command of the experienced and soon to be celebrated and decorated U-boat Commander, 31-year-old Kapitänleutnant Günther Prien. At just after 01:00 *U47* fired one salvo of three G7e electric motor variant torpedoes; two missed and one struck the ship's bow and parted her Starboard anchor cable. The *U47* crew were nervously waiting for the certain retaliation, but none came. This gave the fervent Prien time to reload his tubes. Around 15 minutes later, *U47* fired another spread of three eels. These slammed into her starboard side around amidships and, crucially, into her aft magazine, causing a cataclysmic explosion. *Royal Oak* sank within 10 minutes, taking with her the lives of 833 sailors. By 01:30, Scapa Flow had consumed the old iron warrior and veteran of Jutland; all that remained floating were flotsam and jetsam mixed with oil-covered survivors floundering on the surface. Prien and *U47* escaped unhindered back to the safety of Wilhelmshaven for tea and medals with Dönitz and Hitler. Winston Churchill said after the attack, 'This episode, which must be regarded as a feat of arms on the part of the German U-boat commander, gave a shock to public opinion'.[4]

On 10 May 1940, Germany invaded France, Belgium, Luxembourg and the Netherlands. Both Belgium and the Netherlands quickly capitulated under the might of the overwhelming German forces. Also on this day, the First Lord of the Admiralty, Winston Churchill, at the mature age of 66, was to become British Prime Minister, after the ailing Chamberlain resigned, an appointment which would again change the course of world history.

Earlier, Italy, led by the fascist Benito Mussolini, a man the Italian people called 'the chief' or 'il duce', had signed an alliance with Germany, the so-called Pact of Steel. By the middle of 1940, Italy had sided with Germany and also declared war on Britain and France. Norway had surrendered to Germany and around the same time, France signed an armistice with the Nazis, allowing Adolf Hitler to tour Paris, and Jack Boots to stomp all over France and the Channel Islands. Following the fall of France, the remaining survivors of the British Expeditionary Force (B.E.F) and other allied forces were evacuated from Dunkirk in what was named *Operation Dynamo*. This saw 338,000 troops rescued from the beaches of northern France between 27 May and 2 June 1940. During July 1940, the Kriegsmarine U-boats systematically attacked and sank many merchant ships in the Atlantic.

The summer of 1940 heralded relentless air raids inflicted on Britain by the German Luftwaffe. The Blitzkrieg had begun and London, Southampton, Bristol, Cardiff, Plymouth, Liverpool and Manchester were among the key targets. Britain replied with air raids over Berlin. After 114 days of fighting, the RAF triumphed in air superiority by winning the Battle of Britain but as it transpired this was an arbitrary date and the relentless bombing of Britain continued. Consequently, this win was a catalyst for Germany postponing *Operation Sealion*, which was the German code name for their impending invasion of Great Britain. However, they only intended to move it to the spring of 1941. German U-boats continued to ravage the Atlantic and the Western Approaches at will, sinking vast amounts of allied shipping. Something had to be done to repel the U-boat menace. A plan to enable RAF Coastal Command squadrons to detect, track and attack U-boats from the air was being hatched by an RAF officer working alone on a project code-named 'Leigh Light'. The war continued in earnest as fascist Italy invaded Egypt and soon afterwards signed another pact with Germany and Japan. Throughout October 1940, Germany continued to sweep across its border countries like a lava flow, consuming all it reached with ferocity, and brutal tenacity.

During November 1940, several British U-Class submarines, which had been laid down in 1939, before or around the start of the war, were being commissioned into service. The impact this class of small boat would have on the outcome of World War II is now a part of history. This book will go on to document the sacrifices of one U-Class submarine and her crew in particular, highlighting in detail their contribution towards ensuring the peace and freedom we all take for granted today.

2

HIS WONDERS IN THE DEEP

Yard Number 762 was the numeric allotted to a Royal Navy U-Class submarine laid down on 22 November 1939, nearly three months after the start of World War II. The naval architects at Vickers-Armstrong Ltd of Barrow-in-Furness gave Yard Numbers to all their vessels in build; this particular submarine was named HMS/M *Unbeaten* and her signal, or pennant number was *N93* During a submarine's build, it was not uncommon for key members of a boat's crew to stand by their vessel throughout the building process; *Unbeaten* was no different. The naval vernacular when referring to a submarine is 'boat'. Some of the names of those crew members who stood by her early in the build were documented as being Lt. F.B Gibbs, the boat's 1st Lieutenant, her Navigator, Lt. C.W. Taylor, Sub-Lt. C.W. ST Clair-Lambert and Chief Engine Room Artificer (CERA) Rayner. Also among them was the first of only two Commanding Officers to serve on-board the *Unbeaten*, Lt. Edward A. Woodward who joined two days after Frank Gibbs.

Edward Arthur Woodward or 'Teddy' as he was known was Argentine by birth, being born in 1910 to his British parents in Buenos Aires. Teddy's father, also Edward Arthur Woodward was employed as a British Maritime agent working out of an office in Argentina. Owing to the nationality of his parents Teddy was able to choose to hold British nationality by addition. In 1923 Teddy left Argentina to be schooled in Great Britain. Around 1927 the young E.A. Woodward joined the Royal Navy as an Officer Cadet, receiving training at Britannia Royal Naval College (BRNC). Archives searched by the Argentine researcher José Maffeo show that Teddy returned to his birth place twice during the 1920's. He visited Argentina once in 1926 when his occupation was noted as 'student' and then again in 1927 where his occupation had now changed to 'Navy Cadet'. As a British subject Teddy had no obligations to Argentina. However, the British Community Council in Argentina listed E.A Woodward on the 1944 'List of Volunteers Registered by the Volunteers Committee' as being associated with Argentina. The in-depth research carried out by José Maffeo details around 600 Anglo-Argentine volunteers who served in the Royal Navy and Royal Marines. Many of these men were Royal Navy Volunteer Reserve (RNVR) officers and ratings. Teddy Woodward had served on-board four British submarines prior to joining *Unbeaten*. These boats comprised of two R-Class submarines followed by a stint on the T-Class boat HMS/M *Triumph*, where he was First Lieutenant under Lt. Cdr J.W. McCoy. Teddy's first command was the training submarine *H28*.

Lt Teddy Woodward was only 28 years old and married to his first wife when he joined *Unbeaten* as her first Commanding Officer on 14 September 1940. As mentioned Teddy and several other crew members had been standing-by the submarine during her build and would have been connected with *Unbeaten* slightly earlier in 1940 than their actual joining dates. Another U-Class submarine, whose build started approximately 20 days before the *Unbeaten,* and which shared No. 5 berth with her, was *N99* HMS/M *Upholder*. Like the *Unbeaten*, the *Upholder* also had crew standing by during her build, one of whom was the boat's Commanding Officer, Lt. David Wanklyn.

The *Unbeaten* was one of a number of U-Class, Group 1, single-hulled coastal submarines ordered by the Admiralty in 1939 and expertly built by the British ship-builder Vickers-Armstrong of Barrow-in-Furness. These smaller size boats measured around 190 feet in length, or approximately 58 metres in new money. The first three boats of this class were ordered in 1936 and were originally designed to replace the smaller, ageing H-Class submarines as vital anti-submarine training boats. The *Undine*, *Unity* and *Ursula* hulls were eventually laid down in February 1937 and, thanks to some inspired foresight during their build, they subsequently underwent a few modifications. This comprised the fitting of six bow torpedo tubes, four of which were internal and two external, which would enable the U-Class to carry out short offensive operations. Unfortunately, however, this weapon fit caused the bow to look large and bulbous. On the casing of *Ursula*, a small gun deck was installed forward of the conning tower to accommodate one 12-pounder gun, requiring the hull and mounting to be reinforced. The gun type was later switched on *Unbeaten* to a three-inch gun during a re-fit in 1942, a change that was subsequently carried forward and implemented throughout the rest of the U-Class builds, with the exception of *Undine* and *Unity*.

After rigorous sea trials, the early Unity-Class boats performed well and demonstrated excellent handling and manoeuvrability. These submarines proved to be cost-effective and relatively easy to produce. During World War II, the U-Class submarine went on to prove that, owing to its size, it was ideal for operations in the North Sea and the shallow waters of the Mediterranean. The fact that this class of submarine could perform well in theatres of operation surrounded by shallow waters, combined with the inevitability of war, prompted the Admiralty to put this submarine type into quantity production. Twelve submarines of this class were ordered without delay.

The design of the U-Class Group 1 submarine did not change much from the original concept, but the majority of the next 12 boats ordered through the War Emergency Programme had their number of torpedo tubes reduced to four prior to build. *Unbeaten* was one of these. The three early Unity-Class boats, *Undine*, *Unity* and *Ursula*, along with four Group 1 boats, *Unique*, *Upholder*, *Upright* and *Utmost*, all remained fitted with six 21-inch torpedo tubes, of which two were external. The reason the fitting of two external tubes was withdrawn on all the other submarines of this class going forward was said to have been to avoid the bow wave formed by the bulbous torpedo cloaking nose when the boat was running at periscope depth. This was said to have made it difficult to keep the boat trimmed correctly, and also the bow wake made it easier to spot from the air. Along with the addition of a larger calibre three-inch gun, the U-Class boats' hydroplanes were also enlarged, which greatly improved boat handling. During the 1940-41 war programmes, another 41 submarines were ordered;

however, of this second group of U-Class boats only 34 were ever completed.

The limited offensive potential of this class of submarine was compensated for by the high rate of production, with a large number of boats commissioned within a short time frame. They soon came off the production line one after another in quick succession. Forty-nine submarines of this type were eventually commissioned in the Royal Navy, all but two having been built in Barrow by Vickers. By the end of the war a total of 19 U-Class boats would be lost on active service. Action in the Mediterranean would claim 13 and the Atlantic and North Sea would add another 6 boats to that deadly count.

HMS/M *Vandal* and HMS/M *Untamed* both sank, in February and May 1943 respectively; however, the *Untamed* was salvaged two months later and returned to service with a new name, HMS/M *Vitality*. Some say the U-Class submarine was one of the most important operational classes of submarine to take part in World War II; the documented heroic record of achievements attained by U-Class crews cannot be ignored. The U-Class submarines' versatility proved very successful when hunting other submarines. This was displayed in the Mediterranean, where five U-Class boats, including the *Unbeaten*, sank a total of eight enemy submarines, comprising six Italian and two German U-boats. During 1939, Vickers claimed they managed to launch an average of one vessel every week; however, from 1940 onwards this weekly number was to increase as the war time requirement for submarines intensified. *Unbeaten* was launched on 9 July 1940 with very little of the pomp or ceremony that was afforded to Yard No. 761, the *Upholder*, which was launched the day before *Unbeaten*.

The VIP (or sponsor, as they are also known) who launched *Upholder* was Mrs Thompson, the wife of Herbert Thompson, who was a Vickers Special Director at that time. During a submarine launch, the obligatory bottle was made to swing by the sponsor by pulling a well-used silver-coloured lever mounted in a dark wood box-type lectern. The lever was connected to wires that simultaneously released the bottle, letting it swing and smash on the boat's knife-edge stem. It was also commonplace during this era for customary words to be spoken by the sponsor or sung by the gathered crowd of guests and onlookers.

These words were often taken from Psalm 107 of the Bible (King James Version), this passage holding a special meaning to sailors:

They that go down to the sea in ships;
That do business in great waters;
These see the works of the Lord, and his wonders in the deep.

The VIP speech usually ended with the obligatory '*May God bless her and all who sail in her*' and then the launch lever was pulled. A powerful trigger would be released at the same time by a dockyard worker, sending the vessel sliding effortlessly down the slipway. It was not uncommon for directors' wives or the wives of local dignitaries to be the sponsors at launch ceremonies and, at times, even other Commanding Officers' wives acted as sponsors. Historically, it has been common for women to launch vessels and, in fact, the common-law wife of Lt. Cdr. 'Teddy' Woodward of *Unbeaten*, Mrs. Barbara Woodward, was the dignitary who launched the U-Class submarine HMS/M *Vandal* at Barrow in November 1942. Ironically *Vandal* was launched from the same berth at Barrow as *Unbeaten*, berth No 5.

The *Vandal,* Yard Number 837, holds the dubious place in Royal Navy history of being the shortest serving submarine to be built at Vickers of Barrow. The *Vandal* incident highlighted the perilous conditions and constant danger that World War II submariners were exposed to, even during wartime training exercises. *Vandal* went missing in late February 1943 while on work-up trials and was thought to be lost forever. Her possible wreck site was eventually found at the bottom of the Clyde in 1995 by the Hunt Class Mine Counter Measures Vessel HMS *Hurworth*. The *Vandal's* supposed location was confirmed by divers in the year 2003, along with a theory behind her sinking. It is possible that the submarine took on water and sank when attempts were made to service the boat's Ottway log that was used to measure the submarine's speed through the water when submerged. Upon diving to the wreck of the *Vandal*, her forward escape hatch was located and found to be ominously fully open.

Being launched only a day apart, the *Upholder* and *Unbeaten* would continue to be inextricably linked during World War II, as would the *Unbeaten's* affiliation with a Royal Navy Lieutenant who was a member of the crew standing by a new T-Class submarine HMS/M *Truant* during her build at Barrow between March 1938 and May 1939. His name was Lt. Donald E. Ogilvy Watson. No photographs of the *Unbeaten*'s launch are known to exist; in fact, photographs of *Unbeaten* in general are extremely hard to find. No VIP was recorded as having been the sponsor at her launch. Written by hand in the launch book under the section titled 'Ceremony', it simply states 'None'.[5] However, it would be safe to surmise that the crew who stood by her during the very quick seven-month build would have been there. Also, the Vickers' key directors and any dockyard workers who wanted to see their charge enter the service without any problems would have congregated on the slipway to witness the spectacle. To allow the *Unbeaten* to proceed down the slipway, a pair of release gear were triggered, the force on each trigger being around six or seven tons. The starting rams, consisting of thirty-ton jacks, were not required during this launch and the *Unbeaten's* slipping was said to have 'commenced easily'.[6] The Vickers launch book details all submarine launches, Yard Numbers, and other incidental information including weather. On *Unbeaten's* launch day, Tuesday 9 July 1940, it reads that the weather was 'Dull with drizzle, along with a south-west wind and no sun';[7] notwithstanding this inclement weather, the temperature was a pleasant 69° Fahrenheit.

The vast mass of the propeller-less submarine slid down the slipway stern-first into the waiting Walney Channel, slicing into the brown water at a recorded time of 14:30, during high tide. The *Unbeaten's* Union Jack would have been bent on and hoisted up the jack staff erected on her bow. The red, white and blue flag symbolising Great Britain would have snaked proudly in the wind. The two local tugs, Ramsden and Furness, assumed push-pull positions and took the 409-ton boat in tow, cold-moving her up the Walney estuary and into a basin for completion. Here, more weight would be added as propellers and additional equipment was fitted. This would be followed by her commissioning ceremony prior to acceptance trials, and ultimately, she was destined to join the 5th Submarine Flotilla, based in Portsmouth.

Originally, *Unbeaten* was referred to by the number *P33*; each boat had its own unique signal or pennant number during the build. Upon *Unbeaten's* completion, however, the signal number *P33* was transferred to another U-Class submarine laid down on 27 July 1940 and again built by Vickers at Barrow. With the exception of the early Emergency War Programme boats, which were mostly given 'N' numbers and names, the remaining 34 War Programme U-class submarines were given 'P' pennant numbers unless named prior to launch. This would change from around late 1942/early

1943, when all boats would be named. The new *P33* was never given a real name and was only ever known as this. Regrettably, she was sunk during August 1941. After sailing from Malta on patrol, she intercepted an Italian convoy bound for Libya. A massive depth charge attack ensued around *P33's* position, lasting a crippling two hours. This ferocious onslaught was heard by another submarine; after the attack, an attempt was made to contact *P33* but regrettably no reply was detected: she was indeed lost.

Sunday 10 November 1940 was commissioning day for His Majesty's Submarine, pennant number *N93*, or to give her commissioned name, *Unbeaten*. The loving mother of Jan Wright was standing stoically on the windswept jetty like a sentry, at the end of the narrow, steep submarine brow. The excitedly happy little girl left the concerned gaze and encouraging smile of her mother, who flatly refused to venture on-board her husband's intimidating place of work, and was carefully passed down through the sloping forward hatch. Man-handled by several jolly submariners, she was passed towards the Petty Officer and Leading Hands' mess and eventually into the reassuringly strong arms of her father. The then four-year-old Jan Wright vividly remembers her feelings when venturing on-board the brand new *Unbeaten* on commissioning day. Her father was not a very tall man but fit and strong, ideally suited to working in cramped and confined spaces like a submarine engine room, where there was not enough room to swing a cat.

An early volunteer for submarine service, Leading Stoker Geoffrey H.A. Wright was an experienced submariner by the time he joined the *Unbeaten* on 1 October 1940 and was a veteran of several other submarines - the *Thames, L56, Pigmy* and *Odin* to name a few. Geoff Wright was known by the crew of *Unbeaten* as 'Chalky' Wright. Sailors are sometimes given nicknames poached from a famous person possessing the same or a similar surname. Some nicknames are more unfortunate than others, however, like the chap with the surname Ellis who was unkindly given the female nickname 'Ruth' after the infamous last women to be hanged in Britain. Still, this is not as bad as the name given to an acquaintance of the author, whose surname was D'Aeth – the inspired pseudonym donated to this poor fellow was 'Shitty', to the eternal amusement of his shipmates.

The Wright family lived for what Jan said 'felt like months'[8] in Barrow-in-Furness, as her father was a member of the crew who stood by the *Unbeaten* during the latter part of her build and sea trials. Prior to being drafted to the *Unbeaten*, Geoff Wright had been stationed in the Far East during the Sino-Japanese war. His daughter remembers him coming home on leave holding a leather trunk overflowing with gifts, chocolates and sweets that Jan was to share with all the children in the neighbourhood. Jan knew nothing of her father's whereabouts when he was at sea, and any correspondence between her mother and father was restricted to family chat for security reasons. The little girl longed for her father's periods of leave, which Jan said were 'always filled with love and laughter'[9].

Looking up at the *Unbeaten* on commissioning day, Jan remembers the submarine had what sailors call her 'washing line' rigged, meaning the boat was dressed by stringing up the International Code flags in a row. This included bending on and hoisting the Jack and Ensign fore and aft respectively, in celebration of being commissioned. This is known overall as 'dress ship' and conjures up a real sense of ceremony that is usually reserved for special occasions like a monarch's birthday or jubilee celebrations. Down below, families would have been shown around; Jan remembers being carried all the way round the boat by her father and being told not to reach out and touch anything. The lights were dull and everything seemed dark as they ducked and dived around the confines of the submarine; 'it felt like a tight fit'[10]. They dwelled at the Petty Officer and Leading Hands' mess; her father told her this was where the submariners ate, relaxed, played cards and dominoes and, of course, where they competed in every sailor's favourite board game: the addictively competitive 'Uckers'. This game is a cross between Draughts and Ludo and is still played feverously today by submariners and skimmers of the Royal Navy. The *Unbeaten* was no longer just Yard Number 762; she was now commissioned in the Royal Navy and would soon be undertaking trials. After the completion of her build, the fully manned and fuelled *Unbeaten* now had around a 630-ton displacement when she was moved out into her dockyard basin for the acceptance trials.

These trials inherently took place with some key Vickers staff and Admiralty officials present to monitor and ensure that everything worked as it should. The acceptance trial routine for the majority of U-Class submarines built at Barrow was almost always carried out in the same manner. The procedure adopted for a submarine's first diving trial at Barrow was to carry out a dive prior to leaving the relative safe confines of the basin. The boat and crew were moved out into the basin, and when ordered, the main vents from one to six (with the exception of vent number four) were opened, the air in the ballast tanks being replaced by water. Main vent number four was then opened, allowing the boat to sink to about 10 feet below the water line. Number four vent was then shut and the submarine remained at a fixed equilibrium, floating under the water. The crew would then check the entire vessel for leaks. After successful checks were reported, an inclining test was undertaken to check the submarine's stability at depth. This required the moving of ballast in the form of pig iron around the boat from compartment to compartment. Once complete, the submarine would return to the surface. This initial dive trial took around two hours and was vitally important for obvious reasons. Soon afterwards, the *Unbeaten* left Barrow and transited north, arriving in the Clyde area on 19 November 1940. She was escorted to Greenock by a requisitioned yacht known as the anti-submarine vessel HMS *Troubadour*. The next time the *Unbeaten* would go to 'Diving Stations' would be in the depths of Gare Loch.

Most U-Class boats utilised the very deep, seven-mile by one-mile stretch of water named Gare Loch for the all-important diving trials. Gare is a sea Loch that flows south and opens onto the Firth of Clyde. Some areas of the Loch can reach depths of up to 30 fathoms or 180 feet, which is approximately 55 metres deep. The Vickers-monitored sequence of events was to trim the submarine down to the conning tower depth, and then further down to periscope depth, which meant the body of the submarine would be about 12 feet, or around 3.6 metres, below the waterline. If everything was satisfactory, the crew would then continue down to 70 feet, or 21.3 metres, deep. Once at this depth, an emergency test would take place, which involved blowing air into the ballast tanks and allowing the submarine to reach for the surface at a great rate of knots, often violently breaking the mill pond surface of Gare Loch. Back alongside Barrow after what would have been routine acceptance trials for Vickers staff, the submarine would be signed over to the Commanding Officer who would accept the boat on behalf of the Royal Navy. The trials for submarine and her crew were, however, not over.

Once the Vickers staff were landed shoreside, the submarine would continue to carry out exhaustive work-up trials, not only monitoring the submarine's equipment and capabilities but also testing to the extreme the capabilities and limitations of her crew. It is safe to say that several of the crew would have known each other from previous boats on which they served together and they were for the most part experienced submariners, but for several younger crew members this was their first submarine since training and it must have been a very daunting prospect indeed.

Whilst conducting trials, several defects that were common problems among the early Group 1 U-Class submarines, were noticed. Captain (S3), H.M.C Ionides who was situated on-board *Titania* proposed that as the defects were not really urgent, the *Unbeaten* 'should remain on her working-up programme'[11]. On completion, it was then desired to use the *Unbeaten* in the Clyde area for training. She was to berth in Holy Loch and 'remain in this area until the training was completed or until HMS *Urge* had been worked up sufficiently to take over this training duty'[12]. Once relieved of her duties, *Unbeaten* was to return to Barrow, where her faults, which consisted of defective Kingston valves and singing propellers, would be made good. As fate would have it, *Unbeaten* would have to return to Barrow for another reason, for which only the weather was to blame.

3

THE TRADE

The crew of a submarine has to work together like a well-oiled machine, from the Commanding Officer down. Each man has his own areas of responsibility but inherently, with experience and personal pride, or maybe due to a feeling of self-preservation, a more accomplished submariner would know a bit about everyone else's jobs. To be a safe submariner you need to know your submarine safety inside out and then your trade. This is where work-up trials come to the fore and are very important. During the trials, the effectiveness of the boat, structurally and operationally, is tested along with the tenacity of the crew who will be doing things quicker with each practice. Time spent going over and over laid down procedures could, and often will, save lives. Trials and training are a big part of the Royal Navy ethos and were as much a part of naval life in 1940 as they are today.

The *Unbeaten* would remain in the Holy Loch area, utilising Gare Loch for more deep water trials, while Long Loch, located to the east, was often used for torpedo trials. When not conducting work-up exercises, *Unbeaten* would be secured alongside HMS *Titania*, a submarine depot ship. A depot ship is a floating workshop, rest area, and supply vessel. You could buy cigarettes, get a haircut, have a bath, dhobi (wash) your laundry and transfer fuel, ammunition and torpedoes from her to your submarine. *Titania* was an old girl, commissioned in 1915 and soon to be superseded by HMS *Forth. Titania* was destined to become the depot vessel providing advanced training quarters for the crews of the legendary two man human torpedo, known as the Chariot. However, the training would eventually culminate in a failed attack on the Bismarck-Class Battleship *Tirpitz,* owing to poor weather conditions. A future crew member of the *Unbeaten* would go on to play an integral part in the celebrated X-Craft attack on the *Tirpitz* and add another Victoria Cross to the increasing tally that would be awarded to British submariners during World War II. During this Christmas month in 1940, an event involving *Unbeaten* made the weekly résumé of a War Cabinet meeting. On the evening of 5 December, the majority of *Unbeaten's* crew were ashore and only a small duty watch remained on-board. An experienced submariner, Petty Officer Telegraphist Norman Drury, who had joined the *Unbeaten* during build, remembers that night well.

If you were standing on the shore looking at the *Titania*, the *Unbeaten* was alongside the depot ship's inboard side, which was closest to the shore. Submarines would raft up on the ageing depot ship's port and starboard sides, sometimes berthed three deep, with *Titania* reminiscent of a mother hen. Later that night, without warning, a severe gale blew up. Ardnadam Pier was out of bounds due to the very bad weather and there were no boats moving on the Loch; many of the threatened submarine's crew were stranded ashore, feeling frustrated that they could not help. Overnight, as a precaution, the *Unbeaten's* skeleton crew had rigged spring hawsers and additional berthing lines in an attempt to check the submarine's forward and aft movement. During the early hours of 6 December, under massive strain, these lines parted. The powerless *Unbeaten* was now adrift in a wild and windy Holy Loch. The crew who remained on the out-of-control submarine rushed up top and let go the submarine anchor. This had only a minimal effect and the boat continued to drag her anchor down the unforgiving loch.

The stricken *Unbeaten* had no steerageway so the crew made valiant efforts to start the main motors. As these attempts went on, the wayward submarine bounced off the cable of a captured German merchant vessel anchored in Holy Loch. At last the motors were started; the *Unbeaten* now had steerageway and the crew tried to navigate her ahead of another vessel that they thought was anchored. But suddenly she shuddered and the boat stopped moving – the *Unbeaten* had run aground. Unfortunately, the other vessel they thought was at anchor had also run aground in the same spot, just off the point which shelters Ardnadam Bay. About three tidal changes later, after the gale died down, the *Unbeaten* was worked free and proceeded back alongside her mother ship *Titania*.

During the author's research, several documents surfaced that were rescued from a skip some years ago. The worn pages reveal previously unknown information referring to *Unbeaten* and contain summaries of many other World War II British submarine movements. The log expands on many already authenticated events concerning the *Unbeaten* between 1940 and 1942. The National Museum of the Royal Navy now houses these documents, which they call the Port Logs. The origin of the hand-written manuscripts is unknown, but they provide valuable research material. The log says that after her grounding in the Loch, divers were sent down to inspect the boat's hull and to fully assess any damage which may have occurred during her collision with the interned German vessel and her subsequent grounding. The divers reported that there was no damage whatsoever; however, as a precaution, and to fix the outstanding defective Kingstons and non-singing propellers, *Unbeaten* was sent back to Barrow-in-Furness.

The submarine remained on the surface and was escorted to Barrow by HMS *Philante*. She docked down on 17 December. The 80-metre and 1,628-ton *Philante* was built at Gosport in 1937 especially for the English aviation pioneer and yachtsman Sir Thomas Sopwith of World War I 'Sopwith Camel' fame. *Philante* was requisitioned by the Admiralty in 1939 and had a gun welded on her forecastle. She was regularly used for Atlantic duty as a convoy escort vessel. During the final death throes of the Kriegsmarine and in particular the demise of Grossadmiral Dönitz U-boats in early May 1945, *Philante* was tasked to join the 21st Escort Group. *Philante* was seconded in-place of the frigate *K554*, HMS *Redmill*, which on 27 April 1945 was torpedoed, but not sunk. The escort group including *Philante* was positioned off Loch Erinboll to guide the surrendering, black flag flying, German U-boats into the Scottish Loch. Eventually a total of thirty-three U-boats surrendered at Loch Erinboll. Their number ironically included the Type VIIC U-boat *U1105* which had, only days before the end of the war, blown the stern off *Redmill* killing 32 of the frigates crew. After the war, *Philante* was purchased by Norway and used as the Norwegian Royal Yacht for many years, and she still survives today.

Thankfully, upon inspection of *Unbeaten's* riveted hull, it became apparent that her water-tight integrity was not breached and deemed intact. There was, however, a large dent in her 0.5" or 1.3cm thick steel hull, adjacent to the engine room. This damage was inflicted when *Unbeaten* collided with the merchantman. A large steel plate was welded in place as defect rectification. Thirteen days later, *Unbeaten* sailed from Barrow and proceeded to carry out more work-up trials at the request of her Commanding Officer Teddy Woodward. He was said to have been concerned that a number of the crew were very junior and lacked the experience of the senior members. It was decided by Captain (S3), at Woodward's request, to task *Unbeaten* on a period of ASDIC running. Some say ASDIC is an acronym for (Anti-Submarine Detection Investigation Committee) others say it is short for (Anti-Submarine Division-*ics*). *Unbeaten* was again escorted by the *Philante*, but this time she was bound for Dartmouth. By 1940, the ASDIC had already been developing its underwater listening equipment for nearly 20 years since its conception in 1920. During World War I, submarines had used a piece of equipment called a hydrophone to listen underwater. *Unbeaten* was fitted with hydrophones port and starboard forward, and one on the conning tower facing aft.

The advances of ASDIC were to provide the Royal Navy with a more sensitive and directional system for hunting surface craft. Subsequently, to the detriment of submarines, they also provided ships with an underwater searchlight capability that allowed surface vessels to detect and hunt submarines. During the inter-war years, the O-Class submarine *Oberon* was the first boat to be fitted with this new active acoustic listening system. This advance in technology allowed Allied submarines the capability of measuring an enemy vessel's course and speed, along with its distance away from the eavesdropping submarine. This valuable bit of equipment also gave submarines the means of talking to each other underwater while not being heard by surface ships (unless they were also ASDIC-fitted). This underwater listening device needed to be kept a secret for obvious reasons and it would remain so for the early part of World War II. The Type 129 ASDIC dome was fitted on the U-Class submarine towards the bow on the keel, just below and in front of the fuel and fresh water tanks. It is safe to say that ASDIC played a major role in submarine and anti-submarine warfare during the war. An experienced and well-trained operator of the hydrophones and ASDIC listening devices could often confidently identify an enemy vessel by its propeller revolutions, shaft rate and blade count. In order to facilitate the submarine ASDIC operators and allow them to practice this art and also provide the command with detection and evasion training, it was normal and essential for submarines to carry out ASDIC running. This was combined with acting as a target submarine for ASDIC-fitted ships that were also under training.

The *Unbeaten* slipped silently into the Dart estuary after two nights spent at sea since sailing from Barrow, one of them being New Year's Eve 1941. For several weeks, the *Unbeaten* ran between Dartmouth and Portsmouth undertaking valuable ASDIC training. Wednesday 1 January saw the start of another year at war and the commencement of her ASDIC running. *Unbeaten* returned to her new base port of Portsmouth on the following Saturday where weekend leave was granted to all those not on duty. On the Monday, the boat sailed again from Pompey bound for Dartmouth. The home of the Royal Navy was regularly enduring relentless heavy bombing by Goering's Luftwaffe; *Unbeaten* would then spend the week days training, tying up within the confines of the quiet and picturesque River Dart during the week nights, and returning to Portsmouth at weekends. This routine carried on until 19 March when, on completion of this successful training period, the crew were given some well-earned shore leave in Dartmouth.

Attached by head and stern buoys lined out in a trot running up the centre of the River Dart, one of 50 ex-United States Navy, four-funnel Flush-deck destroyers from World War I, was moored. This vessel and the 49 others like her that would be dotted around Great Britain and at sea were negotiated for by Winston Churchill to help in the war effort. They were given to the Royal Navy by America in exchange for a 99-year lease on British bases in Newfoundland, Bermuda, West Indies and British Guiana. By offering these ships to Britain at this point during World War Two, President Roosevelt did not want to be seen by the outside world as violating United States neutrality. However, what is not widely known is that privately Roosevelt thought, when faced by the might of Germany and their Axis allies, a small country like Britain was sure to capitulate. It was feared by America that if Germany occupied Great Britain and her colonies, this would allow German forces to be based in the Caribbean and bring the USA to within Hitler's reach. On the night of 21 March, *Unbeaten* was secured alongside this ageing, run-down destroyer. Many of the submarine crew were ashore, probably frequenting one of the many fine public houses that Dartmouth has to offer. Later that evening, the recall signal '*Papa*' • ▬ ▬ • was repeatedly passed towards Dartmouth by flashing light, either from the *Unbeaten* or the US ship. '*Papa*' (or the Blue Peter code flag) used in daytime means, 'All persons should report on-board as the vessel is about to proceed to sea.' Everyone scrambled back to *N93* at the rush and grabbed what food they could. As the crew came back, some members climbed up to the old World War I destroyer and purloined food in the form of bread along with other victuals from the vessel. This was because *Unbeaten* was new and had not built up stocks of food and as she had been day-running this allowed fresh vitals to be topped up daily as required, with no need to store them. Owing to the urgent nature of this recall, the crew did not know how long they would be at sea without any means of replenishment.

It was not until all the crew had returned back on-board and berthing lines were slipped and the sleek, darkened shape of the *Unbeaten* passed Kingswear castle at the mouth of the River Dart, that their Commanding Officer informed the crew of why they were recalled to sail so urgently. Whilst the crew were ashore in Dartmouth, word had been received tasking the *Unbeaten* to sail immediately and head for the Bay of Biscay. Other submarines in the area were also told to proceed in that direction, including some ageing H-Class boats. The varied flotilla of submarines and ships were told that their quarry was to be the *Scharnhorst* Class capital ship *Gneisenau,* which was described as being a light battleship or battle cruiser. Also in company with the *Gneisenau* was one of the more infamous German naval vessels from World War II, her vast steel forecastle emblazoned with a large swastika: it was the *Scharnhorst* herself.

Unbeaten was one of 22 submarines tasked that day to proceed towards the Bay of Biscay and patrol off the coast of Brest, to be precise. Two fellow U-Class boats, HMS/M *Union* and eventually HMS/M *Undaunted*, were to join in the hunt along with *Unbeaten*. The *Union* was diverted at the same time as *Unbeaten* and, combined with the other submarines and ships, they were to encircle the port of Brest in an operation which would be dubbed the 'Iron Ring'. To explain the reason for the 'Iron Ring' and *Unbeaten's* involvement, it would be prudent to write about the

Scharnhorst's movements prior to this event and how fate nearly brought them together. In early June 1940, the *Scharnhorst* was hit by a torpedo fired from the destroyer HMS *Acasta* which, along with HMS *Ardent*, was escorting the aircraft carrier HMS *Glorious*. The British ships were returning to Scapa Flow from Norway. Spotted by the *Scharnhorst* and *Gneisenau*, a large gun battle ensued; the *Ardent* was sunk and the *Glorious* was badly hit and rolled over. At around the time the *Glorious* capsized, the *Acasta* fired the torpedo which rammed into the side of *Scharnhorst* under her after 'Caesar' turret. Although badly damaged, *Scharnhorst* fought on and severely crippled and eventually sank the *Acasta*.

Thinking the mighty German battle cruiser had been hit by a torpedo fired from a submarine, the *Scharnhorst* and *Gneisenau* did not want to remain in the area for fear of being hit by another torpedo, so both ships departed as fast as they could. They fled the scene, leaving approximately 900 men from the three British vessels in the water. It was a long and agonising three days later when rescue eventually arrived and sadly only a total of 39 sailors were plucked alive, by a Norwegian steamer, from the unforgiving ocean. Two days later, the badly damaged *Scharnhorst* limped into the Norwegian port of Trondheim and underwent emergency repairs. She was then sent to Kiel for more permanent repair work to get her operational and back to sea. Once repairs had been completed, the *Scharnhorst*, along with the *Gneisenau*, attempted to break out into the North Atlantic. However, this was aborted when the *Gneisenau* was damaged in bad weather. On 22 January 1941, both German vessels made a second and successful attempt to break out into the North Atlantic. The *Scharnhorst* and *Gneisenau* then commenced *Operation Berlin*. By the time this two month operation was over, the two battle cruisers had jointly sunk or captured an estimated 22 Allied merchant vessels totalling a massive 113,690 tons.

The two confident and jubilant Captains' of the marauding German warships were ordered to return to a home port as soon as possible. The battle cruisers had been wreaking havoc around the Atlantic unchecked by any Allied forces for months; they had to be stopped. It was assumed by the British that the German ships would make their return to Germany or Norway by the route from which they came. However, Admiral Günther Lütjens had other ideas – he brazenly decided to embark his ships on the shortest route and headed for the German-occupied French port of Brest. As the two battle cruisers approached the coast of France they were spotted by a British aircraft from the carrier HMS *Ark Royal*. The *Scharnhorst* and *Gneisenau* knew they had been seen and altered course north to make it look like they were going to pass to the west of Great Britain. Once the aircraft was out of sight they altered course back onto their original track. When de-briefed back on-board *Ark Royal*, the British pilot reported the two German ships course as being north but did not mention the course they were originally on when first spotted. Lütjens' ruse worked, and combined with bad weather conditions that prevented aircraft spotting them again until it was too late, the unmolested battle cruisers sailed into Brest on 22 March 1941.

By the time *Unbeaten* and *Union* arrived off Brest, both battle cruisers were well tucked up in the French port. Owing to the U-Class Submarines' relatively slow maximum surface speed of 11.5 knots, the submarines did not get there in time. Frustratingly, the *Scharnhorst* and *Gneisenau* sailed straight through the area which was supposed to have been patrolled by the *Union*. The 'Iron Ring' stayed in place, with several submarines remaining on station in rough weather for a long period of time, just waiting. Owing to other tasking, the *Unbeaten* left the area and was back alongside Portsmouth by early April. It eventually transpired that due to heavy RAF bombing, the *Scharnhorst* and *Gneisenau* would not venture out of Brest until 11 February 1942.

4

FIRST VIEW OF THE ROCK

That Friday, *Unbeaten* berthed alongside the pontoons at Fort Blockhouse in Gosport, the home of the Fifth Submarine Flotilla in Portsmouth Harbour. It was 4 April 1941; she had just arrived back at her base port, fresh from her jaunt along with the other submarines of the 'Iron Ring'. *Unbeaten* was put on extended notice and she was to be prepared for sailing to the Mediterranean. The boat had until 12 April for some of the crew to take leave while the remaining personnel embarked stores and munitions prior to being deployed for what was termed Mediterranean service. This deployment to that far off ocean was to be the culmination of the crew's determination, hard work and exhausting efforts in getting themselves and their submarine fully worked up in every aspect for war service. When alongside at Fort Blockhouse, also known as the shore base HMS *Dolphin*, the *Unbeaten's* Petty Officer (Tel) Norman Drury said 'I was living ashore in digs with my wife'.[13] Some of the other crew members would have lived in barrack accommodation provided at Fort Blockhouse. Owing to Pompey (Portsmouth) being the home of the Royal Navy, the Germans saw the town as being strategically important, and ripe for bombing. Several of the targets were later confirmed from captured Luftwaffe maps as being the dockyard buildings and docks, the Portsmouth railway stations, the power station, Gosport bases and barracks, Vospers Shipbuilders in the Camber, and also the Airspeed Factory. The Luftwaffe continually unleashed heavy aerial bombing campaigns over the area. During *Unbeaten's* time alongside, between 4 and 12 April, bombs fell on the city with alarming regularity, often causing a great loss of life and severe damage to buildings and to the city's infrastructure.

The night before *Unbeaten* sailed, there was a particularly heavy high explosive (HE) bombing raid, which decimated a lot of the area. The very next day, Leading Seaman Jack Casemore was due to join the *Unbeaten* as one of their 'swashbuckling crew'. But that fateful night, Jack was on a final run ashore with some of the men from *Unbeaten*, several of whom he was already acquainted with. The lads would have boarded the Gosport Ferry, located near to Fort Blockhouse, and travelled over to Portsea, a regular matelot haunt. They were sat in a pub at the top of Queen Street, enjoying a drink, when the air raid siren signalled the impending Luftwaffe raid, which hit Pompey that night. Jack and his shipmates had several close shaves as the raid unfolded. They ran from location to location, leaving the pub to hide under a nearby Woolworths. As the powerful bombs were dropping very close, they decided to make a dash for the Royal Sailors' Rest, known as Aggie Weston's. It was a good job they did because an HE bomb landed and detonated on the very spot where they had been standing, at the Woolworths store. Jack remembers that night well: 'We began to get the wind up, as it seemed they were targeting us.'[14] Just as the lads moved from Aggie Weston's and headed for the harbour, the building took a direct hit. They were heading for an air raid shelter of which one of the lads knew the location. Upon arrival the police informed the exhausted sailors that the air raid shelter was out of bounds as it had also received a direct hit. Luckily, it seems all the lads in Jack's run ashore did eventually find somewhere to shelter that evening.

Jack can still visualise the images of destruction. He remembers passing the town hall, which still had furious flames licking out of the roof, the next morning; much of the area was completely destroyed. It was reported that 500 people died that night in the air raid shelter. The sailors were very lucky chaps indeed. Some would say that Jack Casemore, individually, was a very lucky man. Jack had joined *Unbeaten* after serving on-board the requisitioned Canadian Pacific Steamship, Montrose. This ship was commissioned in the Royal Navy as HMS *Forfar* and reconfigured to be used as an Armed Merchant Cruiser. On 2 December 1940 the *Forfar* was sunk by a torpedo fired from the Type VIIB U-boat *U99*, commanded by the formidable German U-boat ace Kapitänleutnant Otto Kretschmer. A total of 171 sailors were lost when their ship went down and only 21 soles survived. Jack Casemore had left *Forfar* just before her sinking.

The morning of 12 April saw *Unbeaten* slip and proceed from her berth at Fort Blockhouse. Some of the crew involved in letting go the berthing ropes would have been fell in, lined up in front of the conning tower, with the tallest man forward, and the shortest aft. It would be safe to say that some family members would have gathered to wave off the submarine – wives, mothers and children, all fighting back tears and frantically waving goodbye as the boat glided past and disappeared into the low early morning sun. The boat would eventually be lost from sight as she rounded the Isle of Wight and headed west, down the English Channel. Traditionally, one of the closest vantage points on the Portsmouth side used by onlookers is Round Tower and its shingly foreshore. This tower is situated on the Portsmouth side of the harbour entrance. Plymouth has a similar spot where loved-ones have routinely mustered over many years to wave off warships and submarines. This area is known as Devil's Point.

As the boat transited the Channel on its journey towards the Mediterranean, the crew would have been acclimatising themselves to life at sea on board the fully manned submarine, watch-keeping and sleeping in shifts. The standard daily watch routine in the Royal Navy was and still is split into seven watches. Often when referring to an approximate time in which a specific event took place it would be placed within the timeframe of a watch. For example, 'we dived during the first' meaning between 20:00 and 23:59. However, watch routines on a wartime submarine were usually two hours on watch and four hours off. The relatively short time on watch was due to the concentration required of a submariner when on duty, operating his particular piece of equipment or maintaining a lookout. Surface warships ran a four hour watch routine when not at action stations. However for the purpose of continuity this book refers to watch time frames by their common names. The watches are as follows: Forenoon, 08:00-12:00; Afternoon, 12:00-16:00; First Dog, 16:00-18:00; Last Dog, 18:00-20:00; First, 20:00-23:59; Middle, 00:01-04:00; and finally the Morning watch, 04:00-08:00.

Every inch of the vessel would have been packed with stores including provisions like potatoes, bread, large amounts of tinned food and plenty of dehydrated vegetables. Fresh water was obviously a must and was only for drinking; it was rationed from the outset. Cigarettes were a luxury but of course deemed essential, and packets of them were stowed in any available gap between machinery and instrument panels. The only place to smoke would have been up top, and only when surfaced with the hatches open. It was not permitted to smoke when dived, and this would have been difficult in any case because due to the oxygen-limited atmosphere of a dived submarine, a match would not burn. During this seven day, running patrol, *Unbeaten* covered approximately 1,150 nautical miles on passage between Portsmouth and her planned stopover at Gibraltar. She would have spent some of her time on the surface, charging batteries and allowing fresh air to get into the boat. Time spent on the surface was always dependent on the threat and weather conditions. Around the same time, back in Britain, at the Royal Navy Signals School and at sea, trials of a new piece of top secret equipment called Type 271 were taking place. This was the RDF (Radio Detection and Finding) equipment. RDF was the precursor to RADAR (Radio Detection and Ranging). The potential of this invention would alter the direction of the war in favour of Britain and her Allies and eventually its conception would directly affect *Unbeaten*.

The Bay of Biscay area, locked between the Finisterre and Sole forecast areas, is, by reason of its location, notoriously nearly always rough, so the boat would have crossed this unpredictable Atlantic bay probably submerged for long periods of time. On 19 April, *Unbeaten* surfaced to brilliant sunshine and in sight of Gibraltar. Jack Casemore said 'My first view of the Rock was a sight I will always remember'.[15] The author has sailed into Gib a score of times and always remembers the Rock as being an awe-inspiring vista when viewed from sea. The huge Jurassic limestone mass looms out of the blue ocean like a great leviathan. One can just make out the clean white stucco buildings gathered around its base. The sheer, impregnable, craggy rock walls, partially covered in vegetation, reach up high into the sky. The Rock's 1,400-foot or 430-metre peak is often lost in a ghostly fog or mist caused by warm wind that flows from the Alboran Channel, and is funnelled through the Strait of Gibraltar. Locals call this phenomenon *Viento de Levante* or the Levanter, which means 'to rise'.

That sunny morning, *Unbeaten* tied up alongside the submarine depot ship HMS *Maidstone*; she was alongside, port-side-to, inside the southern breakwater, or 'mole' as it is known. The depot ship was well tucked in at the inner end of the extended sea wall which protects Gibraltar Harbour. As *Titania* was to the 6th Flotilla, *Maidstone* was to the 8th Submarine Flotilla. In 1939, *Maidstone* had taken over from HMS *Cyclops* as the submarine depot ship based at Malta. When the situation in Malta got too dangerous, the crucial and valued depot vessel was moved to Gibraltar. However, this was only a short-term visit and she was moved again to Algiers Harbour for a longer stay. The submarine remained alongside *Maidstone* for four more days, allowing the crew of *Unbeaten* to top up fuel and stores, and to wash their clothes and themselves. It also gave the men a chance to go ashore and sample the sights and delights of Gibraltar. It is well known that the Rock was infamous for having vast amounts of public houses confined within the small area of land which surrounds its lower areas. This was heaven for a well-travelled, thirsty sailor. Gibraltar was, and still is, very popular for another reason: this is its immensely strategically important location, watching over the entrance to the Mediterranean Sea, or as the Romans called it, the *Mare Nostrum*, meaning 'Our Sea'.

Spain had long laid claim to the Rock, which, since 1703, has been held by Great Britain. Supposedly neutral during World War II, Spain never did join the Axis powers; however, the country, led by General Franco, was seen as being politically aligned to the Nazi ideology, and often collaborated with the Germans. Spanish intelligence often worked hand-in-hand with the German intelligence wing named 'Abwehr'. Basically, whichever country had control of the Straits of Gibraltar could secure naval access and egress to the Mediterranean. Elsewhere as morning broke on day 601 of World War II, British forces were rapidly being pushed out of Greece, as German troops crossed the frontier into the country.

At this time, Germany dominated many of the ports and French naval bases which ran down the English Channel and Atlantic coast. This allowed Dönitz to reposition his U-boats, thus enabling him to virtually halve the distance the Wolf Packs had to travel to their Atlantic hunting grounds. The incumbent First Lord of the Admiralty A.V. Alexander said 'the battle of the Atlantic was now opening'.[16]. Several days before this, Hitler had stated that 'in March and April 1941 a naval war would start such as the enemy had never expected'. At a gathering of Nazi Party members in Munich, he went on to rant: 'We shall face her ... wherever British ships cruise, our U-boats will be sent against them until the hour of decision arrives. The time is coming when we can measure our strength again'.[17]

A rested *Unbeaten* slipped from the *Maidstone* on 23 April and sailed out of the protective breakwaters of Gibraltar Harbour and steered a course towards the Mediterranean. *Unbeaten* would not return to Gibraltar for quite some time. She was bound for a patrol off Sicily, and then onward to war-torn Malta. She left the Atlantic Ocean in her wake and transited through the Strait of Gibraltar, a channel measuring 7.8 nautical miles at its narrowest point between Spain and Morocco, and entered into the Alboran Sea.

N93 was now on war patrol footing, only surfacing at night to pick up wireless traffic (W/T) and charge her batteries. She would remain submerged during the daylight hours. During her build, *N93* was fitted with two diesel engines. These powerhouses were built by Davey Paxman & Co. of Colchester, England, to a specific Admiralty design. Founded in 1865, Paxman had a long association with the Royal Navy going back many years. In fact, the company's involvement in building diesel engines for submarines goes back to before World War II. It has been said that Paxman manufactured nearly two-thirds of all the engines fitted in the World War II British submarine fleet.

The U-Class submarine was one of the first British submarine types to be complemented with diesel-electric drive propulsion. Paxman supplied all but two U-Class boats with their engines; the exceptions were the Group 1 boats, HMS/M *Una* and HMS/M *Umpire*, these engines and submarines being built by Chatham Dockyard. *Unbeaten* was fitted with two six-cylinder engines. These were supplied in pairs to each submarine during build. Each engine had an output of 307 bhp, which in turn powered two electric generators. The diesel engines were not directly connected to the propellers. The generators in turn provided the power to the electric motors via two large batteries, which finally drove the submarine's twin propeller shafts. The two electric motors had a combined rating of 825 bhp and were built and supplied by General Electric.

As described, the power provided to the generators would charge the No. 1 and No. 2 batteries. These huge batteries, made up of 112 cells, weighed in at around half a ton each. No. 1 battery was situated forward of amidships directly under the heads, adjacent to the Petty Officers' & Leading Hands'

Mess. The main battery, No. 2, was under the forward part of the Control Room and also ran under the Wardroom. The batteries required continual maintenance. These power cells had to be checked and their specific gravity reading measured regularly. This was a hazardous job as the battery cells, when open, could give off toxic hydrogen chloride gas, which is noxious and can be explosive in large doses. Because of the care required when topping up the cells with distilled water, this task was nearly always carried out alongside. This did mean, however, that due to the battery locations, the crew accommodation had to be dismantled in order to lift the deck plates to allow access to the batteries. When the submarine was at sea the crew would have to carry out a charge on the batteries. This meant the submarine would have to surface to allow the exhaust from the engines to vent in fresh air. This charging evolution was usually carried out during the dark hours. The CO would then issue that famous order ‘we dive at dawn’. It really was very risky to be on the surface during daylight hours.

The transit to Malta saw *Unbeaten* pass along the coast of Algeria to the south of Sardinia, and then patrol between the Tyrrhenian and Mediterranean Seas, off Sicily. Several other British submarines were also operating in these areas. The *Upholder*, which was among the first of the U-Class submarines to reach Malta, was in the vicinity, having arrived at the island on 10 January 1941. By the time *Unbeaten* was on station off Sicily, *Upholder* was already embarked on her third operational patrol out of the besieged Maltese island. She had achieved some success already during this patrol by attacking shipping to the North of Cape Bon at the tip of Tunisia. HMS/M *Usk,* another U-Class submarine, was also operating in an area off Marettimo, Sicily. *Unbeaten*, *Usk*, and *Upholder* were all directed to arrive at Malta on 3 May 1941.

As fate would have it, only the two submarines which were launched a day apart at Barrow would eventually arrive at the Maltese rendezvous. The *Usk* and her 30-strong crew were never seen again. The boat had been tasked around 27 April to move from Marettimo and head 80 nautical miles south towards Cape Bon. *Unbeaten* had moved to the position previously adopted by *Usk*, off Capo Marettimo. When *Usk* did not arrive at Malta on 3 May, she was ordered to report her position. Nothing was heard. Again, on 5 May, *Usk* was called and told to report, but still nothing. By this time the *Usk* was probably sunk. The *Unbeaten* reported hearing heavy depth charging from the direction of Cape Bon early on 30 April – was this an attack on *Usk*? There is a possibility she may have been sunk by a mine, laid as part of a new and uncharted minefield, which was only discovered off Cape Bon two weeks after she went missing.

During his time on board *Unbeaten*, Norman Drury remembers vividly that some of the crew were very young and inexperienced, although through no fault of their own. This inexperience was highlighted one night, halfway through a morning watch. *Unbeaten* was heading for the Pantelleria Straits, between Sicily and the Italian island of Pantelleria, then onwards towards Malta. An Ordinary Telegraphist who had joined the *Unbeaten's* crew prior to sailing from Fort Blockhouse, was on watch on what was his first long period at sea. During his watch, the young lad had missed part of an important signal broadcast from Rugby, a signal in which *Unbeaten* was mentioned. The signal was transmitted in order to give submarines their patrol positions in anticipation of enemy movements. The part that was missed was the most vital: the position that *Unbeaten* was to go to. A decision had to be made about whether to surface and request a repetition of the broadcast or not. It was the early hours of the morning and dangerous to be on the surface. The signal would not have been re-transmitted until the following evening when Rugby knew *Unbeaten* would be on the surface again. Owing to the submarine's speed of advance, a day's steaming would mean that the boat would be well out of position by the next time they received signal traffic. Reluctantly, the Commanding Officer ordered the *Unbeaten* to be surfaced and to ask Rugby for a repetition of the signal; once received she submerged again and moved into her designated position. Drury puts the poor message handling down to the lad being inexperienced, and the fact that the chap was a 'Hostile Ordinary', an affectionate term meaning that he was an HO, short for 'Hostilities Only'[18] rating. These were men who had been drafted to serve on board submarines or warships, but only for the duration of hostilities. So as serious as the incident was, Norman Drury said 'The young lad could not be blamed totally for the incident'.[19]

5

FAITH, HOPE AND CHARITY

Malta in May 1941 was not the safest of places for a submarine, or any vessel for that matter. Bombing raids inflicted by the Luftwaffe Fliegerkorps X, a flight formation which excelled in attacking shipping, combined with the Italian Regia Aeronautica had numbered 58 during the month of January 1941. By the time *Unbeaten* eventually reached the island, the frequency of raids had steadily increased month on month, to a point where there were a total of 97 raids in May. Twenty-six of these were night raids. The chaps on board *Unbeaten* must have thought that to be alongside the Maltese island was reminiscent of being alongside at Pompey, having themselves also suffered sustained bombing raids back home. Located 985 and 820 nautical miles respectively from the ports of Gibraltar and Alexandria, the island of Malta, not unlike Gibraltar, was seen as being very strategically placed. With this, and the coast of Tunisia only 200 nautical miles away, any force based on the Commonwealth island could effectively control the Mediterranean. Winston Churchill summed it up when he stated that 'Malta must be held, or the way to the east would be open.' [20]

Because the island was effectively besieged on all sides, problems arose when attempting to import vital stores and supplies – these stores were much needed to help keep the island's infrastructure stabilised and to support the Maltese population. Also, at the same time, the archipelago was being built up as a military stronghold, and a base was established from which attacks on German and Axis convoys supplying Rommel's North Africa campaign could be staged. Early on, Admiral Cunningham had estimated that at least two vital supply convoys, carrying a combined total of around 80,000 tons of stores, would be needed to keep the little island secure each month. Fulfilling this estimate would prove to be easier said than done.

During the early part of the siege there was very little combat air support. As luck would have it, several crates were discovered lounging in a hangar at Kalafrana, a base in the area of Marsaxlokk Bay which originally opened in 1917 as a Fleet Air Arm seaplane station. Contained within these eight crates were the parts of several dismantled, pre-World War II Gloster Gladiator bi-planes, in their entirety. These vintage aircraft were left on the island by the *Glorious* prior to the carrier embarking on her fateful Norwegian campaign. Four of these old girls were hastily re-built and handed over to the RAF. It is well documented that the Gladiator pilots battled against insurmountable odds, flying these aircraft relentlessly for many months, inflicting much damage. They downed many enemy bombers in return for the loss of only one Gladiator. The remaining three aircraft were given the nicknames Faith, Hope and Charity. Replacement aircraft were dispatched in March 1941 in the form of 21 Hurricanes. These were loaded on board the merchantman *Parracombe*. Frustratingly, during transit, she was mined and sunk, taking all the urgently needed aircraft with her to the seabed.

Two more U-Class submarines had recently joined the Malta Flotilla. They were HMS/M *Urge,* and the boat which had been detached along with *Unbeaten* during the formation of the 'Iron Ring', the *Union*. Remarkably, Lt. E.P. Tomkinson and the crew of *Urge* had already chalked up their first sinking. On passage, as she transited across the Bay of Biscay, *Urge* attacked a 10,500-ton Axis tanker, *Franco Martelli*. The tanker's cargo was bound for the occupied French port of Brest. The fact that she was carrying oil for the German U-boats based in the French port must have made the sinking all the more satisfying. The smaller U-Class boats were deployed to augment the T-Class submarines and replace the bigger O-, P- and R-Class boats, which, owing to their size, did not perform as well in the shallow, clear waters of the Mediterranean Sea.

Saturday 3 May saw *Unbeaten* enter Marsamxett Harbour for the first time. She proceeded up Lazaretto Creek eight days after she had sailed from Gibraltar. The U-Class submarines were commonly berthed next to the old Lazaretto on the south side of Manoel Island, located in the centre of Marsamxett Harbour. The only road access to the island was over a bridge leading from Selima, which was an area liberally furnished with bars. While some boats were alongside, others would be moored about 50 yards off the Lazaretto buildings, attached forward and aft to Admiralty buoys. One of only a few existing photographs of *Unbeaten* shows her alongside the Lazaretto. The picture depicts her tied up forward and aft, her berthing ropes dipped over bollards, which were in fact old cannons sunk into the rock. These types of bollard, made from ancient armament, were quite normal and can still be found today in Devonport Dockyard and in the harbour walls of the old Barbican at Plymouth. There was a single catamaran positioned amidships, keeping the submarine off the old stone wall. The wall in turn supported the vast looming arches of the golden limestone Lazaretto structure. A narrow submarine brow, or walkway, was the only way of embarking or disembarking the boat.

Unbeaten was now to become a member of another band of British submarines which, at that time, were known as the 1st Submarine Flotilla. This Flotilla was originally made up of 12 submarines divided between Malta and Alexandria. Not until September 1941 did the U-Class submarines based at the Maltese island become the famed 10th Submarine Flotilla. Also that Saturday morning, *Upholder* returned to Malta, entering the harbour and transiting up Lazaretto Creek with her Jolly Roger flying proudly, although fluttering conspicuously below it was a Swastika-emblazoned ensign. As the boat slid past the harbour entrance and proceeded up the channel, a closer inspection of the crew who were standing on the casing revealed that several of them were wearing German steel helmets. They were also brandishing a fearsome collection of the Panzer Division's light automatic weapons. This booty had been liberated from a 2,500 ton abandoned Italian merchantman named Arta. She was packed with vital supplies bound for Rommel's Afrika Korp.

Union arrived at the entrance to Marsamxett Harbour on 4 May. Scarily, as she carefully transited down the same approach channel used by

Upholder the day before, a German-laid acoustic parachute mine exploded close to the boat; luckily, it was not close enough to cause any damage to her pressure hull. This goes some way to explaining why there was a gap between *Unbeaten* arriving at Malta and her embarking on her first operational patrol from the island. The harbours were understandably closed for several days due to mines spontaneously exploding near harbour breakwaters and in approach channels. This occurrence would continue to hamper the British submarines as the Commanding Officer of HMS/M *Upright* Lt. E.D. Norman confirmed. Back in late February 1941, the Regia Aeronautica had been actively dropping similar acoustic mines in an attempt to block the Maltese harbours. However, it was said to be common practice amongst British submarines to fire their conning tower-mounted Lewis .303 calibre machine guns into the water about 100 yards ahead of the submarine in an attempt to set off the sensitive mines. *Upright* was one of the first to prove this method, and after passing through the salty mist from one such controlled explosion she received a signal from shore saying 'Good Shooting' [21]. The day before *Unbeaten* would sail for her first patrol from the war torn island, Winston Churchill said, 'Malta, with Egypt and Gibraltar will be defended with the full strength of the Empire.' [22]

Commander G.W.G. Simpson, also known as 'Shrimp', had been on Malta since 8 January 1941. This was not his first experience of the Maltese island, however. Shrimp had been the Commanding Officer of the minelayer HMS/M *Cachalot* and served within the 1st Submarine Flotilla under the command of Captain P. Ruck-Keene, who was an old friend. That was in September 1939. Now forward to January 1941, George Simpson found himself as the Senior Officer Submarines, Malta, and reporting to Captain S.M. Raw, who was now Captain (S)1. Shrimp had relieved Commander R.G Mills and now all the island-based submarines were effectively under George Simpson's direction and ultimately in his charge. It was Shrimp's job to deploy his boats as and when necessary, acting on intelligence information received, or on orders from the Commander-in-Chief, Malta and Captain (S)1. It was initially said to him that the purpose of the Malta submarine flotilla was to sink southbound enemy shipping heading for the Italian army in Libya, effectively cutting off their supplies.

George Simpson joined the Royal Navy in 1915 and by the time World War II began he was an experienced, veteran submariner. He knew only too well the extremely uncomfortable conditions submariners often endured and the perils they constantly faced at sea. Shrimp was described by one of his staff officers as being a little freckle-faced man who was both galvanic and dynamic. He was said to have had a strong sense of justice and humour and also to possess an innate knowledge of human nature. Other people referred to him as having a caustic exterior and also being slightly eccentric, although this is often confused with Britishness. But more often the men found him to be very inspiring. Lt. Norman of *Upright* said, 'Tales of Shrimp must be legion.' [23] 'Dudley' Norman went on to say that 'Simpson was a remarkable man and a brilliant leader, loved by all who served under him.' [24] These comments may have been because Shrimp was renowned for allowing his men to let off steam when alongside, particularly after very stressful patrols. However, Commander Simpson did not suffer fools lightly, and would not tolerate any form of insubordination. One stand-out display of Simpson's unorthodox man management skills occurred at a submarine alongside the Lazaretto base.

The Commanding Officer of *Upright* wrote in his private papers of an occasion when another submarine was due to sail on patrol at 16:00 that day. Just prior to zero hour, the young Commanding Officer of that boat reported to Shrimp that a member of his crew had failed to return on board from overnight leave. The reason for the skipper's concern was that the crewman was one of the boat's key ratings and there were no available replacements to stand in on the impending patrol. Shortly after he made his report to Shrimp, the Commanding Officer was temporarily pleased to see the rating weaving his way up the road towards the base. However, the refreshed sailor arrived at the submarine singing, shouting, and swearing that he was not going on the boat's 'next f***ing patrol'. This ongoing incident was reported to Shrimp, who promptly ordered a clearing of the lower deck of the submarine. Once all the crew were mustered on the jetty, opposite the boat, the drunken matelot was propped up in front of Commander Simpson. Shrimp asked, 'Are you going to join your submarine?' The rating replied, 'I'm not going on any f***ing sub!' Shrimp ordered a heaving line to be tied around the man. Once this was done, Shrimp barked, 'Throw him in.' A dwell of two marching paces followed the splash. 'Pull him out' was the next order. The sodden sailor was again brought in front of Shrimp. Again, the hapless chap was asked, 'Are you going?' and again the sailor responded in the negative.

'Throw him in.' This charade went on with the sailor being thrown in and recovered about four times in all. On the last occasion he was brought in front of Shrimp and was asked, 'Are you going?' Having had a sudden rush of clarity, the rating replied, 'Of course Sir, thank you Sir.' [25]. That was the end of the matter, which, under any other Commander could quite easily have resulted in the man being court-martialed.

The massive responsibility on the shoulders of Shrimp, combined with the personal admiration and affection he held for his crews and their boats, was often tested, especially when a boat was overdue, or at worst, lost. This emotional rollercoaster must have been a constant weight on his conscience. Shrimp spent many a day pacing his office waiting for absent boats he had deployed to return to the relative safety of the Lazaretto. Several of Commander G.W.G. Simpson's submarines sailed from Malta on patrol and did not return; many vanished forever with no known location to this day.

The Lazaretto buildings were originally an old quarantine site built by the Knights of St. John. The Knights Hospitallers, as they are also known, were given the island in 1530 by the Holy Roman Emperor, Charles V. The Knights remained on the islands for a great many years. During this period they turned the island into the most impregnable Christian fortress in the Mediterranean. The island fortress was built to withstand sieges, and it would be within these ancient stone buildings that the crews of the 10th Submarine Flotilla would endure the last siege of Malta in living memory. The Lazaretto's real estate stretched over a quarter of a mile, consisting of a rabbit warren of passageways and rooms. There were several large, arched storerooms which were intersected by courtyards. To allow shelter during bombing raids these storerooms, down in the building's foundations, were dug back deep into the bedrock by Maltese labourers, British military personnel and civilian staff. Before the miners could start digging, the vast storerooms had to be cleared of centuries of detritus. Much work was carried out on the submarine base at the Lazaretto.

Once the re-building was complete, the base would have essential engineering workshops, a sick bay, and even a cinema. Later on in the war, a small chapel would also be shoe-horned into the underground excavations. On the surface the locals and sailors converted the western wing of the Lazaretto buildings into mess decks, and built a vast dining hall with galley. The wardroom was situated on the first floor, where many Commanding Officers often had a view of their commands. This phoenix, built out of the old Leper Hospital, would rise up and eventually be commissioned as HMS *Talbot*. Jack Casemore recounts a time when the mess deck he was living in along with other chaps between patrols, was hit during a particularly heavy bombing raid. They had not noticed before, but on the opposite walls of the accommodation were two arches which had been bricked up a long while ago. These arches were now blown in by the Luftwaffe's bombs. Beyond the open arches, a small room was exposed which contained several sea chests. The chest Jack laid his hands on contained many very old letters written by sea Captains, detailing cargos and destinations. The letters dated from around 1850 to approximately 1880. Many of the delicate envelopes had been stamped with penny blacks and penny blues. When he was a boy Jack had collected stamps, so he knew a bit about them. He stashed a few in his kit bag, but over time he forgot about them. Many of the letters got lost over the years and he gave a few away to his young nephew.

Far away on the other side of the continent, Saturday 10 May saw a brand new Type VIIC U-boat launched from Howaldtswerke A.G. shipyard, at the heart of Germany's ship-building empire. This new but modified version of the successful VIIB type U-boat would become the workhorse of the Dönitz submarine fleet. The boat which entered the Kiel River that day would soon have a rendezvous with *Unbeaten* and a date with destiny. Elsewhere in the world, Rommel had paused for a while on the frontier of Egypt. He had moved faster than his supply lines could go and had to wait for them to catch up. In the Atlantic, German U-boat attacks were multiplying; however, one renegade U-boat Captain already mentioned in chapter one received divine retribution for his sinking of the *Athenia*.

The ninth of May 1941 saw the capture of a Type IXB U-boat *U110,* by HMS *Bulldog.* The German submarine *U110* was commanded by the infamous Kapitänleutnant Fritz-Julius Lemp. The U-boat was boarded and the *Bulldog's* crew managed to gather up all the important documents held on board. Because of this event, Bletchley Park and its code breakers were at a point where they could now read the very important Enigma key 'Dolphin'. The key used to encrypt Enigma messages on board German U-boats was called the Heimisch key. This key was named Dolphin by Bletchley, and soon they would be able to decipher every coded message sent by Dönitz's submarines. This would be a turning point in the war against the *Rudeltaktik*, or Wolf Tactic. In many ways Lemps actions on-board *U30* heralded the terrifying start of the U-boat menace. Consequently the capture of his final command *U110* was integral to their downfall. The element of surprise encapsulated by Dönitz's 'Unterseeboots' was compounded. Fearing his submarine was going to be rammed by the *Bulldog* Kapitänleutnant Lemp ordered his boat to be abandoned. Lemp was last seen treading water with his crew, the next minute he had simply disappeared. Thirty-two of the crew of *U110* survived. It has been suggested by several naval authors that Lemp may have deliberately drowned himself rather than face the indignation of being captured. The Captain of another U-boat *U570*, later re-named HMS/M *Graph*, was captured when he also ordered his crew to abandon *U570* after being attacked by a Coastal Command aircraft. Kapitänleutnant Hans-Joachim Rahmlow spent the rest of the war as a prisoner, regularly being persecuted, and ridiculed for his supposed cowardice by fellow captured higher-ranking German officers. Did Lemp know the fate which had befallen his contemporary and did he want to avoid that humiliation at all costs?

Back in London, the night of 10–11 May was dubbed 'The Longest Night'. The capital city suffered one of its most severe bombing raids of World War II, and the loss of 1,486 lives. This ferocious raid would change the face of London forever. While alongside Malta, *Unbeaten* was fuelled and restored after her passage from Gibraltar. Teddy Woodward, the Commanding Officer of *Unbeaten* would have gone to see Shrimp Simpson to receive his patrol orders. This was a regular pre-patrol routine, and on completion of a patrol the Commanding Officer of the boat would return to Shrimp with his typed-up patrol report. This report would be discussed and commented on by Shrimp, then forwarded to Captain (S)1 for his comments. And finally it would be sent to the Commander-in-Chief, Mediterranean, for his often succinct and to-the-point appraisal of the entire submarine patrol.

6

GUN ACTION

The evening of 11 May 1941, just after 21:00, saw *Unbeaten* slip her berth and leave the wall of the Lazaretto. This would be her first operational war patrol from Malta. For *Unbeaten's* crew this tasking was what they had trained for all these months. *N93* was under orders to proceed towards patrol area 'Victor'. All the hard work and personal sacrifices made by the men, and their families, culminated in this precise moment. As the little boat moved out into the calm, moonlit, open water the crew would have been highly aware that anything could happen out there, quite literally anything.

The boat steered a course of SSW on passage to its maiden patrol area. Overnight the transit was quiet; the crew would have been getting used to being on patrol, and beginning to establish a watch routine. 12 May passed without incident, with the exception of five explosions being heard some distance away. Finally, the next evening, after travelling roughly 155 nautical miles, the submarine arrived at area 'Victor', which lay approximately 30 nautical miles off the coast of Khoms in Libya. Khoms is a town just to the east of the North African country's capital Tripoli. *Unbeaten* was now well within the enemy convoy routes, just waiting and listening. The submarine was deliberately positioned here to cause havoc with the German and Axis supply routes that ran up and down the coast of North Africa. At around 09:00 on 14 May, Teddy Woodward looked through the periscope and sighted the 13-metre dark rocky promontory, extending three cables off the Libyan coastline, marking the area of Ra's al Hallab. The submarine was now only 6.5 nautical miles from land. After the boat's position was fixed, she proceeded towards Bintil Rock. This rock was a reporting point for British submarines in patrol area Victor, utilised because it is a conspicuous, pointed rock that is never awash. At 13:23, it is recorded in the submarine patrol log that masts of a possible convoy were sighted very close inshore, moving eastwards.

The hunt was on; *Unbeaten* closed her quarry as fast as she could, only to have her speed of approach hampered by a Tunney, which is a small fishing vessel. The submarine had to navigate around the oblivious little boat, passing it only 600 yards away. The requirement to manoeuvre, and the time taken, made a closer attack now out of the question. However, the enemy's course and speed were accurately assessed and it was decided to attack the largest vessel at the rear of the convoy. The masted ships were approximately one nautical mile from the shore and transiting the five fathom line, which means the water was only 30ft or 19m deep; this was shallow water in which to be safely operating a submarine. The enemy convoy was made up of one armed trawler, one two-masted schooner, a 500-ton Dutch schooner and two three-masted schooners, the biggest of which being a 1,100-ton vessel. Extensive research of the Italian Navy archives by the naval researcher Platon Alexiades shows that in all probability the vessels concerned were the schooners *Alas, Trio F,* the *Rita* and *Neptunus*. These vessels would have been carrying supplies for Rommel's North African campaign. The convoy of schooners was escorted by the Italian gunboat *Mario Bianco* and was transiting from Tripoli to Benghazi. *Unbeaten* had been waiting patiently for the right moment to strike. An hour and a half later the opportunity came.

A salvo of three torpedoes was fired at a range of 4,500 yards – an ideal range was around 1,200 yards. Each torpedo was individually aimed using a combination of the Commanding Officer's mathematical skill and the on-board Submarine Torpedo Director Mk II, or 'Fruit Machine' as it was known. This piece of equipment was operated by the third hand, Sub-Lt. J.C. Varley. Its purpose was as a torpedo control calculator, and on board a U-Class submarine it was positioned above the boat's wheel, in the control room. The Fruit Machine calculated the director angle, giving the command a better appreciation of direction and timing when firing the torpedoes. After firing her spread the submarine immediately altered course and opened the distance between the target and her own torpedo tracks, for the obvious reason that all tracks lead to home. The crew would have waited silently, listening for the impact of the torpedoes finding their mark. The anticipation, mixed with a fear of reprisal, must have been palpable. At last a very faint explosion was heard – a whole three minutes after the first torpedo was released. The chaps in *Unbeaten's* engine room, where Chalky Wright worked, said they heard another explosion a full five minutes after firing, although those men in the control room with watches timing the torpedo runs heard nothing.

Twenty minutes after the torpedo salvo was fired, *Unbeaten* was ordered to come to periscope depth to assess the situation. The convoy was now bunched together but the armed trawler or gunboat was seen to be coming towards the submarine, although, thankfully, it was moving at a slow speed. She was probably unaware of her submerged attacker's position. On first look it appeared that one three-masted schooner was missing, but the Command on *Unbeaten*, including the No 1, Lt. Frank Gibbs, were sure the torpedoes had missed and that the explosions were of no consequence. Still keen to put some space between them and their prey, they took the boat deep, and opened to a safe distance in the hope of coming up for a second look. Once at periscope depth, the Navigating Officer, Lt. Charles Taylor, looked again through the periscope and was now sure there was only one three-masted schooner when there had been two. Visibility was better now; the convoy could be seen clearly, and now only four ships filled the lens. No wreckage of the doomed schooner was visible, and the depth was deemed too shallow to investigate further for fear of being spotted by aircraft in the clear water. No vessels were reported by the Italians as being sunk in that area on that date. It appears that the torpedoes passed by the convoy at some range as they do not appear to have been seen by the vessels in the convoy.

Unbeaten slipped silently back into the deep to reload. Buoyed after the possible success of yesterday's attack, *N93* checked and fixed her current position by sighting Sidi Bu Fatimah, bearing 230° at four nautical miles. She then proceeded westwards along the rugged dusty coastline of the Gulf of Sirte. Most of the day was spent transiting down the coast within her allotted patrol area. At around 17:00 a smaller 800-ton schooner was spotted; reservedly, *Unbeaten* did not attack as the vessel was not full of cargo, but instead she watched inquisitively as the vessel anchored in Khoms Roads. Teddy Woodward had another plan of attack in mind: 'Gun action'. The audacious Woodward decided to close towards Khoms Harbour at dusk and attack the unfortunate schooner with good old naval gunfire from *Unbeaten's* 12 pounder gun. Gun drills were one of the evolutions which the crew had practised many times during the submarine's work-up trials. Now they would be doing those drills in anger, against a real target, and for a real purpose.

As dusk came *Unbeaten* surfaced, but trimmed down, and like a crawling leopard she moved stealthily, slowly, ever closer, at all times being aware of what was around her. The plucky little boat got as close as 1,500 yards from Khoms Harbour, allowing Woodward to observe the target through the periscope. The vessel was a normal merchant schooner of the type utilised by the Axis to run ammunition and other supplies. It was assessed by the Command that this schooner displayed no signs of it being a 'Q' ship – the nickname for an armed vessel dressed to look like a harmless merchantman – but it was still deemed a legitimate target. The British had employed the 'Q' ship tactic during World War I and in his book *The World Crisis*, Winston Churchill would write, 'Our two principal devices for destroying the German submarines were the Bircham Indicator Nets and the Decoy Ships, afterwards called the 'Q' Boats.' [26] Shortly after the outbreak of World War II the same ploy had been established again to try to help combat the German U-boat threat. However, this great old British tactic would be turned back on the Royal Navy and Allied forces with many German and Axis navies also sailing 'Q' ships. A good scan of the shore revealed there were no visible gun emplacements dug in along the coast, which was a bonus. *Unbeaten* turned and opened from the harbour with the intention of returning to a surfacing position by 20:30.

When she finally made her return, *Unbeaten* closed the Libyan harbour and bumped along the sandy bottom. She eventually sat on the bottom with a shallow 25ft, or 7.5m, on the gauge. She waited for dusk and watched, stalking and patiently observing her unsuspecting prey. Around 25 minutes later than planned, at 20:54, 'Stand-by gun action' was the order. The crew would have moved quickly to diving stations, which is a term used for both diving and surfacing. Still surveying through the periscope, Teddy

Woodward would then have ordered 'Salvoes shoot', swiftly followed by 'Man the gun'. *Unbeaten* blew her tanks and began to surface 1,000 yards from her target and then cautiously crept ever closer.

The gun crew had a well-practised routine for exiting the boat as quickly as possible. The gun on a U-Class submarine was an afterthought and neither a guns crew nor ammunition hatch were added. Because of this, the guns crew had to exit via the conning tower. This also meant that a quick crash dive during gun action was rarely carried out because of the possibility of leaving a man up top, or worse still, the hatch being open and the boat flooding. The process for gun action was thus: at around 40ft the crew would have opened the lower lid or bottom conning tower hatch. Three men would enter the conning tower and several others would be hanging off the ladder which goes up from the control room. When the boat was at 20ft, the 1st Lieutenant would blow a whistle, which was the order to remove the last clip on the upper hatch; the narrow exit hatch would still be under the water but very close to the surface. The pressure inside would simultaneously pop the upper hatch; water would rush in and then very quickly get sucked out again along with the guns crew. They would exit the boat as mentioned, via the conning tower, then climb down the outside, man the gun and bring up the ammunition, which was struck below in the magazine. On this occasion, *N93* swiftly opened fire on the hapless schooner, pounding her with a reported total of 21 high explosive rounds which spewed from the barrel of the submarine's 12 pounder gun. She was firing at a distance of between 700 and 400 yards from the target. Jack Casemore was part of the guns crew and remembers this action well. 'I remember seeing the native crew running along the bowsprit and diving into the sea,' [27] he says.

In his patrol report the ever self-critical Woodward said that had he surfaced earlier or used star shell, which illuminates a target, the result of the gun action may have been more satisfactory. But to illuminate may have facilitated any shore battery to open fire, which may not have been spotted earlier through the periscope. Also, the breakwater at Khoms Harbour was only 500 yards away and may have had armament situated on it. Woodward went on to report that the muzzle flash from her gun was said to have temporarily blinded the Gun Control Officer, Sub-Lt. J.C. Varley and also the Gun Layer. This blindness made the fall of shot hard to observe, but the cracks of splintering direct hits to the target's wooden hull could clearly be heard. It was ascertained that four direct hits and six ricochets were scored. By the time *Unbeaten* checked her fire and left the scene at 20:58, the schooner appeared to be settling by the stern. It was also said that a small boat was seen pulling clear from the stricken vessel. The schooner concerned was later identified as the *Giorgio*. The name of this vessel is shared by several other Italian sailing ships. According to Italian reports, some of the shells fired by *Unbeaten* fell into the town of Khoms and at least three of them failed to explode, and they caused little damage to the town or the schooner, which actually remained afloat.

On 16 May, the *Unbeaten* again sighted Sidi Bu Fatimah, this time bearing 180° at 3.5 nautical miles. She then continued westwards, patrolling along the coast. Around dusk, two large merchant vessels of approximately 9,000 tons a piece were sighted. *Unbeaten's* Command identified the warship escorting the merchantmen as an Italian *Baleno* Class destroyer. It was in fact a *Folgore* Class destroyer. This class comprised the vessels *Baleno*, *Folgore*, *Fulmine* and *Lampo*. These destroyers were a design modification of the *Dardo* Class, and by the end of World War II all of these Axis warships would be sunk. The nervous escort was zig-zagging 40° either side of her MLA (Mean Line of Advance). Teddy Woodward decided to attack the transports from inside the destroyer's protective zig-zagging screen. As the submarine was manoeuvring into an attacking position she suddenly struck the seabed with 35ft showing on the depth gauge. This impact thrust the boat upwards to 20ft. The range of the destroyer was only 2,000 yards away and Woodward felt sure the submarine's position had been compromised. Frank Gibbs, the boats 1st Lieutenant fought to regain the boat's trim. Once *Unbeaten* was back on an even keel they were able to have another look at their position in relation to the destroyer.

They knew it would be close, and it was. The vessel was only 600 yards away, looming large in the periscope view and heading straight for the vulnerable submarine. As the warship's razor-sharp stem sliced through the water Woodward felt sure the ship was coming in to ram them. It was believed that there was only 8ft of water under the keel. *Unbeaten* was immediately turned hard to Port in an attempt to make the impending collision a glancing blow. The submarine's crew raced to close all watertight hatches and doors, and the order 'Stand by to be rammed' was given. Norman Drury recalls that when the Commanding Officer took a quick look through the periscope and saw the destroyer heading straight for them, Woodward said, 'Open the lower lid.' Norman thought the skipper was going to surrender, but nothing came of it. There was no time, the 1st Lieutenant instinctively flooded 'Q', which is the very quick diving tank. The boat plunged down like a stone down into the depths. The crew waited for the crushing impact, the sound of tearing metal and rushing water, but this never came. The 1st Lieutenant's quick thinking had saved the boat and her crew. It was also later concluded that luckily for *Unbeaten*, the destroyer had come to the end of her zig-zag leg and she had turned away. Much to the relief of the boat's crew, the Italian warship appeared not to have seen the submarine at all. To be sure of not being spotted, Woodward waited a full 12 minutes before daring to have an all-round look in the periscope. All was clear, but unfortunately the target vessels were now deemed too far away, and no attack was possible.

Once everything had calmed down, including the crew's pulses, the Navigator and Captain checked the charts they had been provided with at the start of the patrol. Chart No. 3353 wrongly showed that *Unbeaten* should have been operating in 10 fathoms or 60ft (18m) of water during the whole escapade. No shoal was shown on the chart for that area. Woodward wrote in the patrol log: 'During the few critical moments when it was thought the destroyer was coming in to ram, the behaviour of the officers and men was exceptional.' The Commanding Officer went on, 'They carried on their duties in complete silence. Their sang-froid is exemplified by the entry in the rough control room log, written up at the time: "18:50 being rammed."' [28] The *Unbeaten* proceeded northwards to clear the area and surfaced to pass her enemy contact report.

7

ASH CANS & TIN FISH

The eventful first patrol from Malta continued for *Unbeaten* and her swashbuckling crew. Elsewhere the Mediterranean Fleet was engaged in operations off Crete. In the Atlantic, British and Allied shipping losses had been heavy, due to the constant attacks inflicted on convoys by German U-boats. Back in Great Britain, between 16 and 17 May, bombing raids were concentrated on the Birmingham area, and Nuneaton also received a very heavy attack. Other towns and cities were also hit, including Southampton, Plymouth, Leicester and Chelmsford. In the southern county of Cornwall, three aerodromes were attacked. Britain and her allies responded with bombing raids over Berlin, Bremen, Wilhelmshaven and Kiel. It was recorded in the War Cabinet Weekly Résumé (No. 90) that a German officer who was in Berlin at about the same time declared, 'The R.A.F. could be expected to arrive punctually about 23:00 hours.' [29] Shortly before this given time, all cafes and places of amusement were closed and the trams and buses were crammed with Berliners, all hurrying home. The RAF was always renowned for its punctuality.

During 18 May, just off Benghazi and not far from *Unbeaten's* position, a British T-Class submarine lay in wait. HMS/M *Tetrarch* stalked and sank the 6,000-ton merchant steamer *Giovinezza* with a well-aimed torpedo. The next day, 7,000 Italian troops from the Amba Alagi garrison surrendered to British forces in Africa. Meanwhile at Malta, German and Axis bombers carried out many raids over the course of the month. Luqa Aerodrome was a regular target and was bombed twice on the 20th and again on the 21st by large formations of Luftwaffe aircraft. Grand Harbour and Valetta were again targeted, with much damage to buildings reported. One would find it difficult to decide where is safer for a submariner: alongside or at sea. Shortly after this air raid, however, things started to ease on the bombing front, though only slightly. This could be attributed to the Luftwaffe Fliegerkorps X being removed from Sicily and re-positioned to support the German invasion of Russia.

Late May 1941 saw the German battleship *Bismark* sink the British Admiral-class battle cruiser HMS *Hood*, with great loss of life. Action during this period was not limited to surface vessels. Plenty of sub-surface action involving the Malta submarines was also taking place. As morning broke on 28 May, a landing party from the submarine *Upright* carried out an audacious attack on a railway line four miles south-west of Punto Stilo Light, near Calabria. They were successful in blowing up the tracks, slowing down supply routes for some considerable time.

On 30 May, HMS/M *Triumph* torpedoed an Italian armed merchant vessel in Benghazi Harbour and not long afterwards she sank three other vessels in the Gulf of Sidra, near where *Unbeaten* had been operating on her last patrol. The U-Class submarine HMS/M *Unique* also notched up another addition to her Jolly Roger by sinking a 1,000-ton merchant vessel in Lampedusa Harbour. Meanwhile, back on patrol with *Unbeaten*, the next two days – a Saturday and Sunday – passed without incident. During this time, the visibility was poor and the boat remained around the area of Ra's al Hallab Lighthouse, quietly submerged until after dark. Once darkness cloaked the sea, she surfaced to charge her batteries and patrol throughout the night, just five nautical miles offshore.

In the early morning half-light of 19 May, the lookout spotted a distant but bright light. *Unbeaten* closed at full speed, on the surface. It was starting to get light so the boat dived for dawn, to avoid being seen, but continued to close the light source. Forty-odd minutes later, through the periscope, the light was identified as being that of an Italian hospital ship similar to a known 8,000-ton vessel called the *Galilee*. This ship had been torpedoed by the U-Class submarine HMS/M *Utmost* back in mid-February 1941. However, *Galilee* was salvaged from that attack and limped back to port for extensive repairs. She was now in the sights of another U-Class boat. The submarine tried to close the vessel to positively identify her. The visibility was down to one-and-a-half nautical miles, and soon after it was first glimpsed, the hospital ship was lost in the fog. Later that same day, *Unbeaten* was in position off Tagiura, Libya, when another vessel was sighted through her periscope. It was thought the ship in question was a lone *Baleno* Class destroyer. The contact was in fact the Italian Torpedo boat *Pleiadi.* It appeared that she was escorting a single 5,000- to 6,000-ton merchant vessel, which has since been identified as the *Silvio Scaroni.* The hunt was on; *Unbeaten* started to close and Teddy Woodward ordered the crew to ready three tin fish. Little did they know that the next eight hours would turn into a living hell.

Three torpedoes were fired at a range of around 3,500 yards. The boat was in 14 fathoms, or 25.6 metres, of water. The *Unbeaten* had a level bubble when she fired her first torpedo. Unbelievably, and to the astonishment of the crew, the torpedo exploded only eight seconds later, after hitting the seabed. The tiny submarine was catapulted up to 18ft on the gauge. The second torpedo was fired when the submarine had a 1° aft down bubble. The boat then adopted a large bow down angle and it was felt for certain that her stern had pushed through the sea surface. The crew tried in vain to prevent the third torpedo from being fired but were unable to stop it. All attempts were fruitless – the wayward torpedo went straight down, and also exploded on the bottom. A muffled explosion from the second torpedo was heard two-and-a-half minutes later. The crew listening on ASDIC could no longer hear any HE emitting from the merchantman. Was she hit and sunk? A precursor of what was to come violently threw the boat to Port and Starboard; four depth charges had rained down on *Unbeaten* in quick succession. It was around three minutes after the first torpedo exploded and two minutes after the boat's stern had broken the surface and disappeared again. Although expected, there was little warning as all hell broke loose around the already shaken submarine.

For the majority of the crew, this initial pattern of charges was their first introduction to the devastating anti-submarine weapon called the depth charge, or the *Bombe Torpedini da Getto* (BTG), as the Italian Regia Marina called it. The Italian Navy was very well versed in the design and use of depth charges. Italy's Moncenisio BTG depth charge used in World War II bore a striking resemblance to early British depth charges. The use of the hydrostatic pistol and ball and groove device was used in British depth charges during World War I and it is likely the Italians acquired, copied, and adapted one for themselves. In accordance with her routine for getting clear after firing torpedoes, the submarine was now moving at full speed on a course of 90° to the track of the torpedo. The moment the explosive-packed depth charges made themselves known, all the lights in the boat went out. Reports came thick and fast into the control room. The forward and aft escape hatches were leaking and water was flooding in from the stern glands, which sealed the propeller shafts at the point where they protruded through the boat's hull. Another frightening hazard to which a submariner is susceptible was also reported: the smell of toxic battery gas. The No.1, or First Lieutenant, was working hard to keep the boat trimmed and to relay orders to pump forward or pump aft. A heavy thud signalled that the submarine had arrived on the seabed at 70ft. As for many of the crew, this was Jack Casemore's first experience of being depth charged. In his memoirs, which are held at the Imperial War Museum, Jack wrote, 'We hit bottom, whether a depth charge on top of us pushed us down, I do not know.' [30]

As soon as the noise from the first pattern of depth charges died down, Teddy Woodward ordered both motors to be stopped; the attacking vessel would be listening for any sound which would give away the boat's position. As the motors were stopped the submarine slid down the sloping sandy bottom to a depth of 140ft. All other auxiliary machinery was also stopped. Everything was silent. The special ballast tank named 'Q', or negative, had been blown when the boat was at the required depth during her attempted escape from the torpedo firing position. However, with 'Q' flooded, *Unbeaten* could not rise off the seabed without starting pumps to remove water from the ballast tanks in order to allow her to ascend. To start any type of machinery would immediately give away their position to the hunter listening intently above. This time spent on the bottom, being hunted by the enemy, must have brought an altogether higher level of stress, known only to those who have experienced it. However, the professionalism and tight bond among the crew would see them through. A sailor's gallows humour came into play when Jack Casemore asked if he could use the 'heads', or toilet, to give it its civilian name. The First Lieutenant said he could use the officers' heads. Jack was mid-wee when the officer put his head round the toilet door and said, 'Do it on the side of the pan, you are making HE.' [31] Was the No.1 tense or joking, or both?

Depth charge attacks have been described in many different ways by those who have experienced and lived through one. Sub-Lt. S. Dearnley from the U-Class submarine HMS/M *Universal* used this analogy: 'Being depth charged is like sitting in a tin garbage bin while someone belts the outside with a sledge hammer.' [32] One unknown submariner said that close depth charge explosions cause an unpleasant sound, like broken glass raining down the sides of the submarine. Whatever it sounded like from inside the confines of a steel tube deep under the water, it must have been bloody traumatic. Stoker R.J. Stokes served on board the *Unbeaten* and joined her on the day she was commissioned at Barrow in 1940. Ronald Stokes was on board during all the major action involving the boat, and was mentioned in despatches. Ronald was depth charged many times and said, 'You were in a situation from which there was no escape and you didn't think about it or it would drive you mad. At times it was downright terrifying.' [33] When researching this book the author conversed with the son of Ronald Stokes, who said it was clearly painful for his father to drag back thoughts of this time. He said that the best way his dad could explain to people what it was like to be depth charged was to tell them to watch the classic World War II German submarine epic *Daz Boot*. This was said to be a pretty accurate reflection of what it was like. Gus Britton, the much respected former U-Class submariner and one-time Assistant Director of the Royal Navy Submarine Museum, said shortly before his death, 'I cannot imagine anything worse than being on the receiving end of a depth-charge attack. Once you have endured a few of those every other frightening experience drops into insignificance.' [34] All said and done, one would only know what it really felt like to be hunted and on the receiving end of around 100kg of TNT detonating at irregular intervals all around you, if one had actually lived through it.

They knew she was up there, they could hear her. Could she hear them? Again the depth charges started to fall around the submarine. Between 12:44 and 13:30 a total of 27 depth charges were dropped. Inside the boat the sound was deafening. Norman Drury described this attack in his stiff-upper-lip, understated, matter-of-fact way as 'a bit alarming'.[35] As the submarine lay on the bottom, each charge caused the boat to shake violently. Dust and bits of corking, which is used for insulation, burst off the bulkheads with each blast. 'The high-tensile steel hull of the boat twanged like the string of a bow'[36], caused by the shockwave emitting from each explosive-packed ashcan. A Monthly Submarine Log details daily navigational information, employment of the crew, and engine orders. It also has an area for remarks on attacks, amongst other ancillary information. *Unbeaten's* log shows that throughout this attack, every single depth charge was counted and annotated by a shaky hand, along with a time next to it. Teddy Woodward wrote that 'the hunting destroyer had a very good directional idea of the submarines position.' [37] Each run made by the attacking vessel was straight towards the *Unbeaten*. Luckily, the majority of charges fell short, with the exception of a pattern of five depth charges that straddled the stranded boat. After each pattern the ship would stop and listen, then take off again for another run. Throughout the whole attack the ship was transmitting on a high-pitched sonic frequency. At 13:30 the last pattern was dropped. The hunter sat motionless just off the submarine's Starboard quarter, listening for any sound to indicate that her prey was still alive.

The 'Q' indicator was damaged and out of action, and it was considered too dangerous to blow. Forty-five minutes later, after a long period of silence, it was decided to start the boat's motors and IMO telemotor pump and attempt to slide out on the bottom and escape to the north. This noise was like a red rag to a bull. The destroyer immediately got underway and rang on 200 revs; she closed the submarine, eventually coming to a stop a lot closer to *Unbeaten* than before. Teddy Woodward ordered for the motors to be stopped. He then considered his next move in this very dangerous game of cat and mouse. Woodward wanted to move before dark so he could utilise the daylight to establish his position by using shore fixes. After some deliberation it was thought to be too much of a risk and would without doubt alert the surface vessel of their position. There was also a very real possibility that this destroyer could be joined by another at any time. After weighing up all the factors, Teddy Woodward decided to stay put and lay on the bottom. He was hoping the warship would drift from its position once darkness came, and lose the tiny boat on the seabed. For four hours the destroyer would occasionally turn her propellers, adjust her position and point the ship into the sea, which assisted in her station keeping.

At 20:45, Norman Drury was on the ASDIC set, assisting the young operator sat on the bench. Through his headphones, Drury heard the destroyer up revs and gradually move down the Starboard side of the submarine, from forward to aft. This time she carried on moving and proceeded eastwards. Drury, being an experienced ASDIC operator, was called into the wardroom to discuss his thoughts with the CO. A good Commanding Officer would rely on the experience of his men and Woodward was no different. Drury said he felt sure the ship had moved off. However, in his experience he felt it would be prudent for the submarine to stay put and remain silent until midnight when the attacker's crew would have a watch change. This meant there would be a new operator on the set, listening with fresh, untrained ears. Teddy Woodward agreed with his PO (Tel) and the submarine stayed silent on the seabed. The submarine's duty watch took over and the other crew members were told to turn in and keep all noise to a minimum.

The quietness after the relentless depth charge attack must have been bliss, although death could still be a few feet per second away. The uncirculated air would have been very stale and hard to breathe. Sweat would have been running off their bodies and condensation would have dripped from the bulk and deck-heads, making everything damp. You can imagine that those who smoked would really have liked a cigarette, but they would have to wait. In the early hours of 20 May the pumps were very gently run to lighten the ballast tanks, then 'Q' was slowly cracked open. The main ballast tanks one to six were blown very slowly to lift the submarine off the bottom. To get off the bottom took some time, as Jack Casemore remembers: 'I think we could have been stuck in the mud, but eventually we broke free.' [38] Once *Unbeaten* had left the seabed, her ASDIC operators listened intently for any HE, but nothing was heard. Once 'Q' was blown the crew found it hard to keep trim. The submarine bobbed up to the surface like a cork. Woodward took this opportunity to climb up the conning tower, pop the upper lid and take a quick all-round look. The sweet fresh air would have flooded the boat, rapidly replacing the stale atmosphere contained within. Thankfully all was clear. 'Full speed both'[39] was the next order from Woodward. *Unbeaten* proceeded north to clear the area and headed back to Malta. Teddy Woodward noted in the patrol log after the attack, 'We were able to have a meal and a large proportion of the ship's company turned in and slept.' He went on: 'There was a good deal of laughter, in-spite of the fact that most of us were frightened.' [40] Notably, he mentions that morale was exceptional and, crucially, there were no signs of 'reaction'. [41] It was not unheard of, during sustained depth charge attacks, for men to crack under the extreme pressure, and try to open hatches to get out.

As a result of charges exploding very close and violently shaking the submarine, several defects were reported and noted in the patrol log. About a dozen lights were put out and several light shades broken. The majority of fuse box covers were flung open. Even the amplifier of the echo sounder was thrown from its container. There was a large amount of loose articles all over the deck. Many of these items had originally been secured for sea. A bit more alarming was the fact that the Starboard stern gland had been blown in, and the porcelain insulator was cracked, which in turn caused the wireless transmitter trunk to be flooded. The insulator was vital because this is what the wireless aerial passed through when being raised up and lowered down. Any cracks could cause a leak which could flood the submarine. These porcelain insulators were very hard to come by. In fact, it is documented that the insulators in question were store robbed from submarines that were alongside Malta and fitted to the next submarine under sailing orders. There were many leaks in the air lines, and also, since the depth charging the all-important gyro was not working correctly. If this damage was not bad enough, a couple of major defects which could restrict the boat's operational capability were reported. The submarine's batteries were showing signs of a number of earths, with seven of the cells being cracked. This would require the removal of batteries, which was no easy job.

The ASDIC Dome was also caved in but luckily it was still watertight and clear of the oscillator. As it would transpire, the eager British submarine did not sink her intended target. The Italian torpedo boat did expend all her complement of depth-charges on the *Unbeaten*. The depleted *Pleiadi* then had to play catch-up with *Silvio Scaroni*, which had wisely left the area and proceeded onwards alone. All *Unbeaten's* torpedoes had missed. The *Silvio Scaroni* was later sunk by the British T-Class Group 1 submarine HMS/M *Taku*, off Benghazi, less than a month later on 12 June 1941. A battered *Unbeaten* limped back into Malta, arriving at 07:30 on 21 May 1941. She successfully returned with all hands from her first Mediterranean patrol.

However, all was not in vain. At least the crew could make their Jolly Roger and sew on a crossed guns symbol to signify some gun action. The Jolly Roger is a flag or pennant heavily linked with sea pirates of old. As a general rule all sailing ships held many different flags on board for signalling other vessels when transiting the high seas. Each flag or sequence of pennants had its own specific meaning which could be read at a distance by telescope. This form of signalling is still used by naval ships and merchant vessels around the world today.

The Jolly Roger signal flag was often black or red and may have had a design applied to it or sometimes no design at all. The name Jolly Roger is said to derive from an old French term 'Jolie Rouge', which translates as 'Pretty Red'. It was said that if a privateer or pirate ship raised a black flag, this meant that the ship being attacked should surrender with no resistance, on the assumption and that her crew would be spared. If this was not the case and the vessel being attacked resisted, then a red flag could be raised by the attacker and no mercy would be shown to the unfortunate ship's crew. The use of a Jolly Roger-type flag or pennant goes back as far as the Knights Templar. It is known that the Knights Templar order, based at Malta, were infamous for their piracy and they were known to fly the skull and crossbones. It was common, during the 17th and 18th centuries, for pirate flags to depict the devil, in order to instil fear in men on board vessels that were being attacked. Another nickname for the devil was Old Roger. This emblem eventually morphed over the years into the famed skull and crossbones, which is synonymous with pirate flags seen today.

Much later, in 1910, Admiral Sir Arthur Wilson VC was appointed to the position of First Sea Lord of the Royal Navy. Arthur Wilson was known to be very autocratic, often abrasive, and frequently inarticulate. He only remained in office for two years and then retired after differences on policy matters between himself and the then First Lord of the Admiralty Winston Churchill. It is interesting to note that after several world navies, including the Royal Navy, had adopted the new-fangled submarine, Admiral Wilson was quoted as saying, 'Submarines are underhand, unfair, and damned un-English.' [42] He also said that he would convince the British Admiralty to have the crews of enemy submarines unlucky enough to be captured during wartime hanged as pirates. This statement obviously appealed to a matelot's sense of gallows humour and was later acted upon by a then young Lieutenant Commander, Max Horton. Horton was the Commanding Officer of HMS/M *E9*. His E-Class submarine was the first to fly the Jolly Roger on return to port after sinking the World War I German Cruiser *Hela* and the destroyer *S-116* in 1914.

This fine tradition of hoisting the Jolly Roger stuck and carried on throughout World War I and all the way through World War II. The ritual is still observed today, as it was then, with submarines hoisting a locally manufactured Jolly Roger when entering port, and lowering it on the first night alongside. There soon followed a code of symbols to signify a submarine's success in battle, which was common to all World War II British-made Jolly Rogers. Several British submarines often encountered situations which deserved a new symbol and some were pretty creative. *Unbeaten* was no different. Her Jolly Roger was quite full by the end of her service, as we will find out as the book goes on. Lieutenant Commander Max Horton, hero of World War I, later became Admiral Sir Max Kennedy Horton and Commander-in-Chief of the Western Approaches. He was much respected by the submarine service in which he served.

Teddy Woodward would have gone ashore on arrival at Malta that day to hand in his patrol report. Shrimp Simpson would read the narrative and add his comments and recommendations to the report. It would then be passed to Captain (S1) on board the submarine depot vessel HMS *Medway*. Finally the document and any memorandums would be passed to the Commander-in-Chief, Mediterranean Station for comment. On the occasion of this report C-in-C Med replied with just a short, two-bullet-pointed answer stating that flashless propellant was an important requirement for the 12-pounder gun. However, he followed up this observation with: 'Credit is due to Lieutenant E.A. Woodward RN and the Ship's Company of HMS *Unbeaten* for this successful and coolly conducted patrol in the face of considerable hazard and difficulty.' [43] Captain S.M. Raw, on board the submarine depot ship *Medway,* wrote slightly more and went into more detail about the poorly updated charts held on board the *Unbeaten*. He concluded that a 'special effort should be made to capture a set of Italian charts which should cover the coastal routes of North Africa'[44]. He said that British charts were hopelessly inadequate for the close inshore tactics adopted by British submarines, and that cases of submarine torpedoes striking the seabed in apparently deep water were all too frequent.

Shrimp Simpson's reply was a whole three pages long and went into more detail about *Unbeaten's* attacks on enemy vessels and the attack on her.

Also amongst a detailed analysis of the patrol, Shrimp said that ratings should not be wearing heavy boots and that an application had been made to the *Medway* for the purchase of 300 pairs of sandals, which would be reasonably silent and non-skid, and prevent foot rot. It was also concluded by Shrimp that *Unbeaten's* torpedoes may have struck the bottom due to Servo Motor failure, and a report to this effect was to be forwarded. Simpson summarised by saying, 'The variety of incidents and hazards encountered were dealt with coolly and with good submarine sense, and much credit is due to Lieutenant Woodward in the conduct of *Unbeaten's* first patrol in the Central Mediterranean.' [45] The crew of *Unbeaten* would not embark on their next patrol until 11 June. This gave the Ship's Company and shore staff a period in which to rectify all the numerous defects caused by the depth charging. They would also embark fresh torpedoes to replace the ones which had been expended. This was a hazardous task in itself. Around this time, the *Upholder* was bringing on torpedoes when one of her weapons had what is called a 'hot run'. This was not a good time for the crew of *Upholder*, who were jubilant only hours before after returning from a successful patrol. Being alongside also gave *Unbeaten's* men some much deserved time ashore in Malta, to relax and unwind after their exhausting first patrol. Norman Drury remembered, in an interview he did for the Imperial War Museum many years later, that 'it was not unusual for a submarine to fail to return from its first patrol'.[46] *Unbeaten* was lucky indeed, or was she?

Back in Great Britain during June 1941, Patrick Blackett, a renowned sailor, scientist, and socialist was seconded to the Admiralty as a Director of Operational Research. His job was to head a team whose task it was to develop new procedures and equipment for use in the hunting and attacking of U-boats from the air. His appointment would have a direct effect on *Unbeaten*, although no one knew it yet. Meanwhile, in the Mediterranean, *Unbeaten's* second patrol would also be an eventful one, but unlike her first. This patrol would see one of her crew sail from Malta never to return.

8

WE SHALL COME THROUGH

'When I look back on the perils overcome, and on the mountain waves in which the gallant ship has driven, when I remember all that has gone wrong and remember all that has gone right, I feel sure that we have no need to fear the tempest. Let it roar, let it rage, we shall come through.' [47]

Winston Churchill, May 1941

The regular bombings which Malta was enduring courtesy of the Regia Aeronautica and Luftwaffe were still on-going in early June 1941, but were eased somewhat by the Royal Air Force. On the 6th, more reinforcements eventually made it to the island. The much needed aircraft came in the form of RAF Hurricanes transported by, and flown from, HMS *Ark Royal* in what was named *Operation Rocket*. Such was the urgency to provide air support for the besieged island that many of these aircraft were still in their green and brown paint scheme circa Battle of Britain. This re-supply was swiftly followed by *Operation Tracer*, which saw another 42 Hurricanes land on the island. These aircraft flew from the carrier HMS *Victorious*. A total of 46 Hurricanes took off during that operation. However, two crashed, one ditched in the sea and one went missing and reappeared in North Africa. Four more supply operations would take place during the month of June, and all were vitally important. Despite the death and danger from above, Jolly Jack Tar still managed to get ashore.

Valletta and Selma were favourite matelot haunts. Many submarines had specific bars which they frequented regularly. Bars were plentiful and had names like the Smiling Prince, White Star and the Egyptian Queen. The only way to get to Manoel Island, where the First Submarine Flotilla was tied up, was to cross over a small bridge, leading from a road which had many bars along its dusty thoroughfare. These bars were usually the last stop for some crew before returning back on board their respective boats. This valuable time spent alongside also afforded some crew rotation. *Unbeaten's* No.1, Lt. Gibbs, was relieved by Lt. Aston Dalzell Piper RNR, known to his chums as 'Peter Piper'. Aston Piper had been a merchant Seaman before the war and had joined the Royal Navy Reserve. He once had reason to visit a submarine early in his RNR career and this inspired him to join the submarine service at the start of war. There was also a group of reservists known as RNVR not to be confused with the RNR. The Royal Navy Volunteer Reserve mainly drew members from Hostilities Only ratings. Although in 1958 the RNR and RNVR eventually amalgamated. There was a rather unflattering saying around at the time which was used to comically describe the differences between the three forms of Royal Navy sailor. It went like this: Royal Naval Officers were said to be gentlemen pretending to be seamen; Royal Naval Reserve Officers were seamen pretending to be gentlemen, and finally Royal Naval Volunteer Reserve Officers were neither but pretending to be both. Lt. Piper however was an experienced submarine officer by the time he arrived at *Unbeaten* having joined directly from serving as the Navigating Officer on board HMS *Ursula*, one of the early Unity-Class submarines. This next patrol from Malta between 11 and 22 June was not Piper's first Mediterranean patrol and certainly would not be his last.

Jack Casemore had his regular run ashore oppos or friends; he could often be found drinking with his good pals Thomas G. Sturman and Dickie Dowdell. The last time they had had a run ashore together was in Gibraltar. Norman Drury remembers Leading Stoker Sturman as having fairly recently joined *Unbeaten* after having visited Freetown, Sierra Leone not long before. However, during a night out in Malta, Tom Sturman had complained to Jack of suffering from very bad headaches. Jack told him he should go and see the 'Scab Lifter', or doctor. The next day, Sturman went to the sick bay ashore and saw the Surgeon Lieutenant Commander. He promptly said to the Leading Stoker: 'I know your trouble, get back down the boat and lay off the beer.' [48] The doctor did, however, turn him in and he was sent to Ghain Tuffieha Camp sick quarters. This hospital facility was located on Malta's north coast and had fantastic beaches. Jack said that when he asked his friend how he got on with the doc, Tom Sturman prophetically replied, 'I would rather die first than go and see him again.' [49]

At 13:45 on 11 June 1941, *Unbeaten* sailed from Manoel Island, having had repairs conducted on the damage caused by the depth charging received during the last patrol. Leading Stoker Sturman returned back on board, having told the doctors that he was perfectly well. He had especially requested not to miss the patrol. The submarine sailed to carry out independent exercises and attacks in the company of the Hunt Class Minesweeper HMS *Abingdon*. Early that evening, *Unbeaten* returned to harbour to conduct a compass swing. This was where the boat picked up a buoy forward, and the vessel would swing around the buoy as the tide changed. Fixes would be taken over a period of time by taking compass readings of various points onshore. These would then be used to calibrate the compass. If the compass swing was constrained by time then a tug or small vessel would push or pull the boat around the buoy as required. That evening once the very important compasses were correct *Unbeaten* slipped the buoy and sailed again.

Patrol area 'Mike' was the destination. This area was to the east of Sicily and to the south of the Straits of Messina. During the afternoon of the next day, *Unbeaten* received signal traffic telling her to alter course and head for a group of independently routed enemy ships which were leaving Messina. The boat was told to close as quickly as possible; however, the speed had to be consistent with the charging of her batteries. She eventually reached her required position later that evening. The morning of Friday 13 June broke to clear skies and calm weather. These conditions may sound nice but are in fact perilous for submarines. There were a lot of aircraft in the area and, combined with the weather conditions and sea state, it was necessary for *Unbeaten* to remain deep to avoid detection. She came up every 20 minutes or so for a quick look round and then retired to the relative safety of the depths. One destroyer was spotted, but too late due to the heat haze. Had the ASDIC conditions been better, the Command may have been able to launch an attack sooner but it was now deemed not possible. It is known that sea temperature can also detrimentally affect sound waves passing through the water and degrade the HE; indeed, it has been proved that ASDIC worked far better the colder waters of the Atlantic.

That evening, *Unbeaten* was ordered to retire to at least 25 nautical miles from the coast to charge her batteries. Overnight and into the morning of the 14th, she had to crash dive to avoid detection from an unknown aircraft. At around 01:50, *Unbeaten* surfaced again but by this time her crew had made a grim discovery. Previously that last evening, Tom Sturman had again complained of a headache and was turned into his bunk in the fore ends of the boat. The Coxswain, Mickey Harding, who was described by Norman Drury as 'a raw-boned southern Irishman, and very competent'[50], had given Tom some hot water bottles as some comfort. Norman Drury says he remembers the Coxswain being woken by someone telling him that Leading Stoker Sturman was not well. When they went to check him, Norman touched his hand and the poor man was cold and wet. Norman knew he was dead.

The crew took Sturman to the wardroom and they relentlessly tried in vain to administer artificial respiration. They persisted until 03:00 that morning but his body was quite cold and rigor mortis had set in. Teddy Woodward wrote in the patrol report: 'This tragic experience passed gloom in *Unbeaten* but it is felt that everything possible was done to save his life.' [51] Unfortunately, the submarine was on patrol and would not arrive back in harbour for another nine days. The confines of a submarine were no place to keep a dead body, so Leading Stoker Sturman was to be buried at sea. In fine naval tradition the body was placed into a hammock. The crew searched the boat for lumps of steel, old spanners and the like, to weigh the body down in the water. Jack Casemore remembers helping the 2nd Coxswain Jock Forbes tie the heavy spanners, purloined from the engine room, to the legs and body of Tom Sturman with cod line. The hammock was then stitched up around the body. In the Royal Navy of old, it was tradition that the last stitch would have been passed through the nose of the deceased, through the septum, to ensure the man was properly dead. This may not have been the case that night but this outdated practice was actually recorded as having been carried out during World War II.

Once the hammock was sewn up and lashed, it was transferred up through the conning tower to the bridge. The submarine was trimmed down as low as possible. Teddy Woodward read a short prayer from a prayer book and then, at precisely 04:13 on 14 June, Leading Stoker Sturman's body was lowered into the sea. Once his body was in the water and clear of the submarine, the boat dived immediately and slipped off into the night. Several people had opinions of what caused the death of Leading Stoker Sturman. Norman Drury was convinced it was malaria that killed the unfortunate man. This disease was rife among sailors and Sturman had recently been to a country with high instances of malaria. Because there was no body for doctors to inspect, it was difficult to pinpoint the cause of death. It was the opinion of medical officers that a haemorrhage of the brain had killed the man. This was said to have been aggravated by service in submarines, pertaining to the various air pressures in which he spent his daily life. The whole crew was shocked by his untimely death. On the *Unbeaten's* return to the Great Britain, Teddy Woodward did make it his business to visit with the wife of Tom Sturman. It was understandably a sad time for everyone.

For the rest of this second patrol the weather remained calm with light airs. Because of these ideal anti-submarine hunting conditions, enemy aircraft filled the skies. It was noted in the patrol log that *Unbeaten's* crew had sighted several Italian Caproni aircraft, of which there were many variants. Other sightings consisted of a couple of Caproni CA309 or Ghibli twin-engine transport aircraft, and the obligatory CANT, which was a triple-engine Italian floatplane. Teddy Woodward concluded that the north and south passages usually taken by enemy convoys were no longer being used. He deduced that the convoys were being routed closer to the Sicilian coast, which afforded the enemy better air support and protection from submarine attack. Therefore, to see if they could find any targets of interest, *Unbeaten* moved closer to land and into the lion's mouth. Woodward's decision to move paid off. Early on the morning of 16 June, masts of a convoy were spotted to the east of Taormina, and they were heading southwards. It was said the convoy consisted of three small merchant vessels and a liner. The liner was thought to have been either the Italian passenger liner, now troop ship, *Oceania* or her sister ship *Neptunia.* These vessels were said to each have two masts and one funnel and a displacement of between 19,000 and 20,000 tons. The possible liner was moving at high speed and zig-zagging violently, causing her to heel over drastically.

Woodward had to make some quick calculations in his head and relay a firing solution to the torpedo officer. The liner's unpredictable and erratic movements made formulating any firing estimates difficult. Four torpedoes were fired in a spread equal to three times the target length and set at a depth of between 14 and 16 feet. The tin fish must have hit something, or so the crew thought. At 5 minutes and 50 seconds, and 5 minutes and 56 seconds consecutively after the torpedoes were let loose, two loud explosions were heard. The running range of the torpedoes fired was approximately 7,500 yards. Not long after the torpedoes were fired, HE was heard, approaching fast. A pattern of nine depth charges was dropped by what was described as a single screw anti-submarine trawler. Owing to the large amount of enemy activity in the area, from the air and sea, it was decided that *Unbeaten* would remain deep and clear the location.

By midday, *Unbeaten* was 10 nautical miles from the initial attack position. Woodward wanted to come up and take a peek through the periscope. Shortly afterwards, at 12:15, two heavy explosions erupted close to *Unbeaten*. It was hoped that this was the liner in her death throes. Sadly, this was not to be the case. Extensive research of the Italian naval archives by naval researcher Platon Alexiades concludes that the convoy attacked at long range by *Unbeaten* on 16 June 1941 consisted of the merchant vessels *Spezia, Trapani* and *Livorno*. These vessels were escorted by the armed merchant cruiser *Citta di Genova*. This merchant vessel was used as a troop ship and did indeed have two masts and one funnel. When comparing a photograph of this ship with the *Oceania* and *Neptunia*, the three vessels look very similar. Unfortunately, it was reported later that all four torpedoes fired by *Unbeaten* had missed. An escorting aircraft, most likely a CANT, did drop two bombs and claimed to have hit the attacking *N93*. These were probably the two explosions that rattled the submarine at 12:15 but thankfully *Unbeaten* escaped undamaged. The *Citta di Genova*, however, was eventually sunk towards the end of 1943 by the British submarine HMS/M *Tigris*.

Unbeaten remained well clear of the area all of the following day and night. On 18 June 1941, she proceeded towards Benghazi, an area taken by Rommel back in early April. However, soon after she set course towards Libya, a message was received telling her to turn around and attempt to intercept the Vichy French destroyer *Vauquelin*. This Axis-collaborating vessel was expected to pass through the Straits of Messina heading southbound. No contact between the ship and submarine appears to have been reported by *Unbeaten* in her patrol log. In a twist of fate, by the end of November 1942, the *Vauquelin* would lie at the bottom of Toulon Harbour along with the majority of the French fleet. They were very deliberately scuttled, sitting upright on the seabed, with their masts and funnels protruding out of the oily water.

As *Unbeaten* approached Malta early in the morning of Sunday 22 June 1941, after concluding her eventful second patrol, she was directed towards Grand Harbour, specifically French Creek and No. 2 dry dock. *Unbeaten* was to have some repairs which required her to be out of the water. Once the submarine was guided into the confines of the dry dock, the giant caisson was placed across the entrance and the water drained out. No. 2 dry dock is similar to other dry docks in the world. When all the water has gone the dry dock looks reminiscent of a large Roman amphitheatre. The many carved rock steps extend steeply upwards, with the height of each step getting wider as they continue towards the top of the dock. *Unbeaten* had only just settled that evening onto the wooden chocks, which supported her when the water had finally drained out, when an important message was received.

Information had been passed to Naval Command which suggested that a large Italian troop convoy was due to set sail from Naples. The catalyst for providing the Allies with this information had started in early June 1941. A brilliant breakthrough in combating the war against the Italian Navy in the Mediterranean had occurred. The secret ULTRA organisation had been able to pass Italian convoy movements to Allied vessels because of the successful decryption of the Hagelin rotor-based cipher machine called the C-38m. The codes of this machine were broken by a team of cryptologists at Bletchley Park housed in Hut 4, led by Bernard Wilson, father of the British TV presenter and motoring journalist Quentin Wilson. By the height of the Mediterranean campaign in 1941, Bletchley was deciphering 2,000 Italian Hagelin messages a day. These messages allowed the Royal Navy Command to successfully place ships and submarines in the path of convoys and intercept and attack at will. The tide of war against the Italian Navy was changing.

The order was given by the Commander-in-Chief, Mediterranean to put all available submarines to sea without delay. The dockyard workers at Malta were definitely a group of unsung heroes who worked tirelessly throughout the siege. The workers comprised a mixture of British civilian engineers, RN personnel and Maltese staff. If it was not for their efforts, often in extreme adversity, many vessels would not have returned to sea. On this occasion the dock was flooded again quickly and the Manager of the Constructive Department, known as MCD, and his staff were particularly helpful in getting *Unbeaten* out of the dock and back to sea in a timely manner. The submarine left the island again on the evening of 24 June, only two days after returning from her last patrol. She would head north to join the submarines *Urge* and *Upholder*, who were already in position. During the first dog watch of the next day, many explosions were heard by *Unbeaten*. These explosions, it was said, heralded the approaching Italian convoy. It was not uncommon for the Italians to drop depth charges ahead of their convoys willy-nilly, in the hope that this would deter a submarine attack – when in reality it just gave away their position. The location of *Unbeaten's* patrol area was approximately 084° from Cape Passero at 42 nautical miles. She was placed there in anticipation that the convoy, consisting of four large merchantmen and five destroyers, may transit through her patrol area.

Later in the evening of the 25th, *Unbeaten* surfaced to take a good all-round look. The visibility was very hazy and down to one nautical mile. The lookouts did sight a small destroyer at a range of around 400 yards. This, they deduced, confirmed in all probability that the convoy was indeed in *Unbeaten's* proximity. However, the submarine was not in a good position to attack, mainly due to the poor weather conditions, so the boat dived. Later that evening and into the next morning, the submarine came up to periscope depth and then surfaced. Once *Unbeaten* broke the flat calm still of the Med, the upper lid was opened and the Commanding Officer climbed onto the dripping wet bridge, followed by the lookouts. A heavy swell was noticed by the crew, a swell which could have been made by fast moving vessels passing close by. The visibility had now increased to two nautical miles and the lookouts heard what sounded like the fast engine of an E-boat. *Unbeaten* was crash dived immediately; all the men up top cleared the bridge and slid down the conning tower ladder as quickly as possible. Slamming the stirrup and clip fastenings in-place as they went, effectively sealing the watertight hatches. None of them wanted to be trapped outside the boat when she went under. At around 04:00 on the 26th, the submarine surfaced again and received wireless signal traffic informing them that the enemy convoy had been attacked only eight nautical miles from her position. Still on the surface, Woodward steered the boat towards the expected course of the convoy to investigate. By the forenoon watch, only an anti-submarine trawler was seen, searching in the distance. The Command decided that the convoy must have passed them by or turned back to Naples. In fact, the convoy was attacked by British Fairy Swordfish aircraft close to *Unbeaten's* position. Two of the vessels were torpedoed by the aircraft, and it seems that the remaining ships turned north-east and were later spotted in Taranto Harbour. Shortly afterwards, *Unbeaten* was recalled to Malta, entering harbour on Friday 27 June at 07:00 and ending her third patrol.

The submarine and her crew would remain alongside for the next ten days. This gave the men time to restore, fix any outstanding defects and, more importantly, have some well-earned rest and relaxation. This was easier said than done on an island which was on the receiving end of one of the most concentrated bombing campaigns in World War II. Malta continued to be the focus of the Axis attention from sea and air. Italian and German bombing raids occurred with tremendous regularity. Shipping lanes were regularly mined by both ship and aircraft-laid mines. The war was quite literally on their doorstep. Throughout the month of June 1941 there were 67 raids, of which 25 were at night. On 30 June, during this tumultuous time, Shrimp Simpson was promoted. He would now be known as Captain Senior Officer Submarines, Malta. The new rank did not change the man; he still had a job to do, and do it he did.

Soon it was time for the submarine and her rested crew to leave Malta and embark on their fourth patrol. Things on the domestic front would be slightly different on this patrol. The boat was only being victualed for one meal per day per man. The reason for this is not known by the author but one can surmise it may have had something to do with the reduced availability of food on the island during the siege. It looks as if *Unbeaten* was trialling this enforced food regime, as Woodward reported back his thoughts on the matter upon completion of the patrol. The boat let go her securing lines and sailed out of the harbour on the evening of 8 July 1941. Her destination was patrol area 'L' – Lima was a rectangle area 60NM by 50NM in the vicinity of Lampedusa. This is the largest island in the Italian Pelagie Islands and lies approximately 95 nautical miles south-west of Malta. That evening, prior to leaving the Malta areas, *Unbeaten* carried out a couple of dummy torpedo attacks on the Minesweeper HMS *Abingdon*. This practice was mainly for the benefit of the newly joined 1st Lt., Aston Piper, who carried out the first attack on the Minesweeper just to keep his hand in. Later that night, the lookouts standing on *Unbeaten's* bridge witnessed a British fighter aircraft shooting down an enemy bomber. The burning aircraft thundered into the sea in the minefield area Q.B.B.95 over 10NM from *Unbeaten*. The impact must have been hard as the patrol log says 'it was decided not to close the crash area as it appeared there would be no survivors'.[52]

When nearing their designated patrol area the crew heard a peculiar phenomenon. It appeared to be a loud hydrophone effect (HE) which surrounded the whole submarine. No one could tell what the weird noise was. During the research for this book the author has come across lots of mentions of strange, unexplained undersea noises heard by submariners – like the aptly named North Sea farts for instance, which submariners often report hearing off the Skagerrak area near Norway. Or a sound like gravel being thrown over the boat, which has been reported in the Med. Whatever it was, it was bloody strange, but analysis of the sound couldn't get in the way of the boat's main purpose, which was to patrol the waters looking for enemy shipping.

On 10 July, she was ordered to intercept a southbound enemy convoy in a given position. The submarines *P33* and *Ursula* were also sailed to form a line with *Unbeaten* across the expected transit route of the convoy. Shortly after getting into position, *Ursula* had to drop out and return to Malta with generator failure. *Unbeaten* and her original namesake *P33* continued the intercept. On the 12th, as usual, the enemy convoy's arrival was preceded by the sound of sporadic depth charging; this was heard all through the first dog watch. The convoy passed close to Kerkennah, which is a group of islands lying off the east coast of Tunisia. The convoy was unfortunately to the west of *Unbeaten*, and out of sight, so no attack was made. Over the next four days nothing really happened. The crew heard some distant explosions and sighted several enemy aircraft at long range. A submarine patrol was not all action and terror. Some days passed without incident and were fairly boring by comparison.

As alluded to earlier, the domestic conditions on board a U-Class submarine were pretty basic. There were only two wash basins, one for officers and one for ratings. The same division goes for the two heads, which a man has to gain special permission to use when the boat is submerged the water. The sequence of events required to use heads was very complicated for the uninitiated. They say a wrong turn of a valve could sink the submarine. The accommodation was not much better. The small Petty Officers' mess, through which young Jan Wright was carried by her father on commissioning day, was where the Senior Rates would sleep and live when not on watch. The Wardrobe or Wardroom where the officers resided was next to the POs' mess and was no bigger. The rest of the crew lived and slept in the fore-ends or Torpedo Stowage Compartment (TSC). They had to share this salubrious location with the food stores, spare equipment and, more alarmingly, the actual live torpedoes themselves.

After dark on the evening of the 14th, the submarine surfaced and made her way towards patrol area X-ray, as directed. The boat remained on the surface until dawn then dived. Closing the coast towards Marsa Sabrata Libya, on that afternoon of 15 July 1941, Woodward sighted two schooners anchored in the Marsa Zuaga Roads, one of which was the Italian Auxiliary Minesweeper *Nettuno*. The two-masted vessels were sheltered by off-lying shoals. Because of these sandbars lurking under the shallow water, a torpedo attack was impossible. However, Woodward was keen to have a go with something. Each ship looked to be about 500 tons and heavily laden with supplies of some sort – a peach of a target. *Unbeaten* retired to deeper water and prepared for gun action. After creeping to within 700 yards of her quarry, at precisely 20:00 the boat surfaced and the guns crew swarmed over the conning tower. It is recorded in the patrol log that a total of 43 rounds were fired. It was said that one schooner was hit 15 times and the other 5 times. Several small Tunney fishing vessels bore witness to the attack and one Tunney was only 20 yards from *Unbeaten* when the stealthy submarine punched through the surface of the sea. Imagine being on board that small boat when, without warning, a dark shape surfaces right next to you and starts spewing out gunfire. The muzzle flash must have been blinding.

Only ten minutes later the attack was over. One schooner was seen heeling over at a 30° angle and looking down by the stern. Woodward believed this vessel eventually sank and that the other was badly damaged. *Unbeaten* dived and cleared the area, heading north. For the rest of the evening the submarine was hunted, firstly by aircraft and then by an E-Boat. The 'E' stood for 'enemy'. However, the German Admiralty referred to them as S-Boats, 'S' for *schnell*, meaning 'fast'. *N93* made her way back towards Malta via a route ordered by Senior Officer Submarines. On the morning of the 19th, *Unbeaten* surfaced when approaching the Malta areas. Without warning and seemingly out of nowhere, six violent explosions erupted around the boat, sending mushrooms of spray high in the air. The cause of the detonations, which rained down from the early morning sky, was in fact six high-explosive bombs dropped from an Italian aircraft. The guilty aeroplane had just carried out a bombing raid on Malta and was jettisoning its pay load, lightening itself in order to make a fast getaway. Notwithstanding this near miss, the charmed submarine and her crew arrived safely back alongside at 07:00. In his report post-patrol, the newly appointed Captain Simpson said that the gun attack on the schooners must have made a satisfactory impression on the audience of Tunnies in the vicinity. Once again the Italian archives are not very clear. They say that the schooners that were attacked on 15 July were apparently local vessels. The names of the two boats were not mentioned in the Italian documents. It was said that only one vessel was hit and three of its crew were wounded, but it does not say if any vessels were sunk. Whether the Italian accounts of the time are to be believed is still open for debate.

Woodward concluded his report on this, the fourth patrol of *Unbeaten* from Malta, firstly by writing about the 'no meat during the day' routine. The menu was said to have been adequate, with plenty of salad and fruit in particular. This may have been because a variety of fruit was grown on the island, as it is today, and was therefore more readily available. The crew may have been able to eat the following fruit: sweet peaches, grapefruit, tangerines, oranges and juicy melons to name a few. Teddy Woodward did caveat this by saying that a variety of tinned fish would be appreciated if available. The report ended with a recommendation that the locally made 'Periscope Height Indicator' proved very useful during the patrol, especially when working inshore in calm weather. A submarine's periscope wake or feather is a dead giveaway of a boat's position and can be seen at a great distance from the air. Anything which reduces this would be very beneficial. Woodward went on to say that 'if this item could be made easily then it should be used in all British submarines'.[53]

Sad times would befall the crew of *Unbeaten* not long after they got alongside. Another U-Class submarine was overdue. Jack Casemore remembered, with some emotion, that *Unbeaten* had only been back at

Malta a couple of days when they heard that *Union* was indeed overdue and had been sunk, taking with her all 32 crew. One of the more harrowing tasks a matelot may have to carry out from time to time is to empty the locker or lockers of deceased shipmates. This removal of a man's kit and personal effects by shipmates or other sailors still happens today. Jack and three others from *Unbeaten* were given the task emptying the stowage's of the Seamen and Stokers from the *Union*. Once they had located the men's lockers within the Lazaretto accommodation, they then had to cut off the locks and start packing the deceased submariners' belongings into their kit bags for the last time. Jack said that when opening the lockers they were often confronted with photographs and letters from wives, girlfriends and mothers, as well as personal clothing and mementos these men had in their possession. Many of *Union's* crew were friends of the chaps from *Unbeaten*. As Jack was going about this unpleasant task he said that he wondered how the poor bastard died and if the *Unbeaten* would very soon face the same fate and if some other submariner would then be stowing his personal things in his kitbag. It transpired that on 20 July 1941, *Union* had unsuccessfully attacked a northbound convoy off Pantelleria. She was sighted clearly under the limped water and immediately attacked by the Italian torpedo boat *Circe* with depth charges and by an aircraft with bombs. *Union* could not escape and was sunk. The consort which met with *Unbeaten* when she sailed from Dartmouth for the 'Iron Ring' back in 1940 was no more.

Unbeaten's following two patrols, numbers five and six, were fairly uneventful when compared to her previous missions. However, some aspects of the crew's activities during these patrols are worthy of note. It was Monday 28 July when *Unbeaten* sailed for her fifth patrol. Only a few hours after sailing did the crew pick up the familiar sound of a recognisable HE. It was undoubtedly the exploding sounds heralding a passing Italian convoy. The submarine was directed towards patrol area 'Juliet'. This location was an area between Pantellaria and Lampedusa. Her main objective was to intercept a fast-moving, northbound enemy convoy. This was described as a large convoy, consisting of three escorting destroyers, protecting four fairly large merchant vessels. Every time *Unbeaten* got herself into a good position for an intercept and attack, the convoy altered course. These changes in the convoy's direction occurred several times over the course of many hours. The Commanding Officer brought the boat up to periscope depth for an all-round look. Enemy aircraft were spotted close overhead. Teddy Woodward did not initially put two and two together until he realised that the aircraft had, in all probability, spotted the submarine, which when seen from the air cast a dark shadow resembling that of a giant killer shark, lurking in the shallow, clear waters. He didn't think he had been seen. He wrongly assumed that because no enemy destroyers were detached to attack the submarine, that therefore *Unbeaten* was invisible. The enemy simply avoided the British boat by skirting around its position after being warned and directed by the aircraft. These tactics had been employed before by the Italians, as reported by *Ursula* and *Upright*. It appeared that the enemy did not consider it in their interest to detach any vessels to hunt the submarine. *Unbeaten* was then ordered to move to patrol area 'Hotel'.

The next four days were uneventful. On 5 August the crew heard distinct HE which continued for 40 minutes. *Unbeaten*, now on the surface, altered course to close the noise. It was around 22:00, the moon was full and the visibility was exceptionally good. But inexplicably, nothing was sighted in the direction of the HE, nothing at all. Woodward did note, with some reflection, that the *Unbeaten's* location was only 15NM from the position they were in on their fourth patrol, the one when they heard that strange all-round HE. This noise has never been accounted for to this day.

During the next couple of days, *Unbeaten* was informed about a convoy heading her way. However, on the evening of the 6th, and much to the frustration of Woodward, anti-aircraft fire was sighted. The submarine altered course to intercept the probable convoy at best speed. She headed towards the AA fire, which lasted for 50 minutes. By the time *Unbeaten* had arrived it was all over. What was left of the enemy convoy had retired to the north. All that remained in that position was a burning wreck. A half-mile area of sea surface was alight. There was said to have been a strong smell of paraffin and floating among the dancing flames was wreckage, consisting of barrels and bits and pieces, strewn everywhere. The successful dusk attack was carried out by Swordfish aircraft from the Fleet Air Arm No. 830 Squadron. The pilots who carried out the attack estimated that two enemy vessels were sunk. The crew of *Unbeaten*, and especially Teddy Woodward, felt robbed. This was the second time the eager submarine had felt denied an attack because of the aircraft of the Malta-based No. 830 Squadron. Such was the competiveness of inter-service rivalry. *Unbeaten* arrived at Malta on 8 August having not fired a single shot.

Once alongside, Woodward handed in his short patrol report. It fell to Shrimp to pass his comment first. It was then sent to Captain (S1) S.M. Raw. He commented: 'LT Woodward's annoyance at being baulked of his targets by successful F.A.A. attacks is understandable' but, as Captain (S) Malta (Shrimp) points out 'it is not possible to arrange the happy state of affairs the *Unbeaten* would like'.[54] The ever-practical Woodward concluded his fifth patrol report by saying, 'Submarine sweaters should be of a dark colour in war time as the white sweaters show up when worn by lookouts at night.' [55] This was of course a very fair comment, and a typical Woodward observation. With the passing of every patrol, *Unbeaten's* Commanding Officer was always striving to improve and adapt procedures to make a real difference. This was the mark of the man and this attention to detail has become apparent during the author's analysis of his well-thought-out patrol log entries.

9

THE DEVIL'S DEVICE

The 'tin fish', 'kipper' or 'eel', as the Germans named it, has been mentioned many times in this book, but with little aplomb. It is correct to say that without some form of offensive weaponry a submarine would be virtually useless during periods of conflict. The weapon of choice for a submarine has an aged pedigree, with the first prototype being developed and produced by Robert Whitehead in 1866. The weapon in question is the infamous torpedo. Whitehead was greeted with a healthy form of scepticism and even opposition early in his career. Some Royal Navy gunnery officers of the day dismissed his invention and called it 'the device of the Devil'.[56] The Royal Navy's relationship with the 'terrible weapon' started in August 1870. The torpedo's British inventor, Robert Whitehead, sailed on board a Royal Navy man-of-war HMS *Oberon* to showcase his latest invention, a new variant of the torpedo. A select band of officers was also embarked to witness the trials for the Royal Navy. One of the officers present has already appeared in this book, being mentioned for his outspoken beliefs about the morality of submarine warfare. The officer in question was the then Lieutenant Arthur Wilson of 'dammed un-English weapon' fame and he who would eventually become First Sea Lord of the Royal Navy. The trials he witnessed of this underwater and therefore unseen messenger of death may go some way to explain why Wilson thought the submarine, and all it stood for, was an underhand weapon and just not cricket. Good old naval gun fire had been the overwhelming show of fire power in the Victorian Navy.

The early British A-, B- and C-Class submarines built between 1902 and 1910 required some form of armament and torpedoes were again the weapon of choice. These boats were designed around the earlier Holland submarine concept. Holland One was the first Royal Navy submarine to be fitted with a torpedo. The subsequent A-, B- and C-Class submarines were known as 'Fisher's toys', a nickname derived from Admiral Sir John Fisher, who was a fierce advocate of utilising a submarine in a war footing. These early British boats were fitted with two 18-inch bow torpedo tubes and carried four 'kippers'. In 1904, the insightful Fisher wrote, 'The submarine will prevent any fleet remaining at sea continuously. It is astounding to me how the very best amongst us fail to recognise the vast impending revolution in Naval warfare and Naval strategy that the submarine will accomplish.'[57] Over the following 108 years the torpedo would continue to be developed with many different variants, while always remaining faithful to the initial design concept. The torpedo is a versatile weapon and can be easily be transported and utilised to inflict death and destruction by launching from aircraft and surface vessels alike.

Around the time of World War II, a single torpedo would have cost the Admiralty approximately £2,000. In today's money that would be around £79,000 per torpedo. This is a huge figure at nearly 40 times what it cost back then – in 1940, £2,000 was a vast amount of money. The torpedo was being manufactured at this time in the RNFT factory at Greenock and also commercially built by the Whitehead torpedo company based at Weymouth, Dorset. In 1940, towards the end of her build, and in subsequent trials, *Unbeaten* was complemented with the Mk. VIII torpedo variant. She carried between eight to ten torpedoes when embarking on patrols. Each weapon had a speed of approximately 40 knots and weighed in at 2,253lbs. The torpedo could travel out to a range of 7,000 yards at this speed and packed a charge of 750lbs of tri-nitro-toluene (TNT) in its high-explosive nose. This HE was sometimes substituted with Amatol. After 1943, Torpex was introduced as an explosive. This Mk. VIII variant of the torpedo was first introduced in 1928. Surprisingly, an only slightly modified version of this was still being used by the Royal Navy as recently as 1982, and played an active part in the Falklands conflict. The Mk. VIII was only withdrawn from the service of the Royal Navy in the early 1990s.

To understand the powerful capabilities of the Mk. VIII torpedo we must understand how it was constructed and how worked. The Mk. VIII was manufactured in four sections. The 6.5-metre weapon was made up of the head, fore-body, aft-body and tail. The whole weapon contained around 6,000 parts. The torpedo was pushed through the water by a propeller which was turned by a shaft in the tail section. The torpedo also had a gyroscopic rudder controller to keep it on course. The propeller shaft was driven by a Brotherhood burner-cycle (BC) engine, which was contained inside the aft-body section. This engine design was revolutionary. It ran by superheating pressurized air by burning a small amount of combustible hydrocarbon liquid fuel. This volatile mixture was then fed into the engine, mixed with more fuel and injected into each cylinder. A torpedo was initially sent on its way by a blast of compressed air. Once clear of the tube it would run on its own BC engine. The aft-body also housed a hydrostatic depth control which was set by the submarine's torpedo man as required prior to firing. The hydrostatic control kept the torpedo at a constant depth. The fore-body section was filled with a compressed air chamber and in front of that was the warhead section containing the explosive charge. This was detonated by a firing pin or magnetic pistol called the Duplex Coil Rod (DCR), which should detonate when the torpedo passed under the steel hull of a vessel. The massive explosion and position of the torpedo was designed to break the ship's back. However, this arrangement did failed numerous times. In some cases the Royal Navy reverted to the older contact-style pistol. But despite its failings the DCR type of pistol remained in service with the Royal Navy until 1943. German U-boat crews also experienced many problems with their version of the torpedo. One of the troubles that plagued the Kriegsmarine in World War II occurred when they also adopted the new magnetic firing pistol. The torpedo and its firing mechanism proved unreliable for several reasons, one of which was that British ships and submarines were regularly degaussed, meaning they were effectively demagnetised and therefore did not set off the TNT-packed warhead. However, they did not always fail, a fact to which the sinking of HMS *Courageous* bears testament.

A torpedo was as dangerous when it was inside a submarine's torpedo tube as it was when it was unleashed towards its intended target. As mentioned in an earlier chapter, *Upholder* had a horrendous torpedo incident on 5 May 1941 while in Malta. She was alongside the torpedo depot replenishing her weapons when suddenly there was a 'hot run' in her number three tube. The BC engine had started on its own. There was no sea water to keep the engine cool; the torpedo would have shaken violently and the noise would have been deafening and very frightening. As the engine got hotter and hotter the crew would have tried to shut it down before the inevitable. The warhead would probably not have detonated but the hot engine would have seized and exploded, sending hot metal parts flying around the tiny compartment as it finally disintegrated. Sadly, this 'hot run' killed Petty Officer Carter and seriously injured Lt. Read, the officer who headed the boarding of the mystery merchant ship *Arta*.

Despite its early design, this chilling device would remain the 'most versatile method of destruction from its conception up to the development of the atomic bomb'.[58] Figures gathered at the end of World War II show that approximately 5,121 torpedoes were fired by British submarines. Of this amount, 1,040 were said to have been certain hits; however, this number may be overstated. What can be said is that without this terrible weapon, 25,706,096 tons of merchant shipping that was sunk would still have remained afloat. But instead it now sits on the sea floor, having taking with it countless lives. This massive figure does not include the military ships, submarines and their crew sunk during World War I and World War II.

Norman Drury said, in a taped interview with Imperial War Museum some years after the war, that 'Any submarine was very lucky to survive up to its sixth patrol'.[59] He also said that it was commonplace for the Commanding Officer of that boat to be awarded the Distinguished Service Order in recognition of his and the crew's successful completion of that number of patrols. During mid-afternoon on 18 August 1941, *Unbeaten* sailed again from Malta, embarking on patrol number six in company with HMS/M *Urge*. *N93* passed *Urge* off Gozo, another small island of the Maltese archipelago; they were each bound for the same patrol area. The two boats met again and communicated by ASDIC. They fixed their positions close to the north of Pantellaria.

On the afternoon of the next day, one of the Telegraphists on board *Unbeaten* received a message from Senior Officer Submarines ordering them to proceed north-west to intercept a convoy. Early in the last dog watch, the crew of the submarine sighted funnels. As the boat closed the potential enemy, the distant funnels slowly grew larger and larger. Soon it was clear from the submarine's periscope view that the funnels were attached to a convoy comprising four merchant vessels, transiting with an escort of three destroyers. Buzzing around the heads of the convoy were several enemy fighter aircraft. *Unbeaten* was swung onto a firing course. The whole attack took place 15NM from Pantellaria and only lasted 13 minutes, but the evolution was severely hampered by rough weather. The submarine's attack periscope kept getting washed down and identification of the enemy vessels was hard, especially at a range of 6,500 yards. Woodward aimed at the two lead ships, one of which he recognised as *Oceania.*

A dispersed salvo was fired. This means the first torpedo was fired at a point half of the ship's length ahead of the target. The second tin fish was fired a sixth of the ship's length astern from the bow. The third torpedo misfired, much to the frustration of the boats crew. A fourth torpedo was fired just ten seconds after the third was supposed to have left the tube and was aimed at the stern of the target. Five minutes and 25 seconds later, a large explosion was heard by *Unbeaten*. As per the boat's standard operating procedure she dived deep and proceeded to clear the tell-tale torpedo tracks. The crew fully expected a counter attack. When it came, it was in the form of just one destroyer. A total of 22 depth charges were recorded as being dropped in the submarine's vicinity; some of these were very close and caused a number of rivets to start leaking in the Torpedo Stowage Compartment (TSC). At around 19:50, the submarine came up to periscope depth for an all-round look. Nothing was sighted. It was hoped that they had hit something.

Torpedo safety forks were a pre-firing safety feature of the Mk. VIII torpedo and often kept by crew men and engraved as trophies. The fork was inserted aft of the torpedo to stop the premature running of the propellers and unshipped before firing as part of the pre-firing routine. One of *Unbeaten's* torpedo forks marking this attack still exists today and reads: *19th August 1941 6.000 Merchant Vessel*. This does not, however, mean a ship was sunk; only that a torpedo was fired in anger. Being close to Pantellaria Teddy Woodward decided that it was too risky to hang around and wait for the enemy to send out reinforcements, so they cleared the area. The naval researcher Platon Alexiades has looked through the Italian archives and confirmed that the enemy vessels concerned were the elusive *Oceania* and her sister ship *Neptunia*, along with the *Marco Polo* and the steamer *Esperia*. These ships, carrying troops and supplies, were heavily escorted by the destroyers *Vivaldi, Da Recco, Gioberti,* and *Oriani*. A lone torpedo-boat, the *Dezza*, was also on station. The exact escort at the time of the attack is uncertain but it has been said that the destroyers *Maestrale, Grecale* and *Scirocco* of the 10th Destroyer Squadron arrived soon after the attack. It appears that Woodward may have grossly overestimated the merchant vessel's speed as the torpedo tracks were sighted by an escorting CANT Z aircraft as having crossed far ahead of the convoy. *Oceania* and her twin escaped – this time.

Early in the morning darkness of the next day, *Unbeaten* sighted another submarine also on the surface. It was believed to have been the *Urge*. Shrimp had instructed his Captains not to fire on submarines at night. Teddy Woodward tasked the signalman to challenge the mystery boat with flashing light. If it was *Urge*, she did not respond. Woodward was concerned. A similar situation had happened to *Upholder* earlier in the year. The time it was taking to identify the submarine could have given what might be an enemy boat valuable minutes to get into a firing position and attack *Unbeaten*. Leading Telegraphist P. Birnie, listening on ASDIC, did successfully pick up the HE of the submarine, giving its range and bearing relative to *Unbeaten*. It is possible that the ASDIC operator identified the boat by her HE, which was why Woodward decided not to fire, or did something not feel right? This was not the first time this situation had occurred between the Malta submarines.

The following incident has been written about in the past by several authors, including Jim Allaway, and ex-*Truant* rating Sydney Hart. The story is always attributed to the two submarines it involves. However, because this account also concerned *Truant's* Torpedo Officer, Lt Donald E. Ogilvy Watson, a future Captain of *Unbeaten,* it is worthy of inclusion in this book. The day was Wednesday 12 February 1941. *Upholder* sailed that morning for her second patrol out of Malta. Around the same time, *Truant* had been patrolling the Benghazi areas for several days, and her crew were looking forward to ending their patrol off Tripoli and then heading back to Malta. It would not be long before *Truant* would be crossing the Atlantic and joining HMS/M *Pandora.* Both submarines were to conduct a re-fit at Portland Maine, on America's east coast.

During the evening of the 12th, the Officer of the Watch on the bridge of *Upholder* spotted a submarine. Wanklyn ordered *Upholder* to slowly approach the unknown vessel. Wanklyn studied the silhouette intently through his binoculars. He whispered, 'It's a U-boat.'[60] *Upholder's* torpedo tubes were already loaded and Wanklyn knew that no British submarines were supposed to be in the area apart from *Upholder* herself. He also knew that these areas were hunting grounds for Axis U-boats, waiting to pick off any British or Allied shipping heading towards Malta with valuable, much needed supplies. *Upholder* was moved to within 1,500 yards of her quarry and adopted a good attacking position. The Commanding Officer was well known for his instinctive sixth sense; maybe Woodward also shared this gift. 'Challenge with flashing light' was the next order from Wanklyn. If *Upholder's* Captain was wrong, giving away his boat's position could have had disastrous consequences. Just before the first signal was flashed, Wanklyn identified the vessel as a T-Class submarine. The signalman carried on and flashed the boat. There was no reply. This was repeated three times with no response. Even closer now, Wanklyn was satisfied that the boat was in fact a T-Class and he ordered the crew of *Upholder* to break off the attack. It was not until long afterwards that the crew of *Truant* found out just how close they had come to being on the receiving end of a spread of torpedoes, fired by one of the top submarine aces in the Royal Navy. Leading Stoker Sydney Hart, who was on board the *Truant* along with Lt. Donald Ogilvy Watson would always be extremely grateful to the keen eyesight of David Wanklyn. As he said in his book, *Submarine Upholder*: 'The chances of a submarine escaping unscathed from such an attack would have been infinitesimal.' [61]

It was a catalogue of events that led to *Truant* being spotted on the surface by *Upholder's* Officer of the Watch that night. The *Truant* had earlier crept up a swept channel towards Benghazi Harbour. After spotting some shipping entering the harbour, it was decided by *Truant's* Commanding Officer to fire four torpedoes. The weapons were set at shallow depth settings, designed to travel over the enemy minefield which was in place to protect the harbour. They were hoping to hit the unsuspecting enemy vessels. Suddenly, and almost immediately after her torpedoes had been fired, *Truant* was rocked by a massive explosion. A torpedo had hit a mine. *Truant* made good her escape into deeper water. Owing to the explosion, her radio was now out of action and beyond repair, along with several motors. Later that day she was surfaced to allow the crew to inspect the damage. Her three-inch-thick jumping wire, which was also used as an aerial, was parted and dragging down the boat's casing. After escaping this foray, *Truant* moved to her Tripoli patrol area where an enemy convoy was spotted.

This time, *Truant's* Command decided to engage with gun action. After firing off 17 rounds, *Truant* dived and tried to escape, going deep. Inevitably, the depth charges caught up with her. Dropped in patterns of fours, sixes and eights, the high-explosive charges rained down on her. After escaping again, the crew of *Truant* were still intent on hunting the convoy. They caught up with the vessels and fired another salvo of torpedoes. Two successful hits were heard and again *Truant* was ordered to go deep. Again the depth charges rained down on her. This lasted for several hours but remarkably *Truant* and her crew survived. The boat still had another 14 days on patrol, but because she had expended all her 15 torpedoes, and lost one from a tube during depth charging, it was decided to return to Malta. However, with no radio they could not contact Malta to inform them of their advanced ETA. Four days after the last depth charge attack, *Truant* was then spotted by *Upholder* at night on the surface.

Without knowing how close the crew had come to certain death that night, *Truant* was bottomed off Malta until dawn. When she surfaced and passed her recognition signal by flashing light, she then safely entered Lazaretto Creek and alongside. Once the near miss was discovered, the matter was looked into, but with no real outcome. Sydney Hart offers up some defence by saying that the searchlights of Malta and the sound of an air raid in progress may have been why the *Upholder's* flashing light were missed by those on the conning tower that dark night. We will probably never know. *Unbeaten*, however, arrived safely at Malta on 21 August 1941 at 07:15. An hour before getting alongside, the boat had to take evasive action and dive because of enemy aircraft in the vicinity. Over the next few months, enemy aircraft would prove troublesome to submarines approaching Maltese harbours when returning from patrols.

10

HMS TALBOT

The month of September 1941 arrived at a very poignant juncture for the band of Malta-based submarines. It was at the beginning of this month that the boats of the 1st Flotilla became the famous 10th Submarine Flotilla. Although Shrimp Simpson was still in command of the Maltese Flotilla day to day, both Simpson and the boats would ultimately remain under Captain S.M. Raw (S1), based at Alexandria. This appeared not to have bothered Shrimp. He said in his book *Periscope View*, 'It made no difference whatsoever whether I was Commander Submarines Malta, Captain Submarines Malta or Captain (S10) of Malta.' [62] Although George Simpson was still operationally answerable to Captain (S1) he did say of Raw: 'Fortunately for both of us, never once in two years did he interfere with my operational independence.' [63] Shrimp was happy with this arrangement because as he said, it assured his old friend Captain (S1) 'devilled all my paperwork' [64] and not the Commander-in-Chief's staff.

Around the same time in September 1941, the bomb-damaged, makeshift submarine base at Manoel Island, set up in the confines of the old Lazaretto, was officially commissioned. The buildings had been adapted, with accommodation and workshops having been built; the whole area was a hive of activity. The shore-based site was commissioned HMS *Talbot*.

Simpson wanted the buildings to remain incognito. One of the few ceremonial items that signified the existence of the submarine base was the Perry buoy, or life ring, hanging on a limestone wall. The ring had the name HMS *Talbot* painted on it. Most naval establishments have one or two of these life rings at their entrances. Simpson did not want the White Ensign to be flown over the Lazaretto for obvious reasons.

Shrimp said in his book that Ju87 dive bombers would pull out of their bombing dives, which were targeting the dockyard, and fly right over the old Lazaretto. It was said the enemy aircraft would fly so low that 'the pilot's goggled helmet and hand gestures could be seen clearly.' [65] The Junkers Ju87 was more commonly known as the Stuka. This is short for 'Sturzkampfflugzeug', the German word for dive bomber. The feared two-seated aircraft produced a terrifying noise when dived from height towards its intended target. The shrill scream was inadvertently made by the aircraft's diving brakes. Infamously, it was Stukas that fired the first shots of the Second World War and dropped bombs on Polish defensive positions near the Dirschau Bridge, now known as Tczew, on 1 September 1939.

It was the evening of 24 August, after only three days alongside Malta, when *Unbeaten* sailed on her seventh patrol. She would not return until 4 September. The boat was tasked to an area covering the southern approaches to the Straits of Messina. She was placed in a position to patrol off Cape del Armi, relieving fellow U-Class submarine *Ursula,* which had returned to Malta eight hours before. *Unbeaten* was on the lookout for a southbound Vichy convoy. The convoy was spotted and investigated and the information logged. *Unbeaten* then withdrew to the deep. The next couple of days saw the submarine patrol close to the Calabrian coast. The weather was flat calm and the boat remained deep, listening. During the first dog watch on the 28th, Woodward ordered the boat to periscope depth. As the Commanding Officer swivelled the periscope around, scanning the ocean, he sighted a destroyer moving to the east. Woodward watched. At 16:38, only eight minutes after the destroyer was first identified, a familiar shape was spotted close inshore. Teddy Woodward knew straight away what it was. Because all eyes had been on the destroyer, the U-boat was not seen until *Unbeaten* was 2,800 yards abaft her beam.

The CO had identified the enemy submarine as an Italian Balilla Class, which was a large ocean-going cruiser-type submarine; a prime target. *Unbeaten* was moved into a firing position and at 17:08 a dispersed salvo of torpedoes was fired towards the enemy submarine. The enemy boat was now 3,000 yards away. Unfortunately, the Italian submarine dived as the tin fish passed over her. All four British torpedoes exploded as they ploughed in the beach, adjacent to their intended target. Italian archives reveal that the large unescorted submarine was called the *Adua* and was one of 17 Adua Class Submarines. She was on passage from Pula to Messina. The torpedo attack was not observed by the lucky enemy submarine, although they must have heard the four distant explosions. Her luck would not continue, however; just over a month later, on 30 September 1941, she was sunk in the Western Mediterranean by the British destroyers HMS *Gurkha* and HMS *Legion*.

In the late afternoon of the next day, a 2,000-ton schooner was sighted through the periscope. Woodward ordered *Unbeaten* to close and investigate. The now clearly visible four-masted sailing vessel was stationary. The ship was constructed of what Woodward described as two large deck houses amidships and another on her poop deck; she also had very high bulwarks. It was deduced that this Italian flag-flying vessel was suspicious. Owing to enemy destroyer activity on the surface and the notion that the enemy vessels were sweeping the area looking for submarines ahead of an impending convoy, Woodward concluded that the stationary vessel was a 'Q' ship and that she was orchestrating the hunt. Teddy Woodward wrote in the patrol log that because of this constant sweeping, and taking into account the Senior Officer Submarines, Malta's directive – stating that 'submarines should keep one salvo for enemy heavy units' [66] – no offensive action was taken. *Unbeaten* silently cleared the area.

Early in the morning of 30 August, the lookouts standing on *Unbeaten's* bridge sighted a red flare. The glowing illumination was hanging in the sky and estimated to be about 2NM away. In the post-patrol report, Simpson noted that the flare was described as being similar to the type previously used in 1940 by groups of German U-boats off Terschelling, one of the West Frisian Islands in the northern Netherlands. It would not be long before *Unbeaten* would find herself even closer to a German U-boat, but with much more dramatic consequences.

Around mid-morning, the four-masted schooner was spotted again in the Messina Strait. This time she was not alone. She was working closely with a two-masted vessel which had also been in the vicinity the previous day, but farther away. It seemed that the ships were working together, passing information to sweeping destroyers. *Unbeaten* stalked these two enemy vessels for most of the day, watching her prey intently, but not giving away her position. Just before the end of the first dog, at around 17:45, *Unbeaten* was in a position only 700 yards from the larger of the two schooners. The intended target, the four-masted, topsail schooner, was now stopped dead in the water, a sitting duck. 'Fire three, fire four', would have been the order from Woodward. The two torpedoes would not have taken very long to travel the short distance between *Unbeaten* and her hapless target. Both the individually aimed torpedoes slammed into the wooden hull of the schooner. Woodward said in his report that 'the vessel was blown clean out of the water; such was the force from the two tin fish.' He went on to say, 'The reason two torpedoes were used was to ensure that no retaliatory action was taken against *Unbeaten.'* [67] The British submarine cleared the area, leaving a reported seven survivors clinging on to wreckage. One lifeboat was seen to still be afloat. The other 'Q' ship had made good her escape. *Unbeaten* did search for the absconding vessel but it eluded her.

The four-masted schooner attacked on 30 August 1941 was V51/Alfa (373 GRT), this being the standard tonnage. Captain S.M Raw S(1) said, 'It was probable this 'Q' ship was the same one which hunted HMS *Unique* after the British submarine fired upon her but missed on 30th July.' [68] As with several of the reported sinkings of enemy vessels by submarines in the Mediterranean during World War II, there are inevitably some discrepancies entered in the reports from both sides involved. The surviving crew members of V51/Alfa reported that they had been attacked off Augusta Roads, an open anchorage outside Augusta Harbour. However, *Unbeaten's* patrol log states that the attack took place in or near the Messina Strait; the two locations are approximately 60NM apart, but the times of the two reported attacks were only five minutes different. This attack by *Unbeaten* was included in secret War Cabinet Weekly Résumé (No. 106). In the Mediterranean paragraph the résumé said, 'H.M. Submarines have continued their attacks in the Central and Eastern Mediterranean. *Talisman* fired on two motor lighters off Benghazi on 30 August, hitting both and probably sinking one. On the same day *Unbeaten* torpedoed and sank a large schooner near the Straits of Messina.' [69]

The remainder of this patrol was pretty uneventful. *N93* returned to Malta, passing Dragut Point at the entrance to Maramxett Harbour on 4 September and then alongside the old Lazaretto to officially become a member of the

10th Submarine Flotilla, Malta. Shrimp Simpson summed up *Unbeaten's* seventh patrol by writing in the patrol log, 'The manner in which the Italian 'Q' ship was watched, stalked and sunk, shows skill and determination which I am used to expect from Lieutenant Commander Woodward.' [70] Although it was common for the command to get praised, the crew rarely did in these reports. This sign of the times was also true of medals. It was seen as if the command took it for the team and then passed the praise around. Of course, most submarine commanders knew only too well that they were really only as good as their crew – although the sometimes superhuman skills of many submarine Captains lends credence to what Shrimp Simpson was once quoted as having said during a local broadcast, transcribed into *The Times of Malta* in September 1941:

'Each man in a submarine must not only know how to do his job, but also understand the diving mechanism of the submarine, and the position of every important valve, since one mistake on the part of any member of the crew may cause the vessel's loss. But statistics show that in no other profession is the success or failure of a powerful unit so dependent on the judgement or skill of one man – the Captain.' [71]

When the submarines were not deployed on a patrol, Shrimp ensured that the boats, when in the confines of Sliema Creek, were strung out in a crescent-shaped trot, secured forward and aft. This was so a stick of enemy bombs could not fall along a line of submarines and wipe them all out. The sailors could still get to shore via a floating gangway. This way of securing the submarines had been in place for a period of time and worked well. However, later in the war, tactics would change in an attempt to prevent the boats from being bombed. These tactics would include passing smoke over the moored vessels in an attempt to hide them when viewed from the air. The year 1941 lurched from one patrol to the next for *Unbeaten's* crew. The average time spent at Malta between patrols was said to be seven to ten days, but it was often much less. It has been interesting to note that during the research for this book, several accounts written by those who were there vary in their historical accuracy where dates and times are concerned. This is only to be expected because of the time period that has elapsed, combined with the inevitable fog of war. However, the correct dates and times can be supported by the boat's patrol logs and other official documentation. The author is not for one second questioning the content and integrity of what has been reported by crew members. Because of their testaments it is relatively straightforward, with a bit of research, to line up an eyewitness report, which may have a date discrepancy, with the actual event which is usually officially logged.

Courtsey of Paul Lazell son of Bill Lazell

Aerial photograph of Manoel Island Malta: Sliema Creek above, Lazaretto Creek below

Courtsey of Paul Lazell son of Bill Lazell

Unknown British T-Class submarine leaving the Lazaretto base: Malta 1941

Courtesy of the Ogilvy Watson Family

Lieutenant Donald E. Ogilvy Watson DSC

Courtesy of Mr Derek Bayne

Ordinary Seaman Herbet H. Bayne

Courtsey of Mrs Margaret Donothey née Piper

Leading Telegraphist Albert E. Piper

Courtsey of Mrs Jan Brenton née Wright

Petty Officer Stoker Geoffrey H.A.Wright DSM

Photograph from Authors collection

Photograph from Authors collection

Photograph above: Torpedoes being prepared onboard HMS *Medway*

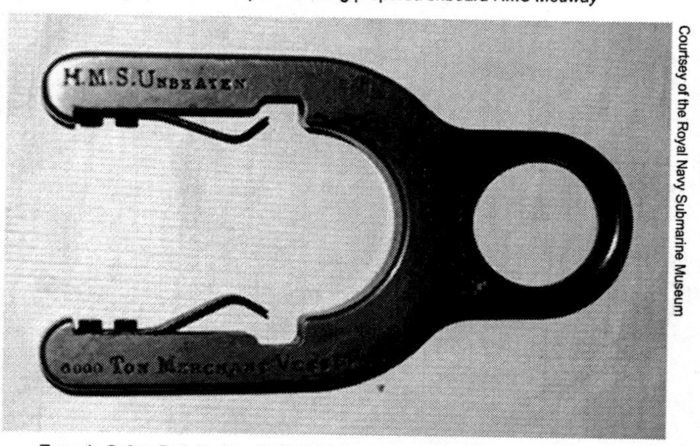

Courtsey of the Royal Navy Submarine Museum

Torpedo Safety Fork fired by HMS/M *Unbeaten* at *Silvio Scaroni* 19th May 1941

Courtsey of Paul Lazell son of Bill Lazell

Downed ME 109 crash lands on Luqa airfield after being hit by Bill Lazell's anti aircraft battery

Courtsey of Paul Lazell son of Bill Lazell

27th Battery, Royal Artillery: Bill Lazell bottom left with the Lewis gun across his shins

Courtsey of the Royal Navy Submarine Museum

Half of *Unbeaten's* crew visiting Hove, the submarines adopting town mid 1942 (Fig 1)

Courtsey of The *Argus* Newspaper

Hove Warship Week: A poster advertising the appeal to raise money for HMS/M *Unbeaten*

Courtsey of the Royal Navy Submarine Museum

HMS/M *Unbeaten*: Alongside Plymouth for fitting of IFF and 291w RDF, September 1942

Courtsey of the Royal Navy Submarine Museum

The Last Photograph: *Unbeaten* at Holy Loch inboard of HNMS/M *Dolfijn*, 22 October 1942

Courtesy of Mrs Jan Brenton née Wright

HMS/M *Unbeaten* Control Room (Geoff Wright second from right at back)

Courtsey of the Royal Navy Submarine Museum

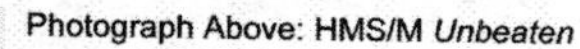

Photograph Above: HMS/M *Unbeaten*

Alongside Gibraltar 21 April 1942.
Unbeaten's crew were the last people to see HMS/M *Upholder* on 11 April 1942

Courtsey of the estate of Mrs Barbara Woodward

Photograph Left: Gibraltar April 1942

Left: Teddy Woodward. Centre: Mr R.G. Casey, British Minister of State,Later Lord Casey, Governor General of Australia. Right: Lord Gort, VC, Governor of Gibraltar

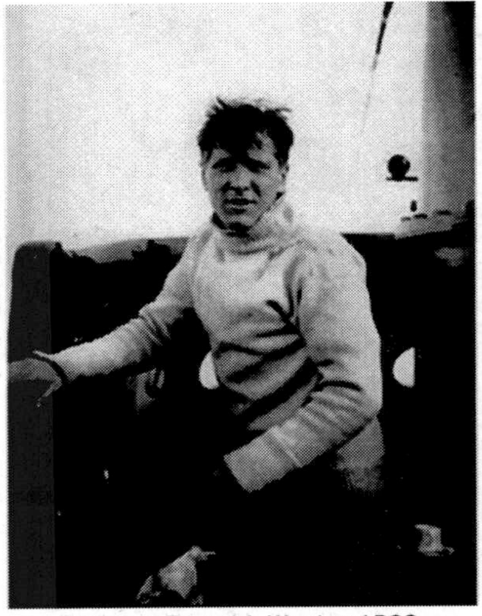

Courtsey of the estate of Mrs Barbara Woodward

Lieutenant Edward A. Woodward DSO

Courtesy of Mrs Desiree Roderick MBE

Special Commando, Lieutenant Richard F. Broome

Courtsey of Jack Casemore

Jack Casemore (Far Left) and shipmates on-board HMS *Forfar* April 1940

11

LET NOTHING PASS

The eighth patrol in mid-September 1941 would see *Unbeaten* almost halfway through her eventual total number of patrols from Malta. This short four-day patrol would see the boat deployed to a position 27NM north of Ras Misurata on the Libyan coast. This patrol was to be a fairly uneventful one for the crew of *Unbeaten* when compared with previous manoeuvres.

The more astute reader of World War II British submarine literature would not fail to have noticed, however, that *Unbeaten's* apparently innocuous, unremarkable, eighth patrol coincided with a significant moment for submarine action in the region. It was during this very patrol and well within the proximity of *Unbeaten*, that Lt. David Wanklyn, Commanding Officer of *Upholder*, achieved what the author Cdr. Richard Compton-Hall RN described as 'arguably the most skilful attack ever made by a Submarine Commanding Officer'.[72] This attack would eventually lead to Wanklyn becoming a recipient of the Victoria Cross, for his and the crew's actions. The thrilling story of the *Upholder* attack on *Oceania* and her sister ship *Neptunia* has been told by many authors in the past and is now firmly part of the *Upholder* legend, and rightly so.

However, this book is about *Unbeaten*, and it would only be right and proper to tell the story from Teddy Woodward and his crew's perspective. It was not the first time Woodward had come across *Oceania* and *Neptunia*; *Unbeaten* had fired a spread of torpedoes towards the sisters on 19 August 1941, but missed. The Italians had learnt a lesson from the British that transporting troops and supplies in fast-moving liners was the way ahead; this tactic had been used with great success by the British in the Atlantic. The faster liners would outrun the slower, stalking U-boats. The author's late grandfather, a 'Desert Rat', bears testament to this swift passage to the war zone. Enter the two Italian liners *Oceania* and *Neptunia*, vital assets in reinforcing the Axis armies in Libya; they had to be stopped at all costs.

A trio of British U-Class submarines, comprising *Upholder*, *Upright*, and *Unbeaten*, was tasked to patrol an area about eighty miles east of Tripoli. Fellow U-Class boat *Ursula* was positioned at the rear, patrolling off Homs. The submarine Commanding Officers concerned were mustered together prior to sailing, and Shrimp Simpson laid out the plan. The Royal Navy had been passed intelligence either by decrypted Hagelin cypher or HUMINT (Human Intelligence), informing them that a fast Italian convoy was bound for Tripoli from Italy and it would be approaching from the east. Once the submarines had reached their patrol areas, Wanklyn placed himself on what he deduced as being the enemy vessels' probable course. As the Senior Officer, he spread out his force of U-Class boats and maintained their relative positions by use of ASDIC. *Upright* took up station 5NM north and *Unbeaten* was placed 5NM south. At 03:07 on 18 September, Woodward spotted and identified a distant funnelled vessel out at a range of 12,000 yards, approximately 6NM. The target of interest was displaying all the hallmarks of one of the elusive *Oceania* Class liners. She was seen to be escorted by five very active Italian destroyers which were thought to be sweeping the vicinity.

Woodward immediately ordered *Unbeaten* to alter course. His boat then closed the target and surfaced at full speed. Woodward wrote in *Unbeaten's* patrol log, 'The range was obviously far too great to get in an attack as the vessel could only just be seen as a small dark smudge through the binoculars.' [73] Around four minutes later, a second shape was spotted at a greater distance of 8NM; no escorting destroyers were visible around this vessel. At 03:13, *Unbeaten* tried to pass an enemy contact report via SS/T (Submerged Sound Telegraphy) towards *Upholder's* position. This form of short range communication was often used for submarine-to-submarine transmissions during the war. It is possible that this attempt to contact Wanklyn's boat was unsuccessful, because around a minute later another attempt was made by *Unbeaten* to pass the report to *Upholder;* this time by W/T (Wireless Telegraphy). Unfortunately, the relay switch was defective. The crew on board *Unbeaten* worked hard and fast to rectify the problem and by 03:24 it was fixed; it was a loose contact. The message was eventually passed – a whole 29 minutes after the initial failed report. Woodward was very frustrated, especially as the radio set was tested just before surfacing and it was said to be correct. The weather was very poor that night and the sea state was rough. At the same time as *Unbeaten* tired to pass her important message, Lt. Tubby Crawford, on board *Upholder,* was the officer of the watch. He was standing on the windy bridge, soaked with sea water, which would have been launched over the conning tower of the trimmed down submarine. Crawford remembers being relayed the message received from Woodward; it simply said: 'They're coming, boys!' [74]

Woodward had reported the convoy as bearing 350° at 5NM from *Unbeaten's* ordered position. Owing to her location down on the southernmost point, *Unbeaten* was the farthest away from any possible enemy contact. The best Teddy Woodward could hope for was to follow in the convoy's wake and see if they could pick off any disabled ships. Back on board *Upholder,* still on the surface, Wanklyn fought against the long swell and tried to judge just the right time to fire his fish towards the perceived course of the two liners. A spread of four torpedoes was fired from a range of 3,000 yards, with the boat yawing heavily. To compound the situation, *Upholder's* gyro compass was broken and Wanklyn had to rely on his magnetic compass. Two torpedoes fired from *Upholder* had hit their targets. One torpedo had slammed into *Oceania's* propellers, stopping her dead in the water. The second fish had punched a gaping hole in the side of *Neptunia,* fatally wounding her. Another vessel also in the convoy tried to make good her escape. This vessel was the *Vulcania.* However, early that morning, as she escaped the scene, *Vulcania* would be fired at by *Ursula* from a long distance. The torpedo would miss.

At 05:01, *Unbeaten* received a message from *Upholder* confirming the hits. Woodward and his boat headed at full speed towards the area of attack in the hope of being able to take a shot at the damaged vessels. Around an hour later *Unbeaten* was dived. At 06:52, Woodward was looking through the periscope when he sighted the masts and funnel of a large merchant vessel. *Unbeaten* closed at best speed. As they got closer the vessel was observed as being stopped in the water. At 12,000 yards away, the ship was identified as being an *Oceania* Class vessel. In the same area another large vessel was sighted but this ship was not seen again. The vessel was *Neptunia*. Woodward got the submarine to within 6,500 yards. It was noticed that several destroyers were surrounding the remaining liner, which we now know was the stranded, powerless *Oceania*. One destroyer looked to be alongside the stricken vessel. *Unbeaten* approached the target cautiously at a dead slow speed. Unluckily, at 3,000 yards, one destroyer got very close to *N93* and forced her to go deep.

Seeing that the liner was still afloat, Wanklyn in *Upholder* closed for the kill. Unknown to Wanklyn, Woodward was also closing on *Oceania* from the other side. Just as *Upholder* reached an optimum firing range and position, a destroyer caused Wanklyn to order *Upholder* to go deep; in a similar situation to that of *Unbeaten* earlier. What happened next is the stuff of submarine legend. Because *Upholder* was now so close to *Oceania* as to allow the boat to come up and fire, Wanklyn decided to pass underneath the 20,000-ton liner, come up the other side, turn the boat to a firing course and let her have another two torpedoes. At 08:49, one very loud explosion was heard by the crew on board *Unbeaten*. This was followed a minute later by another ear-splitting explosion. Woodward wrote in the boat's patrol log, 'It was thought that *Unbeaten* had been detected and was being depth charged.' [75] It was around nine minutes later that the crew on board *Unbeaten* heard a rending noise permeating through the water. Woodward rightly concluded that it was the sound of their target breaking up. *Unbeaten* only stayed deep for 21 minutes and then came up to periscope depth for an all-round look. The bloody destroyer was now only 200 yards away. After a quick look through the periscope Teddy Woodward presumed the target had now sunk. Meanwhile, up on the choppy sea surface, the escorting enemy destroyers were busily plucking survivors out of the water. Hundreds of German Afrika Korps troops were sliding down lifelines to get off the sinking vessel. Woodward and *Unbeaten* closed and watched for a while, as did Johnny Wraith, CO on board *Upright*. A large number of troops – some say 5,000 or more – were said to have drowned that night. The historical documents written by all sources involved in this attack provide a researcher with a wealth of information.

As it transpires, Simpson was not best pleased that his highly trained and competent submarine COs did not take full advantage of the preoccupied, defenceless destroyers as they were rescuing survivors. This was not the first time boats under his overall command had withdrawn while target enemy vessels picked up survivors. However, Shrimp did not say anything to his submarine commanders. He felt their jobs were stressful enough without the added pressure of being ordered to attack the enemy with their pants down at every available opportunity. Moreover, Simpson did not want to lose the complete faith, trust and respect he had earned from his men by chastising them for their compassionate actions. The individual Captains could have, had they wished to, fired on the vessels, but they chose not to. This type of wartime humility was not just limited to British submarines during World War II. In fact, these types of incidents were not unheard of and several are documented in survivor reports from British and Allied merchant seamen on board vessels sunk in the Atlantic campaign. The seamen reported that sometimes, after their vessels were torpedoed and sunk, the attacking enemy U-boats would surface and drop off drinking water and supplies to the poor souls left in life rafts or on Carley Floats. Ultimately, these men often faced a slim chance of being rescued. After the war, one U-boat commander freely admitted that during one such merchant vessel sinking by his U-boat, he even transmitted the stranded crew's position, before hastily clearing the area.

Soon afterwards, *Unbeaten* made good her exit from the location of the attacks. For a further hour the crew could still hear the distant explosions of depth charges, numbering over 200. It seems the destroyers were still hunting the protagonists of the attacks, who were by this time well clear of the area. Several hours later the submarine was ordered to proceed back to Malta. *N93* arrived back at the Lazaretto base on 20 September, safe from her eighth patrol and without having fired a single torpedo. Owing to the amount of platforms and the complexities involved in the attacks on the two Italian liners, Simpson's covering letter to this patrol report encompassed all four submarines' individual patrol reports. This combined command summary was included in with *Upholder's* patrol report number 14.

12

SPECIAL COMMANDO

It would only be three days later after returning from her last outing that *Unbeaten* and her crew would depart on their ninth patrol together. During this relatively short time in Malta the men would have been very busy. Despite the incessant air raids, which totalled 52 in number over the month of September 1941, the submarine had to be made operationally ready for her next patrol. The Commanding Officer usually went ashore, leaving it to the 1st Lieutenant to oversee the preparations for sailing. One evolution which the crew did not have to undertake this time alongside was the replenishment of torpedoes. This re-supply could be time-consuming, disruptive and, as mentioned in a previous chapter, dangerous. *Unbeaten* still had her full complement of torpedoes after her last foray. Vital commodities like food, fuel and water needed to be embarked for the next patrol. Food and fuel stocks were in very short supply on the besieged island. However, it seems the Malta submarines were given special concessions. The submarines' top priority was to stop the Italian supply convoys reaching North Africa; everyone understood this and the boats did manage to get replenished, although food could be a bit scarce.

It was not uncommon for Simpson to stand down his Commanding Officers and let them have a rest. To allow this to take place, Shrimp had several spare COs at his disposal. Teddy Woodward was stood down for this subsequent patrol. Simpson, being the man he was and appearing to be a great judge of character, once said of Woodward, 'It suited him to play the game of war in reverse.' [76] What Shrimp meant by this was that as soon as the boat was back alongside Malta and the patrol report handed in, the young Teddy Woodward would dart ashore to the nearest watering hole and then migrate further afield. He would thoroughly enjoy himself to the maximum. Shrimp said of his exploits: 'The pace he set himself would have put most men in hospital.' [77] However, beyond all Teddy's foibles, Simpson knew that Woodward was a quality submarine Captain, a natural. Not unlike David Wanklyn, Teddy Woodward also possessed exceptional mathematical ability, and as Shrimp said, 'a particularly good eye for a periscope attack'.[78] The CO of *Unbeaten* would be awarded the DSO (Distinguished Service Order) for his actions on board *N93*. He would eventually steer his boat and crew safely through 17 Malta patrols, but sadly not the war. After the end of hostilities, Simpson cryptically wrote of the man, 'Woodward alone survived the war.' [79]

Enter Lt. Compton Patrick Norman, or Pat to his friends. C.P. Norman was a spare CO and would be sailing in command of this ninth *Unbeaten* patrol. However, it was not as if the very capable Lt. Aston D. Piper couldn't command the boat; he often did. Sometimes Teddy Woodward would return on board after his absentia, drive the boat out of harbour, and then Aston would take over. It was said that you would not see Teddy again until the boat was at her patrol position. This time at sea, there were two additions to the submarine's usual complement. Embarked on board for this patrol were two unassuming army chaps. It would not have been divulged to *Unbeaten's* crew why these two men and a fold-up canoe were on board until they had sailed – although to the submarine's crew it would have been obvious. For *Unbeaten* and her crew this patrol would also, should the occasion arise, become a sabotage operation. The officer and corporal were members of the newly formed and highly trained Folbot or Folboat section, the word 'Folbot' being an acronym for folding boat.

Lt. Richard F. Broome and Cpl. Harry (Joe) Slater were both written up in the submarine log as being soldiers from the South Lancashire Regiment. They were embarked on board *Unbeaten* specifically for 'rail sabotage', should the opportunity present itself, but only after *Operation Halberd* was completed; this took priority. The British-led naval operation 'Halberd' was undertaken to ensure the safe passage of a much-needed convoy bound for Malta. The convoy left Liverpool and the Clyde on 16 and 17 September 1941 respectively, arriving at Gibraltar on 24 September and eventually reaching the besieged island with vital supplies on 28 September. It was *Unbeaten's* job, along with other U-Class boats from the 10th Flotilla, to take up specific positions during the operation, so the British submarines could harass the Italian Navy if the need arose. They were also placed in the transit areas to report any attempted Italian attacks on the convoy during its final stage. This was the crucial time when the capital ships of force H had departed the convoy off Skerki Bank, which is approximately 43NM northwest of Sicily. This departure would leave the convoy under-defended. *Operation Halberd* was completed successfully, although several ships were damaged by air attacks courtesy of the Regia Aeronautica. The Halberd aspect of the patrol was uneventful for *Unbeaten* and her crew. It transpired that no enemy targets had been sighted and there was no opportunity for an attack.

Unfortunately, any cloak-and-dagger operations were also a non-starter. The usually calm Mediterranean weather had changed for the worse and it was deemed unsuitable for Folboating. This was compounded by a sickness suffered by Lt. Broome. This 'no go' would have been the submarine CO's call, as the Folboat men would have been under his charge when on board the submarine; although it was probably agreed by both parties that it was too rough to mount Folboat operations. It was not the paddling of a Folboat in rough weather that was overly hazardous; it was getting the boat into the water from the casing of a yawing, wave-lashed submarine.

The clandestine operational merits of the folding kayak-type canoe, first made by Johannes Klepper in 1906, were suggested to the Admiralty by a keen canoeist, Lieutenant Roger J. Courtney, of the King's Royal Rifle Corps. Jumbo Courtney would soon become a leading figure in the newly formed Special Boat Section. Around the same time, in mid-1940, the possibility of utilising the Folboat canoe for military use was also proposed by Lieutenant G.M.D. Wright RN. Lt. Wright was a submariner and engineer serving on board the T-Class Group 1 boat HMS/M *Triumph*. Wright made his proposal in writing to Captain G.C.P. Menzies, who commanded the 2nd Submarine Flotilla between January 1940 and December 1941. Soon afterward, these suggestions were aired to Flag

Officer Submarines, Vice Admiral Max Horton. Permission was then sought for one such canoe to be obtained for trials, to assess its suitability.

Lt. Broome and Cpl. Slater were just two of the men chosen for service in the Folboat Section, as it was then known. The origins of this waterborne canoe section have come to light in a document classified as 'Most Secret'. The document is titled 'Past, Present, and Future Activities of the Special Boat Section'; it was found within the papers of Commander Harold Wilkinson Goulding DSO RNVR. These papers were kindly passed to the Commando Veterans Association by the granddaughter of Commander Goulding DSO. The documents indeed show that in July 1940 a proposal was made for the use of collapsible canoes for 'landing agents on enemy territory and for special reconnaissance and sabotage work'.[80]

Towards the end of that year, and buoyed by the folding boats merits, the Admiralty procured several more canoes from Folbot Folding Boats Ltd. As time progressed, more Folboats were ordered and different variants were designed and manufactured to meet the ever-changing requirements, as the Admiralty realised the potential of this versatile craft. The Goulding documents go on to say that 'a section, consisting of 2 officers and 15 other ranks, with ten canoes was formed and trained at Arran' [81] and that 'in 1941 the first Section was formed at Alexandria under Major R.J. Courtney MC'.[82] It is known that the newly-formed No. 1 Special Boat Section ran from bases at Alexandria and Malta. Roger Courtney had always intended that one day his Folboats would be deployed from submarines to carry out operations along the North African and Italian coasts. On 13 April 1941 the Folboat section was embarked on board the submarine depot ship *Medway*, moored at Alexandria. The unit's name changed from the Folboat Section to the Special Boat Section. The section was assigned to the Royal Navy and came under Captain (S1) S.M. Raw.

Just to confuse the reader a bit more, back in 1940, a Force X was formed. It was made up of four officers and sixty ordinary ratings. The majority of the men were from 'B' Company No. 1 Special Service Battalion, which was destined to become the famed No. 2 Commando. They were trained off the coast of Scotland in the use of Folboats. Their consort vessel during the training was the submarine HMS/M *Thunderbolt*, which was originally commissioned as the Group 1 T-Class submarine HMS/M *Thetis*. On Thursday 1 June 1939, *Thetis* was accidentally sunk with the loss of all hands and several Vickers staff. She was salvaged and re-commissioned as

Thunderbolt. Lt. Broome and Cpl. Slater joined 'B' Company and were members of Force X, having been selected from Independent Companies that had been entered for Special Service. Eventually, both men would become members of No. 2 Commando. It was with Force X that the two men served together in the new Special Boat Section. They ran from Malta on board British submarines, and ultimately ended up on *Unbeaten* for a single patrol.

Shrimp Simpson was first acquainted with the Special Commandos back in early January 1941. An officer from the Liverpool and Scottish Regiment arrived at Shrimp's office one evening and introduced himself as Captain Taylor. The kilted officer cheerfully announced that he had with him the aforementioned three other officers and sixty men, along with a mass of stores, consisting of Folboats, explosives and weaponry. Simpson followed Taylor out of his office and was duly acquainted with the other commandos of Force X. He was first introduced to Lieutenant Walker, who was said to have been an Essex farmer in a previous life. Another officer stepped forward called Dudley Schofield, whom Shrimp said looked 'not long from school'[83] and finally, Lieutenant Richard Broome, whom Simpson said had been a Midlands businessman before the war. This left Captain Taylor himself, who had worked as a timber merchant in civilian street. Taylor went on to explain to Shrimp that the team of officers and men had been trained extensively in the use of canoes and demolition explosives. He continued by saying that for his men the primary role in this theatre of operations was sabotage. They were to attack shore targets and generally wreak havoc amongst the enemy. So it was, not long after this meeting at the old Lazaretto, that the Special Commandos were frequently embarked on board Malta submarines during patrols, waiting for any opportunity to strike deep in the heart of enemy territory.

To launch a Folboat into the sea from a submarine required the boat to be stopped dead in the water and trimmed down so her ballast tanks were slightly awash. The canoe would be brought up to the gun deck from below via the torpedo hatch. Forward and after control lines would be bent on the bow and stern of the Folboat. A dry turn would be taken with each control line. These turns would be taken around the forward and after stanchions, which support the safety guard rail encircling the 12-pounder gun mounting. The Folboat launch position would be on the leeward side of the submarine where practicable, as this offered more protection from wind and an inclement sea state. The two cordage lines would then be surged simultaneously, thus lowering the canoe into the water. The Folboat crew would then gingerly ease themselves off the overhanging gun platform one at a time and, with the aid of two knotted manropes, slide into the waiting canoe.

A collective of Folboats was commonly known as a 'Cockle'. This is where the most famous exponents of this war canoe derived their nickname, the 'Cockleshell Heroes'. It is very likely that the fledgling Folboat Section, which included Lt. Broome and Cpl. Slater, would have been issued with the two-man collapsible Folboat MK 1 or MK 1*. The former had a length of 16ft 8in and a beam of 32in. The MK 1* was just under a foot longer, but with the same beam. These fledgling Folboats had a rubber skin on a collapsible wooden frame. The early Folboat design could carry two men and kit, but was hard to pass through a submarine hatch.

It was not until much later, in 1942, and in preparation for the daring *Operation Frankton* raid, that the Folboat's beam was specifically modified with the introduction of the MKII variant. This allowed the craft to be easily passed up and down a submarine's torpedo re-supply hatch. This evolution was in fact tested on board *Unbeaten* herself in June 1942. The soon-to-be operational commander of *Operation Frankton*, Major Herbert 'Blondie' Hasler, conducted trials to see if the craft could be passed through *Unbeaten's* forward torpedo hatch. There were various marks of Folboat designed and used during the war. This MKII type was the predominant version used on submarine operations in World War II. However, many variants were developed. Needless to say, great care had to be taken when moving the craft onto the casing, in case the rubber skin got inadvertently ripped, making the Folboat redundant.

Back to 1941, *Unbeaten* was in a submerged position 2NM from Cape Bruzzano at around midday on 25 September 1941. The reconnaissance of beaches and possible targets for Folboat operations was undertaken. The majority of the next day saw *Unbeaten* remain under the water. There was a lot of aircraft activity in the area and also a pair of enemy minesweepers passed them only 2,000 yards to the north. During the afternoon of this day, Lt. Broome was turned in sick with suspected sand-fly fever, or to give its proper name, pappataci fever. This fever is common in the Eastern Mediterranean and North Africa and usually lasts up to or over three days.

The evening of Tuesday 30 September saw *Unbeaten* surface to charge her batteries. Richard Broome was still not fit to land and the swell had increased. It was jointly decided that the only day left to carry out the Folboat operations was the next day. The submarine returned to the coast of Cape Bruzzano and reconnoitred a stretch of railway line from Siderno Marina to Cape Spartivento. It was thought that this would be a good location for a sabotage attack. Norman then carried out reconnaissance of the railway line between Locri and Cape Bruzzano. Deploying Folboats after dark was obviously the preferred option for the vulnerable submarine and the Folboat crew; however, during the first dog watch it was noticed that there was very heavy surf all along the coast. The idea of any Folboat operations was dismissed. To further compound the difficulty of any possible operation, there were only one-and-a-half hours between moon set and the end of dawn, and this was reducing every day.

Not wanting to waste the reconnaissance carried out on the railway lines the day before, Lt. Norman ordered *Unbeaten* to surface. At 10:32 the crew found themselves just 1,000 yards off Cape Bruzzano. The guns crew made ready the gun and fired. Simpson said in his summary of Norman's patrol report: 'It was decided to smarten up the shore defences by a brief bombardment.' [84] The main impetus of the gun fire was directed towards the entrance of the railway tunnel under Torre Bruzzano. The order to shift target was given and the gun layer moved target and aimed towards a Home Guard hut between tunnels. A small landslide had occurred and this had caused some Italian military to come running out of the guard house. No direct hit on the hut was achieved but the enemy were seen to be fleeing up the hillside. Only seven minutes later, *Unbeaten* dived to clear the area. Twenty rounds were fired from her 12-pounder gun. Only minimal damage was achieved, however. But it was said that trains would have been delayed for between two to three hours due to landslides on the track. Simpson said at the end of his report on this patrol: 'The bombardment diversion did much to amuse and encourage *Unbeaten's* Gun Crew, though big results cannot be expected from a 12 Pounder.' [85] Lt. Norman safely brought his charge and her crew back to Malta. The boat arrived off the outer mine swept channel on 6 October, where she then entered Marsamxett Harbour and secured. Lt. Broome and Cpl. Slater got their land legs back after what was for them a disappointing operation, but would be the first of many such excursions undertaken with the Malta Submarines.

13

AWAKEN A SLEEPING GIANT

The following nine days spent in the confines of Marsamxett Harbour allowed the men of *Unbeaten* to go through the well-practised ritual of resupplying food and commodities. The boat's magazine was also replenished, with the crew striking down stocks of 12-pounder, three-inch gun ammunition, replacing those expended on her last patrol. The German and Italian combined bombing raids over Malta continued unabated during October 1941. The besieged island was attacked from the air no fewer than 80 times over this month. Twenty-four of these raids were at night. From now until the end of 1941 the bombing raids inflicted on the people of Malta would increase as the Axis leaders attempted to tighten their stranglehold on the tiny island. However, Axis convoys were also suffering frequent attacks and great losses, predominantly orchestrated by the Malta submarines. The pickings for the Malta-based British submarines were quite rich. There were far more Axis convoys transiting the Mediterranean than the Atlantic.

The Führer was concerned about the large amount of Axis shipping losses and, more importantly, the damaging loss of vital supplies and men bound for Rommel's Afrika Corps. Back in early August 1941, Hitler had offered Mussolini 20 German U-boats to augment the Italian submarines operating in the Mediterranean. Flag Officer U-boats Vizeadmiral Dönitz was not at all happy with this pledge. He was rightly concerned that any removal of U-boats from the Atlantic campaign would have a detrimental effect. However, towards the end October, having been overridden by the Commander in Chief Navy, Dönitz, under a directive of Hitler, had despatched an initial group of six German U-boats from the stormy Atlantic to the mild *Mittelmeer* or Mediterranean. The Kriegsmarine U-boats flooded through the Straits of Gibraltar. Another group of six U-boats transited the Straits around 7 November 1941 in order to support and enhance the submarine capabilities of the Regia Marina. A further group of six U-boats remained at short notice in French ports. Once the news that several German U-boats were now at large in the Mediterranean eventually filtered through to the British Admiralty, they thought it wise to suspend any further convoys, for a while at least. This deployment of U-boats in the Mediterranean could tie in with the suspected submarine red flare spotted by *Unbeaten* at the end of August. Maybe the *Unterseeboots* had been in the area earlier than anyone had ever believed. The U-boats where predominately deployed to isolate Malta specifically and attempt to stop any Allied convoys getting to or leaving from the island with lifesaving supplies, fuel and ammunition. However, the confined waters of the Mediterranean were not favoured by the Commanding Officers of the large German U-boats. The predominant U-boat deployed in the Mediterranean was the Type VIIC; the larger Type IX ocean-going boats were far too big and could not easily and effectively operate in these shallow waters. These Type IX U-boats were kept in deeper waters, patrolling west of Gibraltar. This is where the smaller British U-Class submarines definitely had the advantage.

Although the enemy were attempting to do their best to stop supplies getting to the island, vital stores, fuel and ammunition were still getting through. This even included 126 passengers, who were transported to Malta via submarine, along with other essential commodities, courtesy of the hard work carried out by the larger and older P- and R-Class boats and a few of the newer T-Class submarines. This heroic lifeline to Malta was dubbed the 'Magic Carpet' service. The names of several of the submarines nominated for Malta relief operations were HMS/M's *Proteus, Parthian, Regent, Rorqual, Traveller, Thrasher* and the River Class submarine HMS/M *Clyde.* This list is not exhaustive and other submarines certainly took part in these gallant operations. The inside of *Clyde* was totally stripped out for this task, leaving her with one defensive torpedo tube. Although there were three supply runs in 1940, the majority of the replenishments took place during June 1941 through to November 1942. In total, these larger British submarines transferred their much-needed cargos to the besieged island of Malta a total of 41 times, for the best part unseen by enemy air patrols and shipping. When the war was over it would be estimated that these vital missions supplied many thousands of gallons of petrol and kerosene, not to mention tons of mail and stores. The most essential of items for the Malta submarines was also delivered courtesy of the Magic Carpet: the all-important re-supply of torpedoes. The Devil's Device was not only destined for the submarines; some aircraft types based on the island also deployed the torpedo as a weapon.

The majority of torpedoes awaiting use were stored on board the submarine deport ship HMS *Medway*, moored at Alexandria. As previously mentioned, the Malta relief submarines were members of the 1st Submarine Flotilla based at Alexandria – this was the port they ran from up to the point they were forced to move to Haifa, owing to the advancing German army. This monumental movement of men and machinery also saw the destruction of confidential papers or anything that would benefit the Germans. This quick exit from Alexandria in mid-1942 is historically known as 'the flap'. However, once moved and established again, the fantastic Magic Carpet service continued to run.

Back to 1941 and Teddy Woodward was again in command of *Unbeaten* after his short respite. The boat was now embarking on her tenth patrol. It was Tuesday 14 October. This was to be one of the shortest patrols undertaken from Malta by *Unbeaten*. She sailed in conjunction with *Upright* and *Urge*. Each submarine had its own position to patrol and individual orders to follow. *Unbeaten* was dispatched to intercept three Italian *Navigatori* Class destroyers. By the evening of the second day nothing had been seen or heard. *Unbeaten* returned to Malta and arrived during mid-morning on the 16th.

Unbeaten's patrol number eleven lasted exactly eleven days. The submarine was sent to patrol an area between Cape Passero and Messina. The *Ursula* was to the east in an area off the Calabrian coast. They were in these positions in an attempt to intercept enemy vessels transiting to the Sicilian port of Augusta. This patrol provided plenty of enemy shipping contacts but an equal amount of defending enemy aircraft was also spotted. On 25 October, the *Unbeaten* closed the coastline of Taormina and Puteoli. The British boat was tasked to survey the shore, looking for possible locations for future landings or sabotage attacks. It was initially proposed to employ the 12-pounder gun by firing on a railway train stopped in Taormina Station. However, this attack was not conducted owing to a shoreside enemy gun emplacement being spotted only 5.8 cables (approximately 1,074m) away from *N93's* position. Fortunately for the train, no other location afforded *Unbeaten* a good firing position. *Unbeaten* slipped back into the deep. Her tactical retreat left the enemy locomotive and its passengers totally unaware of how close they had come to being attacked. The 26th saw the boat patrolling the coast again, this time off Murro di Porco, Sicily. It was a fact of submarine life that many operations at sea could be quite mundane affairs for the crew and a large proportion of their time was spent on watch or asleep. Not all the time on a patrol was spent being frightened to death. It was not until 06:33 on the 27th, when *Unbeaten* was at periscope depth, that a lonely, dark, object eventually loomed into the submarine's periscope view.

A very keen-eyed Sub-Lt. J.C. Varley spotted the conning tower of what the command concluded was an Italian *Gemma* Class U-boat at a range of 6,000 yards. Every British submarine had on board current editions of *Jane's Fighting Ships*, a recognition manual for ships and submarines. There is also a separate book for the recognition of aircraft. These very informative books of reference are still used by the Royal Navy today to establish the origins of a vessel or aircraft. The books show a picture of the vessel or aircraft concerned and occasionally a silhouette, along with a written description and armament fit. Sometimes the differences in vessels can be very minor and crews can be forgiven for believing an enemy vessel to be one of a different class. Given the rough weather this morning, this sighting was commendable.

The unescorted enemy submarine was cutting through the surface at a speed of approximately 12 knots. Teddy Woodward instantly went into auto. The Commanding Officer assessed the length of the enemy target to be around 200ft and steering a course of 340°. Woodward ordered the depth settings of the torpedoes to be set between 8 to 10ft. Exactly 10 minutes after J.C. Varley had spotted the Italian submarine, *Unbeaten* let go a dispersed salvo 'B', consisting of four MK VIII torpedoes. The British submarine was 3,500 yards from its target. Woodward individually aimed each torpedo. The first was aimed one submarine length ahead of the target. The second torpedo was fired directly at the bow. The third was aimed at the stern and the final, fourth torpedo powered towards a position one length astern of the target. Given the high sea state, this dispersed salvo 'B' was said to give a better chance of one or more tin fish hitting their target. The CO followed the progress of the torpedoes making their way towards the enemy by looking through the high power periscope. Teddy could just make out nine crew members huddled on the Italian conning tower. The enemy submarine was not far from the relative safety of the Port of Augusta and the oblivious crew were probably getting ready to enter harbour and bring their boat alongside. Although all four torpedoes appeared to run correctly, they all missed. The crew on *N93* rushed to reload the tubes but were now too far away to catch the Italian U-boat. With this patrol completed, *Unbeaten* arrived at Malta early in the morning of Thursday 30 October 1941.

Whilst delving into the Italian archives, naval researcher Platon Alexiades discovered the identity of the Italian submarine attacked on 27 October 1941. It was almost certainly the 600-ton *Sirena* Class submarine *Topazio* on passage from Leros to Augusta. The British torpedo attack was not observed by the Italian submarines crew. It is worthy of mention that after the end of World War II the eventual fate of the *Topazio* came to light, drawing alarming parallels to that of *Unbeaten*. The Italian submarine vanished around 10 September 1943. Two days prior to her disappearance Italy had surrendered to the Allies. It was not until the war had ended that it was revealed a British aircraft had attacked what they thought was an enemy submarine on the surface and sank it. The British attack was said to have taken place on 12 September, four days after the Italian Armistice, in a location south-west of Capo Carbonara in Sardinia. This was within the area of *Topazio's* last known position. However, the reasons for the loss of the Italian boat are still open for debate today. Back at Malta in October 1941, Simpson wrote in his report of *Unbeaten's* last patrol, number eleven: 'This is the eighth sighting of U-boats by the Tenth Submarine Flotilla since the 1st of August, whereas none were seen from the 1st January and the 1st of August.' [86] Enemy submarine activity was clearly hotting up; and *Unbeaten's* crew would soon have their first successful submarine versus submarine attack to add to their Jolly Roger.

The submarine remained at Malta for the next for the next 15 days. During the week days, when in harbour, hands were employed in their respective compartments maintaining or cleaning the area; or alternatively, painting and provisioning the boat. These tasks took place between 08:00 and midday. At 13:15 the hands would 'turn to' again until being secured around 16:00. Evening rounds would be at 21:00, when the Officer of the Day (OOD) would walk around the boat checking for cleanliness and securing for sea preparations, etc. It was also a good chance to gauge the morale of the crew. It appears from the *Unbeaten's* monthly log, which is broken down into days, that the crew were usually given what is called a 'Make & Mend' on a Saturday. This is a naval term for making and mending your clothes. Alternatively, if one had no making or mending to do, one could get ashore. Basically, it was an official-but-unofficial afternoon off. This practice still happens today, but with much less making and mending. A Sunday routine would be similar. Hands would clean the boat from 08:00 to 09:15. Then, on completion of cleaning, everyone would be mustered in what was called 'divisions'. At 09:30 sharp, with all the hands mustered, church would take place. It was usual at the end of church to be able to get ashore. However, if the boat was under sailing orders and was slipping the next morning, the submarine's routine would change. This change occurred because after the men sailed they would be going straight into sea watches. Day would become night and vice versa. To combat the inevitable lack of sleep when adjusting to the change of routine, the boat's log shows that 'pipe down' or 'hands to bed' could, on occasion, be around 10:30 in the morning on a day prior to sailing. Of course, a duty watch would still be awake and conduct rounds of the boat and other day-to-day duties.

Patrol number twelve was said to be uneventful and disappointing for *Unbeaten*. She was sent to relieve *Ursula* off Misurata and was positioned there to try to intercept enemy shipping transiting from Tripoli to Sirte or from Tripoli to Benghazi. Nothing much was sighted on this patrol. Simpson put it down to the enemy now deciding to use Benghazi as its main port of disembarkation of stores and troops. On the evening of the 26th, *Unbeaten* altered course and headed back towards Malta. Around 21:05 that night, a small spherical mine was spotted and its position logged. These types of mine were just one of the many hazards to a submarine and her crew. The boat returned to the Lazaretto at 07:30 on 28 November.

The last patrol of 1941 for *Unbeaten* was patrol number lucky thirteen. This fairly lengthy patrol would see the boat sail on 7 December and not return until the 22nd. *Unbeaten* was positioned off the Gulf of Taranto and formed a patrol line with fellow U-Class submarines HMS/M's *Utmost* and *Upright*. During 12 December the three British Submarines adopted positions close to Taranto Harbour. At around midnight the sea was calm and there was no wind. Woodward decided to take *Unbeaten* in a little closer towards the harbour than had been originally ordered by Captain (S). It was hoped they would sight enemy mine sweepers at dawn and thus establish the routes of the enemy mine swept channels into and from Taranto Harbour. Teddy Woodward ordered both engines to be stopped and the crew maintained a listening watch. Not long afterwards, as *Unbeaten* was floating silently and motionless on the surface, one of the lookouts on the bridge noticed a red light glowing intermittently. Teddy ordered the submarine to close the light at a very slow speed, he knew they were getting close to the harbour, but in all reality he did not fully know just how close. Suddenly and to the shock of the bridge crew, huddled on the darkened submarine conning tower, they clearly saw the face of an Italian sentry light up as he took a long drag on his cigarette. The chap was standing on the end of the breakwater which guards the harbour. Realising how close they were and how lucky they had been not to be spotted, Teddy withdrew his boat out into safer water and opened to around 6NM from Taranto Breakwater.

After the 14th, *Unbeaten's* consorts changed and were relieved by *P31* and the Polish-crewed submarine N97 named ORP *Sokol* (Falcon). This submarine was loaned to the Polish Navy by the British in early 1941 and was originally commissioned as the U-Class submarine HMS/M *Urchin*. ORP stands for Okręt Rzeczypospolitej Polskiej or in English, 'Ship of the Republic of Poland'. *Unbeaten* remained on station until ordered to return to Malta on the 19th. This had been an eventful patrol for other submarines of the line but not *Unbeaten*. She was caught out several times by zig-zagging vessels and the weather was particularly bad with rain squalls and reduced visibility hampering her sighting of the enemy. It transpired that on occasion the adverse conditions did allow the enemy to pass right through the line of British submarines without a credible Allied attack. However, *P31* did manage to fire at an enemy cruiser but missed. In direct contradiction to the poor weather on the surface, Woodward said the

ASDIC conditions under the water were very positive. It was said that good HE had been heard when only smoke from a vessel could be seen.

In his closing statement of this patrol, Teddy Woodward praised Leading Telegraphist P. Birnie for his 'efficiency and keenness in the operation and maintenance of his set'. He went on to say, in the third person, 'Had it not been for the Commanding Officer's complete confidence in Birnie's ability on the night of the 16th December, surfacing at such close quarters to the enemy destroyers would have been a hazardous operation.' [87] The experienced Jock Birnie had only joined the complement of *Unbeaten* in the summer of 1941, and was already proving to be a very competent ASDIC operator. Birnie is one of only a few crewmen to get mentioned in the official patrol reports. He was said to have been a U-Class veteran who had joined from *Upright*. No stranger to tragedy, Birnie was said by some to have been a survivor of the accidental sinking of the early U-Class submarine *Unity*. In describing Jock Birnie, the ever-articulate Jack Casemore said he was 'short and scruffy and had hair and a beard which was grey to fair and his beard stuck out at right angles to his face; but on the ASDIC set he was faultless'. [88] A good ASDIC operator could determine life or death for a submarine crew. This was another patrol which had, on the whole, been uneventful for the crew. The Commander-in-Chief, Mediterranean Admiral A.B. Cunningham wrote of this report, 'The determination and offensive spirit displayed by Lieutenant Commander E.A. Woodward, Royal Navy, throughout this strenuous patrol were most creditable.' [89]

Those who know their military history will also note that the date on which *Unbeaten* left Malta for her thirteenth patrol coincided with a major turning point in World War II. At 23:18 on 7th December 1941, *N93* surfaced to flash up her generators and charge the batteries. This time up top gave the crew a chance to get some fresh air flowing through the boat. The telegraphists also picked up some signal traffic. A priority broadcast was received ordering the commencement of hostilities against Japan. Imperial Japan had earlier in the day provoked the United States of America into World War II by attacking the US naval base at Pearl Harbour, Hawaii. Prophetically, Japanese Admiral Isoroku Yamamoto is purported to have said after the attack: 'I fear all we have done is to awaken a sleeping giant and fill him with a terrible resolve.' [90]

14

SHOOT THE SUN

Christmas 1941 came and went for *Unbeaten's* crew, almost like any other Yuletide period. But of course it was not the same as a good old Christmas at home on land in Great Britain. Even a Christmas spent at sea sailing on the Quatuor Maria, the four seas which surround the fair British Isles, would have been preferable. Another event happened on Christmas Eve that year, although *N93*'s crew wouldn't have known anything of it for a long time. 24 December 1941 would see the death of one of *Unbeaten's* ex-crew members, Lt. F. Gibbs, who was relieved by Aston Piper as 1st Lieutenant. Frank Gibbs had left *Unbeaten* to take his own command. Eventually, he became the Commanding Officer of HMS/M *H31*, an ageing H-Class submarine. Frank found himself back amongst the blockading vessels of the long-running 'Iron Ring'. Many British submarines and ships were still waiting for the marauding sisters, *Scharnhorst* and *Gneisenau*, to break out of Brest. The weather in the English Channel was foul. *H31* had sailed from Falmouth to patrol an area north of Cape Finisterre. The last view of *H31* was seen by the crew of her escort vessel in the proximity of Wolf Rock, which is 4NM south-west of Lands End in Cornwall. The H-Class submarine detached to continue her patrol alone. On the evening of Christmas Eve, *H31* was ordered to report her position. Nothing was ever heard from Lt. Gibbs or his submarine again. Some say she was mined in the Bay of Biscay. However, there was a thought amongst experienced H-Boat Commanding Officers that the weather was to blame for the demise of *H31* and her 21 crew. Rear Admiral Ben Bryant CB, DSO, DSC recounted in his book *Submarine Command*: 'Submarines are susceptible to pooping, that is a following sea coming up over the stern and smothering you.' [91] It was said the little H-Boats were prone to this phenomenon and that many H-Class COs kept one foot on the conning tower hatch when on the surface during bad weather.

The weather back at Malta on Thursday 25 December was wet and muggy. The seemingly never-ending aerial bombardment of Malta had continued right up to and including the day of Christmas Eve. A 22-aircraft attack on Grand Harbour took place the day before Christmas day. The attacking aircraft comprised JU88 bombers and many escorting fighter aircraft, including the feared Messerschmitt ME109s. The number of raids during December 1941 had increased alarmingly to a total of 275 for the month, 100 of which were at night. There was to be some respite, however: no air raids were recorded over Malta on Christmas Day itself. Jack Casemore remembers that all the boats of the Tenth Submarine Flotilla were back at the Lazaretto base for Christmas Day. However, things were not all peace and goodwill to all men. Jack said, 'Unfortunately I got into a fight over our Christmas dinner and had two bottom teeth knocked out.' [92] In naval tradition, the Christmas meal is usually served to a Royal Navy crew by their officers. The men of *N93* would have sat down for their Christmas meal in the relative comfort of the dining halls at the Lazaretto. A small duty watch would have remained on board the submarine. Although the food was rationed and in ever-decreasing supply, the scran would still have been good. The base purser would have been scrimping a bit here and a bit there all year to make sure the Christmas meal was adequate. By Boxing Day, however, the peace was shattered. It all started again; the Luftwaffe mounted a high level bombing raid on the island, and many bombs were dropped, causing a large amount of devastation over a wide area, including the three airfields.

New Year's Eve 1941 saw a violent attack on one of the first minesweepers to be based in Malta. This vessel was a regular escort of *Unbeaten* and other submarines of the Tenth. HMS *Abingdon* was one of the Hunt Class minesweepers whose role it was to keep the swept channels around the Maltese harbours clear. This enabled vital supply ships, warships and submarines to safely go about their business without fear of being mined. On 31 December the 750-ton *Abingdon* was busily sweeping an area just off the coast of Malta. A distance away, clustered in an attack formation, an enemy air raid was approaching. Once the 34 aircraft were overhead, a pair of escorting Luftwaffe ME 109s broke off and strafed the minesweeper. *Abingdon* immediately ceased her sweeping duties and hastily made for harbour. Seeing the fleeing target, three ME 109s again turned towards the vessel and went in for another attack. This time the gunners on board *Abingdon* were ready. They responded with volleys of fire from her quick-firing four-inch gun forward and her 12-pounder gun aft. She also had two .0303 machine guns trained on the sky. The determined minesweeper was credited with shooting down one of the attacking ME 109s. The price paid was seven injured crewmen, three of whom were seriously wounded.

With the jovialities of Christmas and the horrors of New Year behind them, a toothless Jack Casemore and the rest of the *Unbeaten* crew sailed on 4 January for their first patrol of 1942. It was dusk as *Unbeaten* slipped silently from Lazaretto Creek, gracefully sliding between the guardians of Marsamxett Harbour, Fort St Elmo and Fort Tigne, and ultimately reaching out into open water. In company with *N93* were the submarines *Thrasher* and *Sokol*. The two British boats and one Polish boat were ordered to form a patrol line, spread 10NM apart, across the entrance to the Gulf of Taranto. *Unbeaten* arrived at her allotted position on the 6th and remained there for the next three days. The weather was very bad. It was windy and this made the sea state a four on the Douglas Sea Scale, with a swell of five, which is defined as being moderately rough. Not nice weather to be on the surface.

It was just after midnight on 9 January when one of *Unbeaten's* telegraphists received a broadcast from Captain (S10). This fortuitous message from Shrimp Simpson instructed *Unbeaten* to proceed to area 'Juliet'. This patrol area was south of Messina and west of Spartivento, Sicily. At around 20 minutes past midnight on the 12th, a signal of things to come literally flashed before the lookout's eyes. The now familiar sight of a red *fallschirmleuchtkungel*, or parachute flare, was spotted bearing 300° from *Unbeaten's* position. Were German U-boats in the area? It seemed *Unbeaten* was not alone in the Straits of Messina. Woodward ordered the boat to dive. The crew listened intently for any HE, but none was heard.

German U-boats were now known to be in the vicinity of Sicily and Italy; some of them were sharing ports with the Regia Marina. ULTRA intelligence suggested that the ports of La Spezia in Italy and the Greek island of Salamis were known to be temporary homes to submarines of the 29th and 23rd Kriegsmarine U-boat Flotillas respectively. This information was gathered by means of SIGINT (signal intelligence) from decoded cypher or HUMINT (human intelligence) from eyes on the ground, or both.

Later that morning, *Unbeaten's* No. 1, Lt. Aston Piper, was manning the periscope as the officer on watch in the control room. It was 10:13 and the ASDIC operator had just detected very audible HE bearing 065°. Piper maintained a good all-round look through the periscope, which had a 040° vertical field of view and on a good day could see up to 3,000 yards across the ocean. Two minutes after the initial HE report, Aston Piper thought he saw something on the horizon; he studied it closely but he was still not 100 percent sure what it was. U-boats patrolling the Mediterranean were purported to have been painted with a camouflage scheme of 'alternate broad diagonal stripes of dark green and light grey'.[93] This may have made them very hard to identify at a distance. It appears that *Unbeaten* was also painted in a disruptive pattern but one which was not as complicated. Photographs show that her pressure hull was black or navy blue with a light grey superstructure. Her periscopes and masts were light grey or white in colour. The No. 1 called the Commanding Officer to the control room at the rush. Woodward, who had been resting in his bunk, leapt into the submarines nerve centre and grabbed the periscope. He pressed his face to the eyepieces and gazed into the lower prism. Teddy's eyes snapped sharply into focus. 'U-BOAT!'[94] was all he said.

In his mathematical mind the CO was already going through a snap attack. The U-boat was bearing 080° at only 1,800 yards. The helmsman was ordered to alter course and come round to a new heading at full speed to get on track. The target was now bearing 123° from *Unbeaten* at just 1,300 yards. The U-boat was heading 237° at a speed of 11 knots, fully surfaced. Woodward ordered the depth settings of the torpedoes to be set at 8 to 10 feet. Only eight minutes after the enemy submarine had been spotted, *Unbeaten* unleashed an individually aimed 'A' salvo of four Mk. VIII torpedoes towards her target. The point of aim was half the enemy submarine's estimated length ahead, one sixth astern of her bow, one sixth ahead of her stern and half a length astern. Not long after the spread of torpedoes had left their tubes, two reassuring explosions rocked *Unbeaten*. The time it took the torpedoes to travel and hit their intended target showed just how close the attack was. Only one minute and five seconds after firing did the first tin fish hit and detonate. Like the first, the second torpedo slammed into the starboard side of the enemy U-boat, only five seconds afterwards. The German submarine slipped under the ocean in a torrent of swirling bubbles, spewing oil and a misty air upwards and out of the sea surface. The *Unterseeboot* sank almost immediately.

Prior to sailing on this patrol, Teddy Woodward had mustered his crew and reassured them about the routine of 'shooting the sun'. This required the submarine to surface during daylight hours in order to establish their position using a sextant and the sun's meridional altitude. A practiced navigator would not take very long to carry out this task, and on completion, the submarine could dive back into the relative safety of the deep. Woodward continued to explain to the men that during this evolution, which would take only around ten minutes, there was really very little chance of an enemy submarine spotting them and initiating an attack. Teddy told his men that there was absolutely nothing to worry about. The lads all felt better after that. This was until Woodward himself sank a German U-boat within eight minutes of it being spotted.

Unbeaten was now at periscope depth in the last location of the doomed U-boat. The euphoria of the hunt and eventual sinking had receded. Yes, the crew were glad to have sunk an enemy submarine, but the other men were also submariners, and each of *Unbeaten's* crew knew only too well the hardships endured by submariners, whatever side you were on. Teddy was looking through the periscope to see what wreckage was visible in order to confirm the sinking. However, Woodward's view was completely dark; he could not see a thing. Aston Piper was called back on the periscope to see what he could see. Almost at once the view was un-obscured. Piper clearly saw the palm of a man's hand move away from the upper prism field of view. Someone on the surface had blocked Woodward's vista and placed their hand in front of *Unbeaten's* periscope. Lt. Piper shouted, 'There's a German up there.' [95]

What happened next is recounted from several witness accounts and from documents and sound recordings held at the National Archives and the Imperial War Museum. Teddy Woodward grabbed the periscope, took one look, and said to the 1st Lieutenant, 'Surface and go full astern as you surface.' [96] This is a very tricky manoeuvre in a submarine and rarely, if ever, practised. This unconventional order was a good one for the man in the water – better than being chopped up by the propeller. Thankfully, Aston Piper managed to pull off the astern surfacing. Even as the conning tower broke the water and rose into the fresh air, the crew on board *Unbeaten* were preparing to venture onto the casing in an attempt to recover the survivor. The submarine was only 4NM from the Italian coast and in sight of Mount Etna.

At 10:36, only 13 minutes after the first salvo had been fired, Lt. C.W. St Clair-Lambert and the second Coxswain Leading Seaman Jock Forbes climbed the conning tower ladder, armed with a heaving line; Teddy Woodward followed. They popped the stirrup clips on the upper lid and clambered out into the sweet, salty air. The hapless submariner was spotted treading water close abeam. Woodward remained on the bridge while the other two men gingerly climbed down the nine ladder rungs, landing on the casing, behind the gun. The weather was still pretty rough up top; it was a dangerous place to be. The enemy submariner was floundering around in a sea thick with oil, while at the same time being buffeted by the wooden slats ripped from the sunken U-boat's upper-deck. The two British crewmen managed to haul the bedraggled German up over *Unbeaten's* fore-planes, along the casing, then up the conning tower to the bridge, where he was passed down the ladder to a waiting Jack Casemore and other crew members. The conning tower hatch was clipped shut and the boat dived immediately. The whole rescue evolution only took four minutes. *Unbeaten* swiftly cleared the area and moved southwards.

The German survivor – now prisoner – found himself stood in *Unbeaten's* Control Room in a pool of sea water, dripping wet and in total shock. Only a matter of minutes before, Ploch had been on watch, standing on the bridge of his U-boat, probably thinking of the next run ashore. The magnitude of his predicament soon overwhelmed the young man and he was violently sick. To this day, Jack Casemore still remembers with amazing clarity that spaghetti was the German's last meal. With *Unbeaten* safely underway, Teddy Woodward was the last man to come down the conning tower ladder. He stepped into the crowded Control Room and as he did so the new prisoner composed himself, snapped to attention and said in German, 'Herr Captain, Geneva Conventions, I claim my rights as a prisoner of war.' [97] The new POW was put in the Petty Officers' mess, where Norman Drury said, 'the man was given a tot of rum to warm him up'[98]. The German submariner said in Pidgin English that he had been on watch as a lookout on the bridge and was standing in front of the U-boat Captain. Ploch said he had been blown off the submarine's conning tower when the torpedoes hit and that he had gone a long way under the water after being sucked down by the sinking submarine. He had managed to kick off his sea boots and shed his oilskins, along with a pair of weighty U-boat Zeiss binoculars. This apparently had allowed him to reach for the surface. Teddy Woodward later examined him for injuries and said the seaman had only suffered a sprained ankle. Aston Piper reiterated how amazing this escape had been by saying, 'the man was shaken but on the whole unharmed by his experience'[99]. He had even managed to climb down the conning tower ladder unaided.

Unbeaten still had over two weeks remaining of her fourteenth patrol. There was no choice; the prisoner would have to remain on board until the boat's return to Malta. Once the chap had settled down somewhat, he started to disclose more about himself and his U-boat to the British crew. His name was Matrosengefreiter (Seaman Corporal) Johannes Ploch. His rate was the equivalent to an Able Seaman in the Royal Navy. Ploch said he was 21 years old and came from Ottrau in Hesse-Nassau in Germany. As Hans Ploch gained more confidence he started to ask questions. He pointed to the boat's depth gauge. He was told that the British gauge was indicated in feet, and that the boat's maximum diving limit was 250 feet. When told there were three feet to his metre, Ploch scoffed and apparently said, 'German U-boats can go down 300 metres. That is how we get through Gibraltar.' [100] Of course, no-one believed him. Three hundred metres! You're having a laugh. The cagy submariner also revealed the name of his submarine as being *U331*. Further interrogation of the German prisoner would not officially take place until *Unbeaten* reached Malta. Even then the interrogation was not wholly above-board, owing to the lack of qualified interrogators.

With the recent excitement behind them, and as the relieved crew settled down for the night, Woodward ordered 'splice the mainbrace'. This traditional naval order can be attributed to the days of sail. An additional tot of rum was issued to crewmembers after completing the arduous and dangerous task of splicing the sailing vessels mainbrace. This evolution, more often than not, took place during the heat of battle. The tradition continues to this day. On-board *Unbeaten* at the occasion of sinking the U-boat Teddy Woodward had ordered the extra rum to be issue to the crew, cementing a job well done. The daily patrol log showed that the Officer of the Watch kept the submarine in the transit state of 'Surface Passage Bridge Con' (SPBC), owing to the prevailing weather conditions. Occasionally, in times of adverse weather, the boat's trim would be adjusted so the conning tower and bridge were just awash. The Officer of the Watch would then con the submarine via the periscope while remaining very near the surface, with both upper and lower conning tower hatches firmly shut. *Unbeaten* closed Murro di Porco and patrolled three miles off the coast. As the sun set on 13 January and the bad weather receded, the boat opened from land and surfaced to charge her batteries.

The next three days were uneventful. There was the odd aircraft sighting and several vessels of only minor interest. Woodward was tempted to take a shot at a tug and tow on the 16th. However, the vessel and its lighter were too close inshore for the use of gun fire. Woodward was also mindful of Shrimp Simpson's directive forbidding the expenditure of torpedoes on small targets of low value; this was born out of a shortage of torpedoes. The 17th and 18th saw the sighting of two larger vessels comprising a schooner and the Italian hospital ship *Virgilio*. The weather deteriorated again by the 19th but early that morning *Unbeaten's* luck changed again for the better. 'HE heard bearing 120°!' [101] The plucky boat and her crew closed to investigate. It was halfway through the morning watch on the 19th and all eyes were on the direction of the HE. The weather was misty with a reduced visibility. Suddenly, bearing 090° at about 2NM, one small, lone, destroyer was sighted. *Unbeaten* was quickly dived. Around two-and-a-half hours later, the funnel of a merchant vessel was spotted at the long range of 10,000 yards. Woodward ordered the submarine to close at full speed. As they got closer and after a quick flick through *Jane's*, the vessel in question was positively identified as the 5,400-ton *Rapido*. However, the enemy supply vessel was still 7,200 yards away. This great distance, combined with bad visibility, meant the ship was deemed out of limits for a meaningful attack. On a positive note, the HE was getting louder as the submarine closed the vessel's position. Four different vessels were heard by the experienced ASDIC operator. A two-engine bomber was escorting the enemy convoy, circling high overhead, scanning the ocean for dark shadows. A submarine in the Mediterranean could expect to remain invisible only if the depth of water was greater than 50 feet (around 15 metres). Luckily, in this case the rough sea state precluded the enemy from seeing anything through the sea surface. Other factors that can affect the visibility of a submerged submarine are the type of sea bed, the height of the searching aircraft and also how bright a day it is.

At around 09:00, there it was, smoking away in the distance. It was the target they had been waiting for. One large Italian tanker, of between 7,000 and 8,000 tons, was sighted. It was escorted by an Italian *Generale* Class destroyer at the short trail. Hans Ploch was at this time being guarded by Jack Casemore. Jack had a revolver in hand especially for this task. Jack said he told the German that *Unbeaten* was 'chasing an Italian ship'. Ploch apparently responded with 'sink the bastards, Italians no good'.[102] There was always a bit of love-hate between German and Italian submariners. The Italians got a tad bitter when the German Admiralty ordered some types of Italian submarine to cut down their tall, highly visible conning towers. Apparently, some Italian boats had four galleys on board, one of which was housed in the conning tower superstructure.

The newly-acquired target was what torpedoes were made for. Teddy decided to attack. Six minutes later the boat's Torpedo Officer unleashed four Mk. IV torpedoes. These were of a World War I variant, stocks of which were being utilised to supplement the newer Mk. VIIIs. One of the main differences with this slower 35–knot torpedo type was that one couldn't alter the depth settings once the weapon was loaded in the tube. Notwithstanding this, after seven-and-a-half long minutes, two distant explosions were heard by *Unbeaten's* crew who were manning the fore ends of the boat. Thirty-five minutes later another very loud explosion was heard. The crew believed that this was the tanker eventually blowing up. Two aircraft had now joined the search for the attacking British boat. These Axis air assets were aided by sweeping enemy destroyers. Teddy thought it wise to clear the area and withdrew at slow speed; thankfully, no retaliation was experienced by the submarine. That evening, *Unbeaten* was ordered the leave the patrol area and return to Malta as she had expended all her torpedoes. Aston Piper said Hans Ploch was 'a bit shattered when he found out we were going back to Malta'.[103] Ploch was led by his superiors to believe Malta was in fact kaput! Neither the name nor the fate of the Italian merchant vessel attacked on 19 January can be found at this time. A much more unpleasant welcome than usual was waiting for *Unbeaten* and her crew upon their arrival back at the small island.

15

IRON COFFIN

Unbeaten and her crew arrived in the Malta areas during the first dog watch on 20 January 1942 and headed for Marsamxet Harbour. Around a month earlier, on 29 December 1941, Lt. Pat Norman had been temporarily standing in command for David Wanklyn on board *Upholder,* just for the day. At around 16:30, both *Urge* and *Upholder* were also approaching Marsamxet after taking part in exercises. Frighteningly, and seemingly from nowhere, an ME 109 hurtled out of the sky while simultaneously firing its deadly twin cannons in the direction of the two submarines. The bridge team on *Urge* had seen the aircraft coming and the boat crash dived. Just several seconds too late, Pat Norman on the bridge of *Upholder* ordered his boat to dive. Then without delay he started following the signalman down the hatch. Unfortunately, one of the five 20mm cannon shells to hit *Upholder* burst in through the bridge, knocking Norman out. The signalman dragged him bodily down the conning tower and went back to shut the hatch. Lt. Norman received several shrapnel wounds but none life-threatening. He was lucky his injuries were not worse. It transpired that the ME 109 which fired on *Upholder* was shot down straight after this attack. The pilot survived and as fate would have it he ended up in the British naval hospital at Mtarfa along with Pat Norman. They even played Uckers together.

As *Unbeaten* made her approach on 20 January she was about 2NM from Marsamxet Harbour and looking to pick up the mine-swept channel. However, owing to a seized alternator (which supplied power to the gyro) the submarine had no Sperry gyroscopic compass. Woodward had to look through the periscope to navigate. Seeing it was all was clear up top, Teddy thought it prudent to surface and proceeded towards the harbour. Suddenly, and without any warning, two yellow-nosed ME 109s popped directly out from the glare of the sun and raced towards *Unbeaten*. As the enemy aircraft closed the defenceless submarine they opened up with their twin 20mm nose-mounted cannons and machine guns. The Messerschmitt ME 109 had a yellow nose and yellow tail rudder so that the aircraft was recognisable to its allies during dog fights. The sight of this fearsome aircraft hurtling towards you at a great rate of knots spewing gunfire must have been terrifying. Teddy Woodward ordered the submarine to crash dive. He then threw himself down the conning tower ladder. Within 30 seconds the boat was submerged. The submarine was hit by about eight cannon shells and machine gun fire. Norman Drury said, 'It sounded like a riveting hammer going over the top.' [104] It was only because Woodward saw them coming that he managed to order the boat to dive quickly and close the upper hatch. *Unbeaten* suffered only superficial damage to her bridge casing, and more importantly no one was injured.

The ME 109s were often deployed to strike in lightning quick attacks. The enemy pilots chose defensive positions like the entrances to harbours and airfields as their targets. By the time you knew they were on you it was usually too late. However, the anti-aircraft guns dotted around the island were regularly successful in shooting these bandits down. Sergeant William John Lazell served with the 27th Battery, 7th Battalion, Royal Artillery based in Malta between 1941 and 1944. Bill was a RDF/RADAR operator with a battery of heavy anti-aircraft guns. Sgt Lazell and his colleagues saw the worse of the siege and relentless bombing of the island. Their task was made more arduous because they had to regularly dismantle the RDF/RADAR station every 48 hours when their position was spotted by enemy aircraft and move to new locations. Whenever he had the chance, Bill used to man the twin Lewis Machine Guns and shoot at enemy aircraft.

Bill Lazell took hundreds of photographs during his time on the island several of which are in this book.

Amazingly, two ratings high up on the conning tower of the U-Class submarine *Upright* claimed to have shot down one ME 109 with one of their bridge-mounted 0.030 Vickers machine guns while the submarine was alongside. After this incident, Shrimp Simpson made it routine that returning boats should surface as close as 1NM from St Elmo Lighthouse. If the CO could not see a red flag flying from the Castile through the periscope then he was not to go up top to the bridge until the boat was past the breakwater. This attempt to prevent a repeat performance did not always work.

The Polish U-Class submarine *Sokol* was twice pounced on only 500 yards from the harbour. It was getting more dangerous every day for the submarines of the Tenth Flotilla. *Unbeaten* did eventually glide into Lazaretto Creek at 17:00, ending her fourteenth patrol. On their Jolly Roger the signalman would have stitched a 'U' shape with a line through it to signify the successful sinking of the German U-boat. The tanker, although not confirmed, also received a place on her black flag in the form of a white bar. Commander-in-Chief, Mediterranean said in his report of this war patrol that a high state of efficiency existed in *Unbeaten*. Praise indeed.

As their first prisoner of war, Hans Ploch, left *Unbeaten* and crossed the gangway, a keen-eyed Shrimp Simpson spotted Jack wishing the young German good luck with a friendly shake of hands. 'Put that man in my report for fraternising with the enemy.' [105] These shouted words must have made Jack Casemore wince. Jack was part of the casing party who slipped the boat when leaving harbour and secured her when returning back alongside. Several of the men had struck up a rapport with the young German sailor; not really a friendship but more of an understanding. An understanding that anyone of them could suffer what Hans Ploch was going through. After all the politics were removed they were all just submariners doing their jobs, albeit for two very different employers with altogether very different points of view. During his time on board *Unbeaten*, Ploch had been employed between decks, scrubbing out and acting as the Chief Petty Officers messman. Simpson said later that Ploch 'needed little encouragement to assume the privileged role of submarine mascot'.[106] Although they were not allowed to, many of the sailors would occasionally give him their tots of rum. Norman Drury remembers the German as being 'quite amiable' and 'quite a pleasant little lad'.[107] It was also said that Ploch would rotate around the boat trying his hand in different positions, for instance operating the hydroplanes or working in the galley. However, Norman caveated this with: 'We knew very well he couldn't do anything to us because he would have damaged himself.' [108]

On leaving *Unbeaten*, Johannes Ploch found himself in front of Shrimp Simpson in the Captain's HMS *Talbot* office. It was explained to him that he would be put into a cell until such time as the RAF could transfer him to Cairo. Unbeknown to Ploch, Cairo would be the location of his first proper interrogation. However, Simpson did not want to let his prize prisoner go without attempting to discover exactly how deep a German U-boat could go. If he could get an answer then this would allow British scientists to develop deeper setting depth charges to combat the U-boat menace. After some conversing and subtle questioning, Shrimp thought he had the answer: 260 metres or 850 feet. Not being content with the answer to this question Simpson now wanted to know more. He wanted to know whether *U331* was the real number of the sunken submarine. In order to question the German further it was decided he would be placed in a cell with another prisoner to see if he would talk. However, the other person was no ordinary P.O.W. The man was in fact a fluent German-speaking coxswain from the Polish Submarine *Sokol*. His name was CPO Ted Domisch. The faux prisoner was dressed in overalls and was to assume the guise of a downed German bomber crew member. Hans Ploch was no fool. The Polish sailor was rumbled straight away. Ploch was transferred to Cairo not long after this charade. Shrimp did in fact receive a roasting via a Major from military intelligence questioning his ad hoc interrogation methods. Shrimp wrote in his book that the Major had mockingly said to him: 'The man had been ruined by us and was completely security conscious.' [109]

Johannes Ploch was eventually transferred to Great Britain for further interrogation by the NID (Naval Intelligence Division). There is an interrogation report dated August 1942 (some eight months after the sinking of Ploch's submarine) in which the prisoner goes into more detail about his U-boat, her movements and her crew. Ploch did not arrive in Great Britain until 17 July 1942. It was noted by the professional interrogators that Hans Ploch had made several false statements during his initial interviews at Malta and Cairo. It was also noted that he was extremely difficult to interrogate due to his level of security consciousness and that fact that the

German knew only too well the advantage of being the only survivor. Eventually, Ploch's claim that *U331* was the German submarine he had been on was disproved. The actual U-boat that Ploch was standing on during those last moments was in fact *U374*, captained by 26-year-old Oberleutnant zur See Unmo Von Fischel, son of Admiral Hermann Von Fischel, who was himself a submariner in World War I.

NID also noted in their interrogation report of August 1942: 'It should be born in mind that Ploch has, during all his interrogations prior to arriving in England, lied circumstantially and vividly, and that he may not have changed his habits entirely.' [110] Luckily, since this report was written, information about the movements of *U374* have become more readily available and the events alluded to by Ploch can now be disproved or at times corroborated. It has been noticed by the author that several aspects of the NID interrogation report are in fact false or slightly misleading. Because of these inaccuracies, the author has drawn little from the interrogation report of Hans Ploch but has instead relied on SIGINT and information collected after the war to compile the movements of *U374*. These anomalies can be corrected by researching the decrypted cypher messages provided by Bletchley Park, which clearly show the boat's movements day to day. Another fantastic and reliable source of wartime U-boat information can be obtained by reading the mass of Kriegsmarine data captured at the end of the war.

Around mid-1942, a Royal Naval Volunteer Reserve (RNVR) officer who worked for the British Director of Naval Intelligence had thought of a daring but brilliant information gathering plan. He presented his idea to the boss. Why not send a unit of specially trained clandestine troops to the front line and intermingle them with regular soldiers? This unit of men could then advance with the troops, sweeping up high-grade intelligence as they went. The idea was seized upon and not long afterwards a band of specially selected men came together to form the infamous 30 Assault Unit. This unit was overseen by the same RNVR officer. His name was Fleming, Lieutenant Commander Ian Fleming to be precise. 30AU achieved many successes during the war in many theatres of operation. However, one of their biggest coups, and the one most pertinent to this story, would come as the war lurched towards its final juncture. It was during April 1945, a month before the war in Europe would end, that 30AU Team 55 stumbled, after some searching, upon one of the biggest hauls of intelligence captured by the Allies during World War II. It was when Team 55 arrived at Tambach Castle, near Coburg in Thuringia, Germany that they were led to a vast library in the castle. It was there that they discovered the entire German naval archives for the years 1868 to 1945. More specifically, this treasure trove of intelligence held everything pertaining to the Kriegsmarine between 1939 and 1945. This valuable information came in the form of KTBs (Kriegstagebücher) collated for the BdU (Befehlshaber der Unterseeboote), or Commander Submarines. Effectively, KTBs were detailed war diaries or logs of every U-boat, specifically complied for the perusal of the German naval command. Some of the details logged would even be passed on to the Führer. The author has noted during his research that the British patrol reports and daily logs available for viewing are comprehensive but nowhere near as fastidiously detailed and as readily available to view today as the German U-boat logs. It transpired that in 1944 all of the naval records had been moved from Berlin to prevent their destruction. Dönitz specifically wanted the records to be kept safe at all costs. It was through these transcripts that Karl Dönitz thought the integrity of the Kriegsmarine would be displayed to the outside world, showing that the German navy conducted themselves properly and, in particular, showing his U-boats in a relatively good light.

The German U-boat *U374* was a Type VIIC, measuring 67 metres long with a displacement of between 769 to 871 tons. She was effectively bristling with armament. The boat was armed with one 3.5 inch gun, one 20mm anti-aircraft gun and five 21-inch torpedo tubes. To feed these tubes she carried 14 eels. *U374* was part of the third wave of German U-boats to enter the Mediterranean on the orders of Hitler via Dönitz. Prior to her deployment to the Mare Nostrum, *U374* was a member of a four-boat Wolf Pack named 'Mordbrenner'. This group was known to have operated in waters south-east of Greenland from 16 October 1941 to 3 November 1941. The Mordbrenner group consisted of *U573*, *U374*, *U208* and *U109*. Records show that *U374* was quite successful operationally and several sinkings can be attributed to this boat. Unno Von Fischel's submarine sank the British freighter *King Malcolm* off Newfoundland on 31 October 1941. It has also been said by some naval researchers that *U374* sank the ex-British merchant steamer originally named *Notton*, which then became known as the French vessel *Rose Schiaffino*. However, this sinking has been logged by the author Jurgen Rohwer as being credited to *U569* off Newfoundland on 3

November 1941. The author concurs with Rohwer and has in his possession copies of decrypted cypher messages from *U374* to BdU stating that on 31 October 1941, *U374* did indeed sink a vessel of an estimated tonnage of 6,000 GRT. This would be consistent with the tonnage of the *King Malcolm*; the *Rose Schiaffino*, by contrast, had a reported estimated tonnage of only 5,000 GRT. Also the sinking of *Rose Schiaffino* was not reported in *U374's* patrol cypher decrypts. On 3 November, *U374* was ordered to return to the occupied French port of Brest for a re-fuel and re-arm. Many of the crew, stand fast those on duty, were allowed a couple of weeks' leave.

In early December, Von Fischel and his boat were tasked to head for the Mediterranean to form part of the third wave of U-boats to enter that sea. They were to join the 29th U-boat Flotilla, based at La Spezia. On the 11th, *U374* was ordered to head for that area in the Mediterranean at high speed on the proviso that she would refuel in Messina. The same day would see *U374* transit the Strait of Gibraltar. It was when the boat was just through the Straits and into the Alboran Sea that Fischel sighted and sank the British anti-submarine trawler HMS *Lady Shirley*. All 33 of the trawler's crew perished. HMS *Rosabelle*, a British patrol yacht, was also in the area and tried to locate the U-boat shortly after the sinking of *Lady Shirley*. Only 21 minutes after the first sinking, *U374* unleashed another torpedo, hitting *Rosabelle*. She sank within 30 seconds. Thirty crewmen, including her Captain, were lost; only nine survivors were plucked from the water by HMS *Sayonara*. A fraught Fischel sent a message saying: 'AM BEING HUNTED BY 4 DESTROYERS. REQUEST IMMEDIATE ASSISTANCE BY AIRCRAFT [*sic*].' [111] Fischel sent another more telling message soon after saying he would like to head straight for La Spezia because his U-boat was suffering from a snapped left shaft in its port diesel and a breakdown of diesel couplings. This damage was probably as a result of the attack by the four destroyers. Flag Officer Commanding U-boats ordered *U374* to head for La Spezia for repairs.

The German boat remained in the Italian port for four days and after repairs sailed again on 11 December for what would be her first and last Mediterranean patrol. The German submarine's designated patrol area was the north coast of Africa. Once the boat was far away from the area of La Spezia she was told to switch to the Crete message service and simultaneously she was placed under the operational command of the 23rd U-boat Flotilla based in Salamis. The enemy U-boat's crew spent an uneventful Christmas and New Year at sea. It was not until around 8 January that Johannes Ploch says the U-boat spotted a British convoy on transit in the direction of Mersa, having come from Benghazi. This sighting ties in with the record of cypher messages received from *U374*. Three very telling messages were sent to *U374* from the Captain U-boat, Mediterranean. The first was sent on the 7th, asking the boat to report on the situation in her designated area and also to provide information on any special experiences and observations. No reply was received by Captain U/B Med. Twice again on the 8th, *U374* was told to report her position and situation. No reply was received from *U374*. The reason for this silence could be attributed to the fact that Ploch said his U-boat had spent several hours stalking the convoy and moving into a good position for an attack. However, during the last dog watch, the stealthy *U374* was detected by Allied destroyers.

Von Fischel immediately dived deep down, eventually arriving at a depth of 187 metres, or 613 feet. Over the next two hours the attacking warships, HMS *Legion* and the Dutch destroyer HNLMS *Isaac Sweers*, dropped over 40 depth charges on *U374's* assumed position. These charges all exploded above the U-boat and they were said to have caused much damage. Ploch said in his interrogation report that the wireless and depth gauges were out of action and the torpedoes were no longer capable of being fired. To compound this situation both propeller shafts were leaking. It is revealing to note that NID, during the section of the interrogation covering this attack, still thought Ploch had lied about the depth his U-boat could go to. The NID interrogator wrote: 'The depth of 613 feet is an exaggeration.' [112] After all the noise had died down and the Allied destroyers had cleared the area, *U374* cautiously surfaced and assessed the damage then headed straight for the safety of Messina. Von Fischel's boat could not contact base to report their location or condition. Von Fischel would have been anxious. He would have known only too well that it was procedure in the German U-boat world that when a boat was unable to be raised on the W/T equipment for three consecutive days, on the third day the crew's families would be informed the submarine was presumed sunk. *U374* remained on the surface during her transit back to Messina. Ploch said that Von Fischel told the crew they would be quite safe on the surface because the weather and sea state were too rough for an Allied submarine to make an accurate attack. On 12 January 1942, *U374* crossed the patrol line of HMS/M *Unbeaten*. Von

Fischel's mistake was to underestimate the skills of a British submariner. This mistake would cost him his life and the life of his crew. In scribbled pen at the bottom of the final *U374* Bletchley cipher decrypts from Hut 8, one handwritten line simply states: 'Possibly sunk by S/M "Unbeaten" 1025/12/1/42 37° 50' N 16° 00' E.' [113] [*sic*]

16

PIER HEAD JUMP

Lieutenant John Dennis Martin was an experienced submariner. He had been in command of two other submarines previous to this current, albeit temporary, drive. J.D. Martin had commanded the submarines *L27* and *H43* prior to finding himself on board *Unbeaten.* This time he was there in the capacity of a stand-in Captain while Teddy Woodward was having a rest. No such breaks were afforded to the remainder of the boat's crew, though. It was around 20:00 on 2 February 1941 when J.D. Martin carefully steered *Unbeaten* out of harbour with all the care someone would show to another's newborn child. The submarine proceeded along the south-east searched channel and out towards open water. The weather was windy and the sea was rough. *Unbeaten* was heading for patrol area 'Kilo', also known as Kerkennah Banks (Bancs Qarqannah). The first five days of this fifteenth patrol were fairly quiet for the crew. Several enemy aircraft were spotted, which often necessitated that the boat be crash dived. The usually calm waters were pretty bad during this period; Martin ordered the submarine to be kept trimmed at around 70 feet during daylight hours. One reason for this was to keep the boat out of the sight of enemy aircraft. Another was to stay out of the inclement weather which ravaged the sea surface. Staying deep allowed for a slightly more comfortable passage.

On the morning of 7 February at around 09:20, a 5,200-ton Axis merchant vessel was spotted through the forward of *Unbeaten's* two periscopes. This forward-looking device was called the binocular or search periscope, the aft one being the attack periscope. The enemy vessel was not alone; she had one escorting destroyer, along with an additional bomber aircraft providing top cover. Thirty-four minutes after this initial sighting J.D. Martin ordered a salvo of four Mk. VIII torpedoes to be fired. The spread was achieved by an individual torpedo firing interval of 14.5 seconds at a range of 3,500 yards. The crew listened intently after hearing the tell-tale whooshes of the torpedoes exiting *Unbeaten's* bow. It was several minutes since the kippers had left their tubes and no hits had been heard; it seemed unlikely that they had sunk their target. Martin said in the patrol report: 'The torpedoes appeared to run correctly.' [114] Only ten minutes later the enemy made a fevered counter-attack which lasted around 20 minutes. J.D. Martin said in his report that 30 charges were dropped in this short time frame. All the charges were said to have exploded pretty close to the submarine. Bits of the boat's bulkhead cork covering were falling off as the depth charge pressure waves pounded the boat. It had been just over an hour since the first charges were dropped; all was quiet now. The submarine's search periscope was raised to allow the Captain to take a look around and see if their efforts had sunk anything.

Martin smartly followed the periscope up, rising from a crouched position, keen to have a good all-round look. However, a patrolling Axis CANT Z.506B floatplane put them deep again almost immediately. Reluctantly, without seeing any proof of a sinking, *Unbeaten* was set on a new course towards the south-eastern corner of her patrol area. The crew swiftly reloaded the empty torpedo tubes. Shrimp Simpson was again not happy with what was thought to be a waste of four torpedoes. Shrimp said in his post patrol report: 'The expenditure of 4 Mark VIII torpedoes on a north bound vessel was hardly justified in view of our extreme shortage at Malta.' George Simpson went on to say: 'However, it was the Commanding Officer's birthday and perhaps he felt particularly confident.' [115]

Research of the Italian archives carried out by Platon Alexiades shows the merchant ship attacked on 7 February 1942 was called the *Bosfore.* She was escorted by the Italian torpedo boat *Calliope* and one Savoia-Marchetti triple-engine aircraft. According to the report made by the crew of *Calliope*, two tell-tale torpedo tracks were spotted heading towards her while a third torpedo was seen making for *Bosforo*; they were all just avoided in time. Valentine's Day 1942 saw *Unbeaten* and her crew arrive safely back at Malta and secure within the confines of Lazaretto Creek.

The sixteenth and penultimate Malta war patrol embarked upon by *Unbeaten* started on 21 February 1942. It was expected that her Commanding Officer would be back on board to take her out of harbour. However, as it transpired, Teddy Woodward had sprained his back whilst ashore – doing what is anyone's guess. So J.D. Martin remained in command for this eventful patrol. Also joining *Unbeaten* on this day was Lt. Basil Charles Godfrey Place. B.C.G. Place was soon to become *Unbeaten's* next First Lieutenant. Godfrey Place would go on to relieve Aston Piper in March 1942. Simpson had previously called for Lt. Piper to come and see him at his HMS *Talbot* office. Shrimp informed Aston that the RNR officer had been selected to attend the next Submarine Commanding Officers' Qualifying Course and that he would soon be flying back to Great Britain. The experienced Piper was very pleased to be given the opportunity to eventually gain his own command. Aston Piper would go on to have a long and successful career in the submarine service. *Unbeaten* was sailed in company with three other submarines on the evening of the 21st. The plan was to head for Misurata and carry out a patrol in area 'Sierra' with the intention of intercepting a reported southbound enemy convoy. The inclement weather conditions made daily life on board the boat harsh. The submarine's transit speed was greatly reduced due to a head sea on the bow which allowed her to make only eight knots. In order to make up time, and ultimately distance, the command also stopped the usual preventative zig-zag plan which was normal procedure during a patrol. This tactic did not work and on the 23rd the boat was still 32 miles away from her required patrol position.

Eventually, Martin was ordered to move the boat to area 'India', which was between Kuriat Island and Lampion Rock; she arrived in the new position on 25 February. Nothing much happened between this date and 1 March. During the first day of March the crew stumbled across the hulk of an enemy ship which showed signs of having clearly been beaten up. It transpired that this vessel had earlier been attacked by Allied aircraft and subsequently torpedoed by the submarine *P35*. *Unbeaten* was closed to investigate. The stranded and wrecked vessel was beached with a list to port and her stern awash.

It was much later, at around 19:30, that the black smoke from an approaching southbound enemy convoy was spotted. The approaching group of vessels consisted of a 7,000-ton tanker in company with two other large merchant vessels and at least one or maybe two destroyers. It was thought possible by the command that this convoy was Vichien. Martin decided to close the screen of vessels and go in for an attack. At precisely 19:38 at a range of 4,000 yards, *Unbeaten* let go a salvo of four torpedoes with an 18-second separation interval. Martin aimed half a length ahead of the largest tanker. After 3 minutes and 43 seconds there was a massive, reassuring explosion. One of the four torpedoes had found its target. The three remaining torpedoes were said to have ended their run. However, the crew failed to hear these wasted weapons explode on the seabed. This was wholly due to the fact that the escorting destroyers instantly went on the defensive and dropped an estimated seven depth charges, blocking out any other sounds. *Unbeaten* went as deep as she could go in the 50 metres (164 feet) of water. The British submarine managed to sneak away silently. The next morning no HE was heard in the area so Martin thought it safe to surface and investigate in the position of the attack the day before. All that remained floating on the sea surface were some bits of wreckage, dirty oil and, surreally, an amount of fresh oranges bobbing up and down.

It was concluded that the suspected Vichy vessel had been sunk. Research shows that the large tanker was indeed a Vichy vessel. She was owned by the French railway company 'Paris-Lyon-Méditerranée'. The 110-metre *P.L.M. 20* was part of convoy S14 on passage from Sax to Bizerta. Also present in the group were *Chateau Latour*, *Sainte Odette* and *Sainte Simone.* These vessels were escorted by the sloop *La Batailleuse* and the torpedo boat *La Bombarde*. After the attack, *La Bombarde* reported having been missed by a torpedo. She then went on to drop five depth charges in the area of the suspected submarine. The sinking of this valuable tanker would see another white bar stitched to *Unbeaten's* Jolly Roger. Shortly after the successful attack on *P.L.M. 20, Unbeaten* was recalled by Captain S10. The submarine altered course and started heading back towards Malta. The crew reloaded the barren tubes with the remaining four tin fish. They had to be ready for any eventuality.

It was the evening of 2 March and *Unbeaten* was on the surface charging her batteries as she continued towards Malta. At around 22:00, a lookout spotted something in the water. As the boat closed the object the darkness receded to reveal a large piece of floating wreckage. It was estimated to be around 35 feet in length and made of all wood construction covered in canvas. It soon became apparent that the crew were looking at a piece of aircraft wreckage. The top side of what looked like the span of a wing was camouflaged with brown circles on a yellow background. The underside was very light blue. Not all of the wing could be seen as some was submerged and no markings of origin were visible. It was thought that what remained of the aircraft had only been in the water a few days. The wreckage was in a position bearing 285° from Lampedusa at 40NM. Simpson expressed in his report that it was the wreckage of an Italian fighter aircraft. The camouflage markings would be consistent with this nationality of aircraft. J.D Martin made a pencil sketch of the wing span in the patrol log. What had happened to that aircraft? Where were the crew? The wreckage was left where it was found and *Unbeaten* slipped back into the dark.

Early in the morning of 3 March a large trawler was sighted within firing range of *Unbeaten's* torpedoes. Martin showed great restraint and did not fire on the relatively unworthy target. He was acutely mindful of the lack of torpedoes at Malta. During the first watch that evening the ASDIC operator detected HE. It was deduced from the operator's experience that the owner of that HE was in fact an enemy U-boat. The British submarine started to hunt the enemy boat. It was not long after, however, that the HE suddenly disappeared. It was likely that the U-boat was on passage and simply outran *Unbeaten* without even knowing it. It was now Thursday 5 March. During the early part of the middle watch, *N93* surfaced and proceeded towards Malta, arriving at 07:00. This arrival successfully concluded what would be J.D. Martin's last patrol on board *Unbeaten.* Simpson ended his report of this patrol by saying, 'This was a well-executed patrol … and no opportunity for offensive action was allowed to pass.' [116]

17

GUGLIELMOTTI

The day before *Unbeaten* would embark on her final war patrol from Malta, another name synonymous with the final days of the submarine would join her alongside at the besieged Lazaretto. Sub-Lt. P.W. Cannon arrived on board on 11 March 1942. Rated Lieutenant in April of the same year Patrick Cannon would eventually go on to become *Unbeaten's* last First Lieutenant. But for now he was working under Teddy Woodward and Godfrey Place. Aston Piper had returned to Great Britain and Place was now the new No. 1 on *Unbeaten*. Godfrey had previously been drafted on loan to the Polish U-Class submarine *Sokol* as the liaison officer serving under Captain Borys Karnicki. Godfrey had a very successful time on board the hard-working Polish boat and this had earned him the Krzyz Walecznych – the Polish equivalent of the Military Cross. It was awarded to him on 10 February 1942 for good services in Polish ships. It was all go for the very able Lt. Place. He had only just been promoted to Lieutenant on 16 January of that year. However, with the sudden removal of Piper back to Great Britain for his Submarine Commanding Officers' Course, B.C.G. Place was effectively 'pier head jumped' to join *Unbeaten*, which means it was a last minute draft for him. The Navy List of early 1942 shows Godfrey Place as being attached to HMS *Talbot* as a Sub-Lieutenant, having joined on 1 September 1941. Also on the list of those officers affiliated to the Lazaretto base at that time were the names of the spare Commanding Officers like Lt. C.P. Norman and Lt. J.D. Martin. At the same time, named above Place on the list of staff was the then Sub-Lt. P.W. Cannon.

With Teddy Woodward back at the helm, the revised crew sailed from Malta for *Unbeaten's* seventeenth war patrol. The submarine moved down the mine-swept channel at around 20:30. As Teddy stood on the bridge watching the blackout-darkened, moonlit shape of Malta dissipate behind him, little did he know that this would be the last Malta war patrol for him, his crew and their U-Class submarine. Fate had something in store for *Unbeaten*, but not before *Unbeaten* would deal out some fate of her own. Prior to the British boat sailing, her command was warned about the possibility of E-boats operating 5NM to the north of the island of Gozo (known by the locals as Ghawdex), which lies to the north-west of Malta. To that end, loud HE was heard in the reported direction but nothing was seen. The submarine's orders were to proceed to area 'November', which was south of the Straits of Messina. Shrimp said in the patrol report: '*Unbeaten* had freedom of action in the area which was well known to Lieutenant Commander Woodward.' [117] The submarine closed the Calabrian coast and much activity was noted in the area in the way of enemy aircraft and minesweepers.

As it would transpire, the next careful positioning of *Unbeaten* on 16 March 1942 was to pay dividends. It was 11:37 in the morning when smoke was sighted on the horizon through the periscope. The weather was very poor with patchy mist. Soon afterwards, the familiar silhouette of a destroyer was spotted. Woodward ordered the submarine to approach the vessel at full speed. Around 13 minutes after the initial sighting of smoke, the faint outline of a merchant ship was seen about 5NM away. The submarine continued to close but Teddy soon realised that an attack would be futile due to the bad weather conditions and the extreme distance of the target. Also, the submarine was well abaft the target's beam, which would have made a shot tricky, if not impossible. As he had done before in this area of the Straits, Teddy positioned his submarine closer to the south-west of the coast. Later in the day and just into the first dog watch, another vessel was spotted. The ship in question had an estimated 11,000-ton displacement.

The large merchant vessel was heavily escorted by three Axis destroyers and three aircraft. It was instantly decided to close for an attack. Woodward chose an attack position astern of the second destroyer and he tried to get his submarine as close as possible. At one minute past 17:00 the destroyer passed only 150 yards ahead of the submerged *Unbeaten*. Five minutes later, 'Fire' was the order. A dispersed 'A' salvo was let loose in the direction of the merchant vessel. The first of four individually aimed torpedoes was fired at a range of 4,000 yards with a depth setting of between 10 and 12 feet. At around 3 minutes and 50 seconds, and 3 minutes 58 seconds later, two ear-shattering explosions were heard. The British submarine would have adopted its well-practised escape routine after firing its torpedoes. As expected, two of the destroyers went into attack mode and saturated the area with depth charges. However, the coordination of the reprisal was not very accurate; the destroyers never dropped more than three charges on any one attack leg. One hour and twenty-four minutes after the first torpedo was fired, the depth charge attack eventually abated. Teddy Woodward cautiously looked through the periscope and saw two destroyers stopped dead in the water, drifting close to the shore, just off Cape Bruzzano. There was no sign of the target. Another destroyer was sighted speeding down the coast towards the stationary enemy vessels, but it was too late, *Unbeaten* was gone.

Platon Alexiades concluded from his research of Italian archive material that the merchant vessel attacked on 16 March 1942 was the *Vettor Pisani*. She was escorted by two Navigatori Class destroyers – *Vivaldi*, and *Malocello* – along with the torpedo-boat *Sirtori*. An escorting CANT Z.501 No. 4 of 184 Squadriglia had reported sighting a torpedo track fired from a distance of about 2,000 metres. The enemy aircraft dropped two 160kg bombs on the origin of the track. However, the result of the enemy counter-attack remained uncertain to the Italians. Indeed, *Unbeaten* had escaped; Teddy had decided it was time to clear the area and reload.

The next day was Tuesday 17 March and *Unbeaten* was in a position to the south of Del Armi. It was 06:33 in the morning and the British boat had only just submerged half an hour earlier, after successfully charging her batteries overnight. It was now 20 minutes before sunrise, but it was still very dark up top and the weather was misty and overcast. Suddenly, a cry of 'diesel HE bearing 130°' echoed throughout the submarine. One-and-a-half minutes later and against the first light of dawn, the recognisable silhouette of a U-boat was sighted through the forward periscope at a range of 2,200 yards. Woodward ordered the submarine to be steered onto a 100° track but when he got there he could not see the target. Teddy gave another order to alter to 130° and then gave the engine order to increase to full speed. Teddy was busy calculating a firing solution in his head. By looking at the target through the periscope, Teddy deduced that the enemy submarine was on a course of 005° at 10 knots. The torpedo depth settings were fixed between 8 and 10 feet. Without any hesitation Woodward fired a dispersed 'A' salvo from a range of only 2,000 yards, while *Unbeaten* was still at full speed and in the turn. The torpedoes were fired from the submerged British submarine as the boat was still swinging round to her new course. This movement allowed the torpedoes to spread from the bow to the stern of the target. Only one-and-a-half minutes after the salvo was fired, a single explosion was heard. The diesel HE stopped simultaneously. There was another altogether familiar sound travelling through the water layers: the wrenching, grinding noise of the U-boat breaking up. The whole attack had lasted only five-and-a-half minutes.

Thanks to the research carried out by Platon Alexiades, the author can describe with some accuracy the movements of the U-boat just prior to her sinking. The U-boat in question was the Italian Brin Class submarine *Guglielmotti*. The events leading up to the sinking of *Guglielmotti* were initially triggered weeks earlier. It had been intimated by the German naval command that several Italian submarines were languishing in the French port of Bordeaux. The German government suggested to the Italian Supermarina that they move their submarines to the Mediterranean and assist in the ongoing Libyan offensive. *Guglielmotti* left Bordeaux on 22 September 1941, passing Gibraltar at the end of that month. After a small patrol, the boat eventually arrived at Messina on 16 October. She was then ordered to transit to Taranto and berth for an extensive refit. Post-refit, several routine trials and exercises took place throughout February and March. The fully worked-up and tested *Guglielmotti* sailed from Taranto at 17:30 on 15 March 1942 and headed for Cagliari, where she was to join the VII Grupsom (7th Submarine Flotilla). As history shows, *Unbeaten* made sure she never made it.

At around 07:20 on 17 March, *Unbeaten* was surfaced in an attempt to pick up any possible survivors from *Guglielmotti's* crew, of whom about twelve were spotted floundering in the water. Woodward wrote in the patrol report: 'Survivors all appeared to be wearing "collar" life jackets.' [118] Although reluctant to leave the poor submariners treading water, Teddy had no choice. Owing to the close proximity of several enemy fighter aircraft, he had to dive *Unbeaten* to save his own crew. This forced him to go deep and clear the area. After the news of *Guglielmotti's* sinking had filtered through to the Italians, a destroyer – the *Francesco Stocco* – was dispatched to the area of the attack. She was tasked to search for any survivors and also attempt to hunt the Allied submarine. At 10:10, Woodward reported in the log that 24 distant depth charges were heard. The Italian archives say only 17 depth charges were dropped without result. The Italians also say that one body was found and that a total of 7 officers and 54 ratings were lost. However, in contradiction to this testament many of the crew of *Unbeaten* would go on to receive decorations and citations for this and the merchant vessel attack the day before. Regarding *Guglielmotti*, it says in the crew's 'Recommendation for Decoration or Mention in Despatches': 'This sinking has subsequently been confirmed by a prisoner captured from another U-boat who was a survivor from this event.' [119] So it seems someone did survive the sinking of *Guglielmotti*, although this revelation is of little comfort to the families of those men who died.

Two days later, having expended her torpedoes, *N93* was back at Marsamxett Harbour, arriving at 08:50. This was a quick turnaround and would still be classed as part of her seventeenth patrol. The men worked hard to reload a full complement of torpedoes. Within 11 hours the unrested crew of *Unbeaten* were back at sea, slipping and proceeding at dusk. Woodward was given orders to make headway towards to a new patrol area. Shrimp told Teddy to concentrate his efforts on an area bearing 165° at 11NM from Del Armi. The British submarine was strategically placed in this area because a vital British convoy was sailing from Alexandria to Malta. *Unbeaten's* orders were to intercept any Axis cruisers which looked like they could threaten this convoy as it made its way towards Malta. However, between 22 and 24 March the weather was atrocious and this kept *Unbeaten* deep. At times it was too rough even to maintain periscope depth. Woodward kept his boat at around 70 feet but maintained a listening watch. It was later confirmed that several enemy cruisers did enter the Straits between these dates but they went unheard by *Unbeaten* and the submarine *P34*, which was also in the vicinity. On the 24th, *N93* was again recalled to Malta.

The fast-moving convoy which *Unbeaten* was supposed to be covering consisted of four ships carrying vital supplies for Malta. The merchant vessels were the *Breconshire, Clan Campbell, Pampas* and the *Talabot*, which in turn were escorted by the British cruisers HMS *Cleopatra, Dido, Euryalus and Penelope*, along with nine destroyers. The convoy did eventually arrive at Malta but it was very battered. During the early part of the convoy, the destroyer HMS *Hurworth* was busy sweeping ahead of the main group when she was torpedoed and sunk. The attacking Axis vessels received short shrift from the British escorts and they too suffered casualties. Shrimp Simpson said of *Unbeaten's* seventeenth war patrol, 'This profitable and well executed patrol has again demonstrated Lieutenant Commander Woodward's excellent judgment at attack and more and better targets seem to be coming his way.' [120] Little did Simpson know what the Luftwaffe had in store for *Unbeaten* in the not too distant future.

18

A DAPPER LITTLE MAN

Air attacks on Malta were increasing in their ferocity. It transpired that some of the supply ships which reached Grand Harbour from the convoy mentioned in the last chapter were badly damaged in air raids on 26 March. The merchant vessels *Talabot* and *Pampas* were hit by bombs. Also during that evening the *Breconshire* was hit. She caught fire and eventually rolled over and sank. Much of these vessels' vital cargo was lost to fire. However, on a positive note, several Spitfire aircraft were landed on the island over a two-day period, having been transported and flown off British aircraft carriers. Also, two Beauforts and three Blenheim bombers had arrived from Gibraltar to augment Malta's air defences. Shrimp was very concerned about the well-being of his submarines. Malta was becoming more and more indefensible. At times, the Malta-based submarines looked like they were the last defence of the island. The Admiralty was reluctant to move the submarines from Malta as this would mean Rommel's supply line could continue unchecked. The Axis bombings were getting much worse and valuable submarines were getting hit. Jack Casemore remembers: 'Sliema was in a hell of a state, buildings were laying in rubble and very few bars were open.' [121]

Over the month of March 1942, Malta had been on the receiving end of 365 air raids by enemy aircraft. Shrimp decided to do something to try and protect his submarines. He couldn't risk getting them blown up alongside the Lazaretto – or out on the trots for that matter. Around 6 March, Captain Simpson had started, albeit reluctantly, to tell his submarine Captains to dive their boats in deep water berths during daylight hours. However, there was almost always one submarine refitting and unable to dive. This boat was kept alongside the Lazaretto and rotated around when refits were completed. Upon *Unbeaten's* return on 27 March, the practice of berthing at the bottom of the harbour was already being adhered to. *Unbeaten* was ordered to proceed up Msida Creek, just off Marsamxett Harbour, to unload her torpedoes and stores. Because the boats would be sat on the seabed all day every day, Shrimp made it a policy that only a small duty watch would remain on board submarines when dived in the confines of the harbour. The submarines' crew were split into three watches. Two watches would reside ashore for the day and one watch would remain on board. These watches would then rotate on a daily basis. The defect rectification work that would usually be carried out on the submarines during the day would now take place at night.

Unbeaten's skeleton crew moved the submarine out of Msida Creek and into Lazaretto Creek. It was here, on April Fools' Day, 1942, that *Unbeaten* was dived. In charge during the dive on that day was Godfrey Place. Also on board was the boat's Petty Officer (Tel) Norman Drury, two seamen, one Engine Room Artificer and a stoker. One of the seamen was Jack Casemore and the other was his mate Duggy Upton. Jack wrote an account of this time and remembers that once the boat's engines were stopped, the submarine gently touched down on the sandy bottom in about 40-50 feet of water. The conning tower was just awash but slightly proud of the water line. Jack said, 'We had breakfast, tidied the boat, then turned in for a well-deserved sleep.' [122]

Shrimp Simpson remembers that 'between 14:30 and 15:00 a heavy raid of Ju88s followed by Ju87s developed on the harbour area…' [123] During this raid, nine Ju88s dropped a total of 65 high-explosive bombs right across Grand Harbour and also across Marsamxett Harbour. Six of these enemy bombs were of the devastating 1000kg variant. Jack, Duggy and a stoker were getting their heads down in their hammocks, tucked up in the fore-ends of the *Unbeaten,* which was sitting quietly at the bottom of the creek.

Suddenly they were abruptly shaken by a massive explosion. The attacking Luftwaffe Ju88s had dropped a couple of sticks of bombs from north to south across the Lazaretto. Both Jack Casemore and Norman Drury have since said in their private papers and recorded interviews that the raid which affected *Unbeaten* took place between 10:00 and 10:40 on that day. This contradicts Shrimp Simpson's statement. However, what was for sure, and agreed by all, was that the bombs landed very close to *Unbeaten*.

Jack Casemore remembers finding himself and his shipmates blown into the corner of the aft port bulkhead by the force of the explosion. Norman Drury, who was in the boat's Petty Officers' Mess at the time, said: 'It picked the submarine up off the bottom and shook it like a dog shaking a rat.' [124] When the submarine settled again, sea water was rushing into the empty torpedo tube space, which had been badly distorted by the bombs. Water was also coming in from the twisted watertight seal around the fore hatch. Luckily, in accordance with procedure, all the watertight doors and hatches had been shut prior to the attack. However, all the lights were out and everywhere was in complete darkness. It must have been terrifying. Simpson had witnessed the attack and saw the bombs hit the water close to *Unbeaten*. Once the raid had abated, a motor boat from *Talbot* raced over to *Unbeaten* to see if her unfortunate crew were all right. Because the conning tower was only slightly awash, Captain Simpson was able to make contact with the crew and tell them to surface. It took a while but Godfrey Place and his reduced crew managed to blow the ballast tanks and bring the damaged boat up to the surface; a miraculous escape indeed.

The first day of April would see 148 enemy aircraft drop countless bombs on Malta; around nine ships and submarines were hit during a day of relentless attacks. The submarine *Pandora* had just returned to Malta after her refit in America with the *Truant*. The *Pandora* had entered Grand Harbour and her crew were unloading a supply of torpedoes at Hamilton Wharf for use by other submarines. The roar of aircraft overhead was the only warning her crew had; she was pounced on in an early raid that day. A bomb went directly down the boat's engine room hatch and exploded. *Pandora* sank in four minutes, with the loss of 26 men. The British submarine *P36* was also badly damaged and rolled over while tied up to the Lazaretto. This happened despite the best efforts of naval personnel ashore attempting to prevent the boat from capsizing.

Unbeaten's time in Malta would end rather indignantly, however. Owing to the damage caused to her torpedo tubes, inflicted by the air raid, the boat was deemed operationally useless. A decision was made by the Admiralty, and supported by Shrimp Simpson, to send *Unbeaten* to Gibraltar to be examined in the dry dock there. On 8 April, temporary repairs were made to *Unbeaten* at Malta. These essential repairs were to make her watertight and seaworthy, although she was still in a very sorry state. On 9 April 1942, *Unbeaten* and her crew sailed from Malta, as they always did, during the early evening under cover of darkness. Out of Lazaretto Creek, past Dragut Point, and once out of the swept channel, she was in open water. Unbeknown to the crew, this would be the last time that *Unbeaten* would ever sail from this brave little island. Malta would remain undefeated throughout the war. The island would hold an unenviable place in history by becoming one of the most fought-over islands of World War II. Malta and its people became well-deserved recipients of the George Cross, awarded to the island on 13 September 1942.

The next forenoon, just a cruising watch remained awake on board *N93*; the rest of the crew were asleep or relaxing. Suddenly, it became obvious that Teddy Woodward had smelt something. He jumped out of his rack and told the stokers to lift the battery boards up. Sure enough, several of the battery cells had spilt, which had probably been caused by the recent bombing. The cells were leaking sulphuric acid, which, when mixed with salt water can create highly toxic chlorine gas. It was common practice for boats to carry electrical short-cutting straps, which Norman Drury said were 'made of copper and as thick as your arm'.[125] These leads had connection terminals on each end and were used to bypass defective battery cells and connect undamaged cells with other good ones. However, the crew did not have enough leads to bypass all the damaged cells and several sulphuric acid-filled battery cells had leaked dry overnight. As luck would have it, in the envelope containing his submarine's orders, Teddy Woodward had read that on 11 March, *Unbeaten* was to rendezvous with *Upholder*, which would transfer some Special Commandos to *Unbeaten* for passage onwards to Gibraltar. Once at Gib, the Army personnel would be landed and continue their journeys. It was thought that maybe *Unbeaten* could purloin some battery leads from *Upholder*.

The night of 9 April was also a significant one for *Upholder*. This was the boat's twenty-fifth war patrol from Malta. David Wanklyn had been on board for nearly all of these patrols, except when ordered to rest by Shrimp Simpson. This night, *Upholder* and her crew were tasked to disembark two native North African agents safely onto the coast near Carthage, on the tip of Tunisia. To facilitate this clandestine operation, two Special Commandos were embarked, along with a Folboat and a rubber dinghy, amongst other kit. They had been on board since the *Upholder's* departure from Malta. The two men were part of the Special Boat Section like Lt. Richard Broome and Corporal Harry Slater, who had embarked on board *Unbeaten* back in September 1941.

Captain Robert A. Wilson DSO, Royal Artillery and Lance Corporal Charles Parker of the Beds and Herts Regiment were the two Special Commandos selected for this operation. Tug Wilson was a slight man and not tall. He was dashing looking but did not look like the typical comprehension of a Commando. Norman Drury described him as 'a dapper little man'.[126] Tug was now well-known to all the Malta submarine Captains and had embarked on several clandestine submarine landing operations during 1941 up to this point. That pitch dark night, Tug Wilson left *Upholder* and towed the two agents towards the drop-off point as they sat motionless in the inflatable RAF rubber dinghy. Tug skilfully paddled the Folboat, whilst at the same time guiding the unwieldy rubber craft across the still water. When they were close enough to land, Tug cut the dinghy loose and the inflatable craft surfed onto the shore. Wilson returned to *Upholder* having successfully completed another mission. *Upholder's* orders on completion of this operation were to transfer Tug Wilson to *Unbeaten* so he could be dropped off at Gibraltar and make his own way back to Great Britain.

Unbeaten was to rendezvous with *Upholder* in the early hours of 11 April in a position 2NM off Lampion Rock, which is approximately 10.5NM north-west of the island of Lampedusa. Norman Drury says of this pre-arranged meeting: 'By ASDIC we called the *Upholder* and he answered but Wanklyn was very, very cagey about displaying where he was.' [127] A few hours before the break of dawn the two U-Class submarines had surfaced, albeit trimmed down and edged towards each other through the half-light. The weather was deteriorating and the boats would soon be diving at dawn. Leaving Lance Corporal Charley Parker on board *Upholder* to go back to Malta with the submarine, Tug paddled his Folboat over to *Unbeaten*. He also brought with him all the battery cutting-out straps the *Upholder* could spare. Once alongside *Unbeaten*, Wilson climbed out of his canoe, which was then unceremoniously passed down the forward hatch, followed by the Special Commando. The two submarines then parted company. This would be the last time any living man would see *Upholder*, along with the most successful and decorated British submarine Captain in World War II and his loyal crew. The submarine, which was launched from the same dock the day before *Unbeaten*, slipped off into the murky blackness. She was last seen steering south to continue her allotted patrol off the western approaches to Tripoli. The next day, 12 April, all communications with *Upholder* were lost. The crew of another submarine tasked in the same patrol line as *Upholder* said they heard heavy depth charging on the 14th. *Upholder* had disappeared. There is much conjecture about what became of *Upholder* and it would not be for the author to surmise what had happened. The story of the supposed untimely demise of *Upholder* has been repeated by many authors, and in a way, this repetition of varying theories strengthens the legend which has become a testament to *Upholder*. It has been said by several submariners who have been depth charged that if you can hear the ominous hydrostatic pistol click of the depth charge, which takes place half a second before it explodes, then it's too close. Did the crew of *Upholder* hear this final click?

A battered and tired *Unbeaten* eventually arrived at Gibraltar on 21 April. She was in such a state with the gassing batteries, etc. that the submarine had to surface the day before they got in and proceed with the rest of the passage to Gibraltar on the surface. The crew of *Unbeaten* did not hear about the loss of *Upholder* for some time. It also transpired that David Wanklyn had invited Tug Wilson to stay on board *Upholder* if he wished, while they completed their patrol. The decision made by Tug to leave Wanklyn's boat that night ultimately saved his life. Tug Wilson left *Unbeaten* in Gibraltar and would, over the course of the rest of the war, become a legend in his field of clandestine expertise. He even had a book written about him, which is well worth a read. Sadly, Lance Corporal Charles Parker also went down with *Upholder*. He would not be the only non-Royal Navy person to go down on a submarine. A news reporter who embarked on the U-Class submarine *Urge* also lost his life along with her crew when she too was sunk at around the same time as *Upholder*.

19

ONCE IS ENOUGH IN ANYONE'S LIFETIME

Eventually arriving at Algeciras Bay on Tuesday 21 April, *Unbeaten* manoeuvred alongside the submarine depot ship *Maidstone*. The plucky boat managed to make Gibraltar with only one-and-a-half cracked and leaking batteries remaining on board. She had left half of one battery in Malta for the benefit of other submarines. Weighted monkey's fists tied on the end of heaving lines were thrown down by *Maidstone's* crew, landing with a thud on the submarine's casing. *Unbeaten's* ropes were bent on, hauled up and secured forward and aft over *Maidstone's* bollard bits. The submarine's crew were all pretty shattered, especially after the bombing inflicted at Malta and the long surface transit to Gib. Lt. Alastair Mars, who was Commanding Officer of the Group 2 U-Class submarine *Unbroken*, remembers Teddy Woodward's boat reaching Gibraltar that day. Mars and the other COs alongside Gib would have chatted and exchanged dits in *Maidstone's* wardroom. There was a bar in the Wardroom and its surroundings afforded some comfort. Mars was keen to get to Malta and get amongst the thick of it; he said of Woodward and his crew, 'Understandably, they were not anxious to discuss their experiences.' *Unbroken's* CO went on to say, 'The slaughter and havoc were too vivid in their minds to be the subjects of chatty conversations.' [128]

The infamous Port Logs, rescued from a skip, tell us that *Unbeaten* remained alongside *Maidstone* until 29 April. On that day, the damaged submarine was taken in hand by Gibraltar dockyard staff and went into a period of 'Docking and Essential Defects' – in 1942, this period of defect rectification was known as D of D, and is known today as D.E.D., which basically means the same thing. The submarine would undergo temporary bomb damage repairs, which would take over three weeks to complete. During this long spell at Gibraltar, the boat's crew took time to sort themselves out and also have a bit of relaxation and recreation. Bars on the island were plentiful; however, things could be a bit subdued as there was a curfew at 23:00 each night. Captain Tug Wilson eventually left Gibraltar a week after *Unbeaten* brought him to the vast rock peninsula. At this time, Tug and *Unbeaten's* crew were still unaware of the loss of *Upholder*. Tug Wilson travelled back to Great Britain, eventually arriving at Liverpool on board the Royal Navy corvette HMS *Gardenia*. The ten-day trip took Wilson through waters teeming with German U-boats that were coming and going from their safe havens in the occupied French ports. Although the *Gardenia* survived this jaunt, she would flounder on 9 November 1942, when she was in collision with another Royal Navy vessel in the Mediterranean, and sank. Captain Wilson was summoned to Northways, at Swiss Cottage, which was where Flag Officer Submarines Max Horton worked from. Horton had told a shocked and saddened Wilson the bad news concerning *Upholder*. Although Tug's mission from *Upholder* had been successful and the agents were providing vital information, the sting was taken out of the tail of the clandestine operation's success with the news of the demise of *Upholder's* crew. Tug passed on a photograph and a handwritten letter given to him by David Wanklyn and addressed to the submarines ace's wife. Max Horton duly passed these last heart-wrenching mementoes to the widow of Lt. Wanklyn VC.

While on the island of Gibraltar it is highly likely that the indomitable Teddy Woodward did a bit of networking. He was pictured with Lord Gort VC, who had commanded the British Expeditionary Force (BEF) and had overseen their retreat from Dunkirk in 1940 during '*Operation Dynamo'*. Gort was then appointed as Governor of Gibraltar and Malta, a position he would hold between 1941 and 1944. However, more importantly, Teddy Woodward met with Mr R.G. Casey, whom, at that time in April 1942 was the British Minister of State. Mr Casey would soon become Lord Casey and take on the role of Governor-General of Australia. Teddy Woodward eventually retired to that antipodean isle after the war. It is widely known that one required a sponsor to be able to permanently reside in Australia.

The repairs to *Unbeaten* would be completed by 18 May; incidentally, this was the date that *Upholder* and her gallant crew were officially reported missing, presumed lost. Back in Malta on 22 April, Shrimp Simpson had made the decision that the Tenth Submarine Flotilla's position at the old Lazaretto in Malta was untenable. It was reluctantly decided by the Admiralty, on the advice of Simpson, to evacuate the Malta submarines and deploy the boats to the relative safety of Alexandria, where Captain Philip Ruck-Keene was now Captain S1. All the Malta submarines arrived at Alexandria with the exception of *N17* – the *Urge*. This U-Class boat had left Malta on 27 April on passage to Egypt. Although it has never been confirmed, *Urge* was said to have been sunk on 29 April 1942. As part of the evacuation, *Urge* was transporting around ten passengers, along with her crew, to Alexandria. There was, however, an unofficial passenger whose existence on board *Urge* was revealed only in 2003. Bernard Gray was a journalist on the British Sunday Pictorial. He was a well-known war correspondent of the time and was often referred to as 'the man who goes everywhere'.[129] Before his departure on that fateful sailing, he wrote to his wife: 'My own darling, I'm going away now on a trip which is dangerous. It's the last thing of its kind I shall ever do. I'm doing this for the children.' [130] The *Urge,* her crew and her passengers were never seen nor heard from again.

Although temporary repairs were implemented and *Unbeaten's* shattered gassing batteries had been shovelled out, the Port Logs reveal what was discussed at a high level on completion of the dockyard work: 'It would be unwise to sail "U" for patrol work until permanent repairs are affected.' The log goes on to say: '"U" should be taken in hand at Chatham about mid-June on completion of HMS/M *Unique* and instead of *Upholder.* [131] So it was that *Unbeaten* left Gibraltar for the second and final time on 26 May 1942. The British submarine set course for Great Britain and the home of the Royal Navy, Portsmouth.

The day after *Unbeaten* sailed from Gibraltar, the T-Class British submarine HMS/M *Torbay* sailed into the imposing rock-sheltered harbour, after successfully ending her eleventh Mediterranean war patrol. She had sailed from the Egyptian port of Alexandria on 12 April and reached

Gibraltar on the 27th. The *Torbay* was also destined to return to Great Britain for a refit. She did not stay in Gibraltar for long. Once refuelled, she sailed only three days behind *Unbeaten* and was also bound for Gosport, near Portsmouth. Much vigilance was required when returning to Britain across the Bay of Biscay. This area of ocean harboured a lot of U-boat activity. German and Italian U-boats were tucked into ports right up the Atlantic coast line of France. The Bay of Biscay was not so much a patrol area for U-boats but more of a transit zone. Enemy submarines would arrive in the bay returning from Wolf Pack operations off the United States and patrols off Newfoundland, Canada. They would need to pass through the bay to get back to their occupied ports. There was even a rumour that German U-boats were refuelling from blockaded vessels alongside Spanish ports like Vigo and El Ferrol and then proceeding back to sea. Unhindered, *Unbeaten* crossed the sometimes hostile Bay of Biscay, reaching the English Channel and her reporting position of Bishop Rock Lighthouse with no reported problems. A day or so before arriving at Portsmouth, *Unbeaten* rendezvoused with the quicker T-Class boat *Torbay* off a Devon peninsula called Start Point. Both submarines would enter Portsmouth Harbour in company on 8 June 1942 to well-deserved pomp and ceremony. Once alongside Dolphin at Gosport, *Torbay* tied up first, followed by *Unbeaten*. It had been exactly one year, one month and 28 days since the boat and the majority of her crew had left Portsmouth back in April 1941. There must have been much rejoicing and relief at returning home and also sadness for those who did not return. The two watches of *Unbeaten's* crew who were not on duty were given weekend leave. Norman Drury said after his return to Pompey, 'I didn't want to go to the Malta again [*sic*] … once is enough in anyone's lifetime.' [132]

It was at Dolphin or Fort Blockhouse that *Unbeaten* paid off. A sizable majority of her crew left the boat at this point, including Norman Drury and Jack Casemore. A skeleton crew would have taken the submarine to Sheerness and into Chatham Docks for her well-earned refit. When you think hard about it, one circumstance really does affect what happens in the future. If the German bomb aimer had not dropped the stick of bombs across the Lazaretto at the precise moment he did then *Unbeaten* probably would not be back in Great Britain and in a refit and, ironically, in place of *Upholder*. It was on 16 June that *Unbeaten* was taken in hand by the Chatham dockyard staff and she entered D of D on 22 June 1942.

Poignantly, six days before *Unbeaten* finally reached Portsmouth, a fledgling RAF Coastal Command flight named 172 Squadron received a signal from No. 19 Group RAF, under the command of Air Vice-Marshal G.R. Bromet, CB, CBE, DSO. The signal read: 'Four aircraft and crews of 172 Squadron will be operational from 15:00 on 02/06/42.' [133] The receipt of this signal marked the culmination of a long period of anti-submarine training for the crews of the Wellington bombers stationed at RAF Chivenor in North Devon. During their training the aircrews were no strangers to exercising with live submarines. In-fact they are recorded to have carried out practice attacks on the British submarines *H34* and *Thunderbolt*. The Air Station log goes on to say that once the training was completed the aircrews were only too eager to 'hunt the Hun'.[134]

During the latter part of *Unbeaten's* time in Malta, a massive government fundraising effort took place back in Great Britain. It was known as Warship Week. In a nutshell, Warship Week was organised to encourage towns and cities to raise money to try to meet the cost of a particular warship or submarine. The figure set was relative to the town or city's size. Once a sizable sum of money was raised, the town or city would adopt the vessel in question. *Unbeaten* would become the adopted submarine of the good people of Hove. This town's Warship week was 14-24 March 1942. The money-raising slogan devised by the people of Hove was: 'Hove Must Save...Unite Now By Effectively Adding To England's Navy.' The first letter of each word when put together spelt 'HMS *Unbeaten*'. The people of Hove managed to raise a massive £521,000, although the actual target, based on the size of Hove, was only £425,000. However, adoption went further than just money. It gave the general public a warm feeling to think that they were doing their bit for the war effort. Schools and churches would provide and donate additional comforts to the crews of adopted vessels. Woollen socks and scarfs were not uncommon items to be donated to the adopted submarine. Schoolchildren would often write letters and cards to the crew to cheer them up. To thank the generous people of these towns and cities, warship and submarine crews would visit the adoptive areas and very often a parade would ensue. Half of *Unbeaten's* crew made such a visit to the Hove Municipal Borough shortly after their arrival back in Great Britain in 1942.

A very rare picture of half the crew was taken on the day of the visit. Fig. 1 shows the men all together, along with two local dignitaries. The names of the men (from left to right, starting at the back row) are as follows:

(1) Ldg Seaman G.D. 'Jock' Forbes (Ty) 2nd Coxswain (2) Unknown Sailor (3) Local Dignitary (4) ERA 4 L. Tiffin, (5) Ldg Stoker J.E.F. 'Pop' Stockwell (Ty) (6) Unknown Sailor (7) Telegraphist F.T. Haddon (8) Unknown Sailor (9) Telegraphist F.W. 'Lofty' Furr (10) Stoker R. Stokes (11) Stoker D.J. Oliver (12) Able Seaman C.G. Smith (13) CPO R.D. Norris Coxswain (14) Lt. BCG Place 1st-Lt. (15) Lt. Cdr. E.A. Woodward, Commanding Officer (16) Mr A.H. Clarke, Mayor of Hove (17) Lt. C.W. St Clair-Lambert (18) PO Stoker G.H.A. Wright.

The abbreviation '(Ty)' signifies a temporary position. Often, men were appointed into acting roles. These appointments were for temporary periods; no-one expected the war to last six years and one day. Back at Hove, plaques were exchanged by both parties to mark the adoption of the submarine. During the crew's visit, Teddy Woodward presented the Mayor of Hove with *Unbeaten's* actual Jolly Roger. However, this most treasured symbol of *Unbeaten's* achievements during her Malta war patrols was lost forever. The Hove Town Hall, where the flag was housed, was badly damaged during a German bombing raid soon after the flag's donation; it was no more. A replica Jolly Roger was given to Hove Mayor's Office in 2007 by the estate of Mrs Barbara Woodward. Over half the crew pictured in Fig. 1 died on board *Unbeaten* when she went down in 1942. Although the loss of *Unbeaten* would have been a serious shock to the people of Hove, the public managed to rally together and raise more money to adopt another submarine – HMS/M *Simoom* (*P225*) was one of the new Group 3, S-Class submarines. Sadly, this submarine was subsequently lost in November 1943 with all hands.

During *Unbeaten's* refit, World War II carried on unabated. Rommel's army advanced and took Tobruk. The aforementioned 'Flap' ensued; 22 June saw what was left of the 1st and 10th Submarine Flotillas make good their escape from Alexandria and head for Haifa in Israel. Another blow was to be dealt to the British submarines in the Mediterranean on 30 June 1942. The VIIC Type U-boat *U372* torpedoed the submarine deport ship *Medway* as she was making for Haifa from Alexandria. The mother hen sank quite quickly, stern first. Some 1,105 passengers and crew were rescued. Thirty men lost their lives in the sinking. Notwithstanding the loss of life, a very important commodity was also put in jeopardy: *Medway* was carrying the lion's share of spare torpedoes. Of the ninety torpedoes on board at the time of her sinking, 47 did bob up to the surface and float clear of the sinking vessel. These were recovered and put to good use. Around a month later, on 22 July, Shrimp Simpson reinstated the 10th Submarine Flotilla at Malta; they were still to run out of the old Lazaretto complex. Earlier, in the month of June 1942, a Wellington bomber from 172 Squadron Coastal Command was patrolling in the Bay of Biscay when the wandering British aircraft stumbled across The Italian Marconi Class submarine *Luigi Torelli* on the surface at night. Squadron Leader Jeaffreson Greswell, flying the Wellington 'F' for Freddy, went in for an attack using a brand new piece of equipment which had been specifically designed to attack submarines at night. Basically, it was a very bright 22-million-candlepower directional searchlight mounted on the plane which illuminated the enemy submarine. Greswell and his crew dropped four depth charges across the target. However, the submarine did survive, although it was badly damaged. This new weapon in the war against the U-boat was called the Leigh Light, after its inventor, Squadron Leader H. de V. Leigh. This weapon would have massive consequences for *Unbeaten* as Great Britain tried to win the longest-running battle of World War II: the Battle of the Atlantic.

Towards the end of her refit, *Unbeaten* was getting crewed up again. New crew members started to join the boat to relieve those who had left prior to the refit. The Port Log shows that the submarine's D of D was completed on 29 August 1942. All the defects had been rectified and it is likely that during this maintenance period *Unbeaten* had her 12 pounder gun upgraded to the more powerful three-inch variant. The boat then sailed for exercise trials. However, the crew of *Unbeaten* soon found themselves back alongside Chatham again due to several defects. The submarine was given a revised date of completion of 5 September 1942.

20

THE HORIZONTAL CHAMP

Prior to her sailing from Chatham, one of the submarine's youngest crew members was allotted *Unbeaten* as his first sea draft. His name was Herbert H. Bayne. Bert was just 17 years old when he walked over the gangway to board *Unbeaten.* Ordinary Seaman Bayne had completed his basic training and just finished his trade training. He was a qualified radio direction finder (RDF) operator, or what today would be known as a RADAR operator. However, at the time Bert joined the submarine she was not yet fitted with RDF. The young sailor wrote to his parents in a letter dated 14 September 1942: 'I've got a ship at last. The only trouble is that up to now she has no RDF on-board, also she is having her engines overhauled so I guess we won't be seeing anything of the sea for another 2 or 3 months.'[sic] [135] Ten days after *Unbeaten's* revised refit completion date, work was eventually finished. The revitalised submarine left Chatham Docks and Sheerness on 17 September 1942 and arrived at Portsmouth on the 18th. She remained in Pompey for just over two days. The day *Unbeaten* sailed from Portsmouth is a poignant one for the author and integral to the conception of this book. This was the day an extended relative of the author's, by way of marriage, joined the crew of *N93*.

Leading Telegraphist Albert E. Piper was 28 years old when he threw his kit bag down the forward hatch of *Unbeaten*. Albert was not an overly tall chap; he stood at 5ft 5in, with auburn hair, blue eyes and a fresh, freckled complexion. Previously, a young Albert had joined the Royal Navy as a boy sailor, second class, in July 1929. After completing his basic training at HMS *Ganges* he went on to serve on board the warships HMS *Renown*, HMS *Rodney* and HMS *Royal Sovereign*, followed by some training on board the warships *Malaya*, *Vivid* and *Delhi*. Albert was also drafted to HMS *Tamar*, which was the Royal Navy shore base at Hong Kong. This was followed in 1938 by a short spell on board the battle cruiser HMS *Enterprise*. Albert was a volunteer for submarine service and entered into his submarine training at HMS *Dolphin* on 11 November of that year. It may well have been the increase in pay that enticed Albert to join the Silent Service against the express wishes of his mother, who had tried to make him promise not to become a submariner; her appeals were not to be heeded, however, and on the completion of his submarine training Albert joined the L-Class submarine *L23*. His new submersible draft was an old World War I submarine. There were only three L-Class submarines left in service at the beginning of World War II. This class only saw operational service for a short spell before being relegated to a training role. *L23* moved around as a training boat for submariners and Albert was part of the training boat's crew. *L23* would be the training submarine attached to many units, including HMS *Titania*, HMS *Ambrose*, HMS *Dolphin* and HMS *Elfin*. Albert remained with *L23* between 1938 and 1942. He did spend a month on board the submarine HMS *Clyde* and then swiftly returned to *L2*3. Leading Telegraphist Piper joined *Unbeaten* in Portsmouth on 21 September 1942 prior to her sailing. It does appear that Albert was 'pier head jumped' to join *Unbeaten* at short notice. It was common to take people from training billets to replace people at sea at short notice; this practice continues today. You don't need to train the trainer. Ironically, the *Unbeaten's* penultimate stop in Great Britain would be Albert's birthplace and the home of his parents – Plymouth.

A day after sailing from Pompey, *N93* arrived at the nautical Devon city of Plymouth, a haunt of the 16th century privateer Sir Francis Drake and home of the 'Janner's mouth organ', more commonly known as the pasty or oggie. The submarine was berthed alongside Devonport Dockyard for the fitting of several modifications. *Unbeaten* was taken in hand by the dockyard staff on 25 September. The boat was moved into a tidal basin and berthed starboard side to. She was to be fitted with the new Type 291W RDF/RADAR and also complemented with IFF (Interrogation Friend or Foe). The IFF only operated when the RDF/RADAR was on. When the IFF received a challenge from an Allied aircraft it would respond automatically by squawking or emitting a code specific to that submarine, therefore identifying it to friendly forces.

The Type 290/291 RDF replaced Type 286, which was used on several platforms – but no RDF had been fitted to *Unbeaten* prior to this occasion. Type 291W was primarily used for air and surface warning for small ships. It was said in a paper written after the war by a member of ASWE (Admiralty Surface Weapons Establishment) that Type 291W had a range of 17,000 yards when attempting to detect a battleship. The detection range was 6,000 yards for a surfaced U-boat and 30 to 35 miles for aircraft detection. This increased visibility was a tremendous leap forward in RDF/RADAR design. The set did present the submarine with quite good early air and surface warning but its bearing accuracy was not great and was not to be relied upon for blind torpedo firing. Around the same time, several Coastal Command aircraft types like the Wellingtons based at RAF Chivenor were getting adept at and accustomed to using the new type of airborne RADAR. This piece of equipment was referred to by the aircrew in operational sortie reports as 'SE', or special equipment. It was in fact called ASV, or Air to Surface Vessel. The ASV Mk. II was a tremendous aid in leading the searching aircraft towards a target vessel. When utilised in conjunction with the Leigh Light anti-submarine device, the combination could be lethal for enemy submarines. Providing the aircraft was around the optimum height of 10,000ft then detection ranges of the ASV Mk. II sets used by Coastal Command were said to be 40 to 50 miles for a battleship. A smaller destroyer could be detected at up to 30 miles and a submarine at much a much shorter range – only around five miles. In the ASWE instructions covering the use of ASV two lines stood out when the author read them. 'If U-boats are known to be about, an unidentified echo first detected at the appropriate range must always be assumed to be a U-boat until proved to the contrary'. Towards the end of the U-boat war, Grossadmiral Karl Dönitz said, 'The enemy has deprived the U-boat of its essential feature, the element of surprise, by means of RADAR.' He went on to say, 'With these methods he has conquered the U-boat menace. The scientists who have created RADAR have been called the saviours of their country. It was not superior strategy or tactics which gave success, but superiority in scientific research.' [136]

The weather while sailing from Portsmouth to Plymouth must have been quite inclement. Herbert Bayne wrote to his parents while he was alongside in Plymouth: 'Since I last wrote to you I have been to Sheerness, back to Gosport I am now in Plymouth' [137] [*sic*]. He went on to write: 'I had a bad dose of sickness coming down from Portsmouth to here, it got me the following nick-name THE HORIZONTAL CHAMP.' [138] It is highly likely Albert Piper would have taken the opportunity to visit his family living in Plymouth. Albert now lived in Blyth with his expectant wife and due to the war, visits to his original home town would have been infrequent. The modifications to the boat were completed on 3 October 1942 and *Unbeaten* sailed from Plymouth the next day. The fact that Plymouth was the last port *Unbeaten* stopped at prior to the boat arriving at Holy Loch goes some way to explaining why Albert Piper's family, for a long number of years, believed that the submarine was sunk off Plymouth. It would have been the last time the family would have seen off Albert and his submarine as she slipped past Devil's Point, around Drake's Island and edged her way out of the western exit of the Plymouth Breakwater and into open water.

On 6 October the submarine entered the Clyde areas and conducted two weeks' worth of working up trials. The crew would have been testing the new equipment fit and training up new joiners. For old hands like Geoff Wright, the PO Stoker, it was just another set of trials. Several of the crew who had served on board *Unbeaten* in the Fighting Tenth at Malta were still on board – like Geoff Wright, Jock Forbes, Francis Haddon and Pat Cannon, to name but a few. It was also during this set of working up trials that the last Commanding Officer of *Unbeaten* would join. There was no better time to join; the new CO, already an experienced submariner, would get to put the newly refitted U-Class boat through her paces over the next two weeks. On completion, *Unbeaten* would return to Holy Loch and come under the wing of the 3rd Submarine Flotilla, now commanded by Capt. H.M.C. Ionides, residing on board the submarine deport ship *Forth*.

Lt. Donald Edgar Ogilvy Watson was first indoctrinated into the arena of all things nautical one year after Teddy Woodward had joined the Royal Navy, albeit at a much earlier age. Donald was only 13 years old when he climbed up the steep gangway of the Merchant Navy school ship HMS

Conway. This old British frigate, originally HMS *Nile*, a 92-gun second rate ship of the line, was not the first incarnation of *Conway*, but was the one attended by Donald. She was berthed within the reaches of the River Mersey between 1875 and 1941 specifically to train young boys for a life at sea. The hulk was then moved during World War II to avoid the blitz of Liverpool. Donald had established himself as a very competent seaman and had worked his way up to the lofty heights of head cadet by the time he left *Conway* in 1932. Soon after leaving the training ship, the Royal Navy offered him a place as an officer cadet. However, Donald had already committed himself to an apprenticeship with the British steamship company P&O. It was as a merchant seaman that Donald went on to consolidate his maritime experience by serving on board SS *Rawalpindi* and SS *Mongolia* consecutively. During World War II, the Mercantile Marine was a good recruiting ground for well-trained seamen. Incidentally, many of the RNR officers who joined the navy had a good Merchant Navy background.

In April 1935, Donald transferred to the Royal Navy. Officer Cadet Ogilvy Watson entered training at Britannia Royal Naval College. Donald became a sub-lieutenant RN in 1937 and shortly after that, in 1938, he attained the rank of lieutenant. He cut his teeth as a seaman officer on board the battle cruiser HMS *Courageous*. It would not be long before Donald would transfer to the secret undersea world of the Submarine Branch. On 14 April 1939, after successfully completing his initial submarine training at HMS *Dolphin*, Donald joined HMS/M *L26*, a 760-ton submarine of the 5th Flotilla, and worked under Lt. Cdr. F.W. Lipscombe OBE. At the outbreak of war on 3 September 1939, Donald found himself at sea on board *L26*. He returned to Blyth on the 17th and got married soon afterwards. Donald's wife reminisced about their happy wedding day: 'There was a shortage of glasses and I found my brother-in-law drinking champagne out of a flower vase, and a large one at that!' [139]

Towards the end of September 1939, Donald was drafted to a new T-Class submarine in build, HMS/M *Truant*. Donald would initially be under the command of Lt. Cdr. R.W. Peers. During the boat's build at Vickers of Barrow, the Ogilvy Watsons' were accommodated in a poorly appointed flat in Barrow-in-Furness. Mrs Ogilvy Watson recalls life at Barrow in great detail, especially the times when situations were harsh for her and others. Also remembered were the many Polish submariners who had escaped their country at the outbreak of war. Many were bereft of their families and had no idea whether their loved ones were still alive. Donald's wife said that these servicemen were 'pretty lost and aching for revenge',[140] a sentiment carried through to those brave Polish servicemen that also served in the RAF and flew during the Battle of Britain, inflicting exact revenge on the German Luftwaffe. In a letter written to the author, Mrs Ogilvy Watson prophetically wrote: 'There was always the submarine that did not return and other losses as well.' [141] Unfortunately, these occurrences were all too common.

The *Truant* had a long and distinguished tenure during World War II and it would be the making of another book if the author was to go into detail regarding all of the achievements of this submarine and her crew. Suffice it to say that Donald Ogilvy Watson was an integral member of her crew. He served on board during many of *Truant's* patrols between 1939 and 1942, even sailing on Christmas Day 1939 for post-repair trials; such was the Admiralty's need to get submarines to sea. One of the most notable patrols in which Donald was involved would lead to the sinking of the Kriegsmarine light cruiser *Karlsruhe* on 9 April 1940, during the submarine's sixth war patrol. *Truant's* Commanding Officer at this time was Lt. Cdr. C.H. Hutchinson. Lt. Ogilvy Watson was the Torpedo Officer on board and was subsequently awarded the DSC for his part in this attack. Donald was also on patrol in *Truant* when France finally capitulated between May and June of that year. On 30 August 1940, Donald's wife was standing with the wife of *Truant's* Third Captain Lt. Cdr. H.A.V. Haggard at the vantage point near North Queensferry, just below the Forth Railway Bridge. Together they watched the submarine sail from Rosyth towards the Mediterranean and eventually Malta.

As alluded to much earlier in this book, it was during this deployment to the Mediterranean that *Truant* had a near miss with *Upholder* that could have been catastrophic. 16 October 1941 would see *Truant* return again to Malta from her refit in America. The boat was soon back patrolling the Mare Nostrum. Donald left *Truant* shortly afterwards in early 1942 and was drafted back to Great Britain to attend a Submarine Commanding Officers' Course. This incredibly testing and mentally draining curriculum is also known as the 'Periscope' or 'Perisher' Course. The course predominately incorporates training for submarine attack. To successfully pass the Perisher Course, a potential submarine Captain must have many skills. The only person on a submarine who knew exactly what was going on up top was the

Captain. He was the one who should be able to sweep the horizon all round when looking through the periscope and then, in his head, work out what the shipping on the surface was doing in relation to his submarine. He also needed to know the limitations of his weapons and be able to process internal data passed to him from various positions in the submarine simultaneously – for example, ranges and bearings passed from the ASDIC operator or navigational information from the officer of the watch. With all this going on, the man must be able too to keep his head when all around him could be losing theirs. Many good officers failed to achieve a pass in this course.

The author had served under many Captains during his General Service career in the Royal Navy. However, one of his most memorable Commanding Officers was actually a submariner. Sir James Perowne was a submarine Captain by trade but was placed in charge of one of the newer Type 23 anti-submarine warfare frigates of the time, HMS *Norfolk*. The author remembers sitting in the operations room manning the 'Bearings only Plot' (BoP). This job entailed plotting the bearings of HE sent in from the sound room and marking them on a perpetual roll of ever-moving graph paper. The Captain would sit, or more often than not, stand in the middle of the operations room, rooted to the spot, surrounded by the many brightly illuminated buttons of the ops room and the green sweeps of multiple RADAR screens. It was a sight to behold, watching the skipper controlling his ship from below the water line, in a room devoid of windows. He did this by using all the information passed to him either visually by looking at the plot or via communications on a headset. He would mentally process the data and then, by analysing it all in his head, he could decide where best to place his ship in order to make an attack while also taking ship safety into consideration. The information would be passed to him thick and fast, with only a short time in which to make a judgement. It was very impressive to watch when you were a young Able Seaman. Sir James Perowne went on to become Flag Officer Submarines in 1996. A position once held by Sir Max Horton.

All entries in the Port Log referring to *Unbeaten* stop abruptly on 23 October 1942. This would be the day that *Unbeaten* sailed from Holy Loch for her final operation. The next chapter is the penultimate one in this remarkable true story. There will be no happy endings; however, it is hoped that these final chapters will provide the families of crew members with a better explanation of the surrounding events which took place prior to the loss of *Unbeaten*. It has transpired that a letter was sent from the Admiralty to some of the bereaved families after the end of World War II. The short one-page note, dated 1945, attempted to explain the disappearance of the submarine and her crew but was it was deliberately vague. Details of the final operation were kept secret for many years until they were eventually released and placed in the public domain in 1972. It is from these 'MOST SECRET' orders that the details of the final chapter are drawn.

21

OPERATION BLUESTONE COMPLETE

It was 22 October 1942 and the location was Holy Loch, Scotland. Sometime on that Thursday, a photograph was taken from the upper deck of the submarine depot ship *Forth*. The unknown photographer was looking down onto *Unbeaten's* rain-soaked casing. This would be the last photograph of *N93* known to exist. The incredibly detailed and clear black and white picture, held by the Royal Navy Submarine Museum, is an epic snapshot frozen in time. There is so much going on in this final image. A bushy-haired rating is seen aft of the bridge, high up on the conning tower, intently working on an aerial with a long screwdriver. A Royal Naval officer in his black peaked cap and shiny black oilskins is resting his forearm on the gunwale and leaning over the conning tower. He is looking aft down the starboard side and clearly appears to be giving orders to someone on the casing below. It is a wet day; the grubby White Ensign flying at the back of the bridge is stretched taut by the strong wind pulling it from forward to aft. The submarine's steering position on the bridge is clearly distinguishable by the old-style ship's wheel which is visible below the gimbal-mounted compass. Three oilskin-clad submariners are standing forward of the new three-inch gun, and in front of them stand another three sailors dressed in full foul weather gear with hoods up – which would have offered some protection against the lashing rain and biting Scottish wind. The men are making up heaving lines to pass back to the incoming submarine. It is not difficult to see what is going on in the photograph. *Unbeaten* has just got alongside *Forth* and has also just received the Dutch U-Class submarine HNMS/M *Dolfijn* outboard. Securing ropes and wires have been passed and the Dutch boat is singled up, awaiting her second lines so she can double up and secure. The crew forward of *Unbeaten's* gun platform are waiting patiently to pass a wooden brow across to *Dolfijn*. The picture captures an everyday working moment on board *Unbeaten*, perfectly.

The *Dolfijn* and *Unbeaten* had been working up together, day-running from Holy Loch. The work up trials and exercises were now complete. Tomorrow would be Friday 23, the day *Unbeaten* would sail from Holy Loch forever. Several days before *N93* was due to depart Holy Loch, Donald Ogilvy Watson received an envelope passed to him by hand. The envelope contained a file of 'MOST SECRET' orders. The front cover of the file was devoid of any explanation of what was inside. The buff-coloured cover had the words 'OFFICE OF ADMIRAL (SUBMARINES)' in red lettering. The only other markings were three red stripes crossing the cover horizontally, one thick between two thin. Officially, there were only ever four copies made of these secret operational orders. The four secret files were distributed, one copy each, to C-in-C Plymouth, Captain F.A. Slocum NID(C), Captain (S3) and, finally, the Commanding Officer HMS/M *Unbeaten*, Lt. Ogilvy Watson. On completion of the operation, Rear Admiral S.M. Raw, who now worked for Max Horton at Northway's, requested that all copies of the file be destroyed and certificates of destruction rendered as proof of their destruction. However, a fifth copy did exist in the form of a draft copy of the secret operations orders. This file had pen amends which were then re-typed into the corrected, formal fifth file. This file somehow missed being destroyed and after the war it eventually found its way into the National Archives, where it laid for decades buried within another file. It was through a chance email conversation with the naval researcher Platon Alexiades that the author came across this elusive document.

Unbeaten slipped from the *Forth* and sailed out of Holy Loch on Friday 23 October 1942, heading south towards the Bay of Biscay. On board the submarine was a special passenger. This person, destined for a one-way trip, was an unnamed agent controlled by NID(C) (Naval Intelligence Division, Section 'C'), also known as G3(C) within the SIS (Secret Intelligence Service). The clandestine SIS unit had many pseudonyms and was often referred to as MI6. The man who coordinated these agents for NID(C) was on the distribution list for *Unbeaten's* operation orders. His name was Acting Captain F.A. Slocum. Forty-eight-year-old Frank Alexander Slocum was an experienced British naval commander and a World War I veteran who had passed for first-class ships and was accredited as being an accomplished navigator within the Royal Navy. However, at the start of World War II, Slocum came out of retirement and was chosen to head an 'Operations Section'. The main purpose of this section was to create and maintain clandestine physical communications with the whole of occupied Europe. Frank Slocum would carve a different career in the Royal Navy and become the go-to man for these types of secret operation. It would seem that because of the demands of the job and the fact that Slocum was integral to many successful outcomes of Secret Intelligence Service operations, he was rated up to Acting Captain. Slocum was very successful in landing agents ashore in foreign lands; this was in no small part due to the accomplished and brave team he had formed around him. He would go on to receive many awards from grateful former occupied countries after World War II.

The orders detailing *Unbeaten's* operation came from the Office of Admiral (Submarines) based at Northway's in London. The code name for the operation was to be 'BLUESTONE'. The sole objective of *Unbeaten* and her crew was to land an agent in the southern approaches to the Spanish city of Vigo, located on the Atlantic west coast just above the border with Portugal. However, before the operation could commence some training had to be carried out, both for the benefit of *Unbeaten's* crew and the agent. The training had to be of a standard that would satisfy Captain (S3). It was apparent that the agent was already proficient in the handling and navigation of a folboat (or folbot). But further training was required in conjunction with *Unbeaten*. This came in the form of practising the routine required for the disembarkation of a manned folboat from the submarine. If the folboat and agent could not be successfully deployed from *Unbeaten* then the operation was not to proceed. However, as we know from past war patrols, several of *Unbeaten's* crew were proficient at getting folboats safely into the water from the boat's casing. In the operation orders, under the section titled 'Preliminary Training', it says that NID(C) would provide the agent with 'a folbot, a luminous compass, a large knife and emergency rations'. The orders go on to say: 'The greatest care is necessary to check that all equipment is in perfect order before sailing.' [142] The agent would also carry a small amount of personal gear.

The sequence of events for this operation have been repeated from the original operation orders and retold in this story. We know *Unbeaten* completed *Operation Bluestone* and it is likely that the scheduled events did take place in accordance with the written orders. Lt. Ogilvy Watson was to drive his submarine to the landing point west of Bayona (or Baiona), which was in the position of 42°6'54N, 8°52'10W, roughly 15 miles (around 24 km) from Vigo, as the crow flies. If the intended destination of the agent was Vigo, not only was it a long walk, but before the agent's feet touched terra firma, the chap had to canoe a fair distance. *Unbeaten's* orders were to disembark the agent out at sea in a position some two nautical miles north-west of the landing point. The orders go on to say the agent 'is to be left to his own devices'.[143] As with most submarine operations, it was at the discretion of the boat's Commanding Officer as to which location was chosen for the disembarkation of the agent within the designated area. There were several limiting factors which Donald Ogilvy Watson would have taken into consideration. One was the weather conditions at the time and another was the possibility of enemy patrols. However, taking all this into account, the orders stressed: 'IT IS OF PARAMOUNT IMPORTANCE THAT THE DISEMBARKATION SHOULD TAKE PLACE UNOBSERVED.' [144]

It is unknown what the final destination or the reason for the agent being landed in this area of Spain was. I am sure the answer lies in another innocuous file buried in the depths of the National Archives. However, one could surmise that the destination was actually the Port of Vigo. Although professing to be neutral during the war it was known that Spain collaborated with the Germans. Outwardly, the Spanish government had rightly embargoed several vessels being used by the Germans in Spanish ports including the Port of Vigo. However, it transpired that these vessels were secretly being visited by German U-boats at the dead of night. The U-boats were being refuelled by the vessels and would also take on board water and stores. The German submarines would then proceed back into the Atlantic and sink more Allied shipping. The vessel names and Spanish ports concerned were as follows: *Bessel*, code name 'Bernado', tied up in Vigo;

Thalia, code name 'Gata', which was alongside Cadiz; *Corrientes*, code name 'Culebra', at Las Palmas in the Canaries; and *Max Albrecht* at El Ferrol. All these tankers were visited numerous times by German U-boats between 1940 and 1944. The port of El Ferrol was also a port to which German U-boats would make for to undergo repairs after air attacks, etc.

The Germans had an entrenched underground supply network operating all over Europe during World War II and it was active even in supposedly neutral countries. This very secret supply service was said to be known as '*Ettapendienst*'. This clandestine supply network had cells located almost everywhere in the world. They operated under the guise of dummy companies and remained almost fully undetected throughout the war. Testament to the organisation's untraceability was an account of an *Ettapandienst* cell which was purported to be still operating in Japan in 1948, three years after the end of World War II.

Back on board *Unbeaten*, the orders in front of Donald Ogilvy Watson said the disembarkation of the agent may take place during any of the four nights after the day of the submarine's arrival off Vigo. The orders were also very specific in stating that attacks on enemy shipping were to take precedence over *Operation Bluestone*, and while the submarine was in the vicinity of Vigo she may be tasked to commence operations against enemy shipping; if this occurred then further instructions regarding Bluestone would be signalled. However, most pertinent was the following statement: *Operation Bluestone* could be cancelled by order of Admiral Submarines or by the Commanding Officer of *Unbeaten* should there be any unforeseen risks to his submarine. It is unclear when *Unbeaten* arrived at her station off Baiona, as her patrol log in which the dates and times would have been annotated were lost with the submarine. However, we do know from a 'HUSH MOST SECRET' naval message that the landing was to take place between 30 October and 2 November 1942.

Unbeaten's CO was briefed that there were several shore defences in the vicinity. Donald was also informed that many of the anti-aircraft batteries in the area would almost certainly have a searchlight capability and that these may be mobile. Vigo Bay was protected by 62 gun batteries located around Silliero and Ferro; they were positioned to fire north. If this was not enough of a deterrent there were several RDF stations located around the area, particularly north of Arosa Bay. The Operation Bluestone Intelligence Summary Appendix 1 to the orders goes on to say that up and down the coast, at various points, coast watchers and coastguard stations were also in position. It is worthy of note that in the operation orders appendix there was also mention of a projected mined area between Ile de Faro and the mainland but positive evidence of mines was not confirmed. However, it does appear that *Unbeaten's* mission was successfully carried out and the submarine's crew sent a W/T message at 19:30 on 2 November 1942 stating that 'Operation Bluestone was Completed'[145] the night before at 23:59. The operation orders show that after landing the agent, *Unbeaten* was to withdraw to the vicinity of 43°N, 12°W, which is approximately 162NM west of Corunna. It was here that the boat was to make the above report.

The British submarine was then tasked to carry out a Biscay patrol. On 6 November the submarine was told to locate an enemy vessel which was reported to be trying to break out of the blockade. Lt. Ogilvy Watson sighted the enemy vessel, which had been badly shot up by aircraft. The submarine's crew reported the sighting and was then told to make for Bishop Rock lighthouse. She was to meet with another submarine that was escorting vessels in that area. This was the last time anyone heard from *Unbeaten*. Research shows the blockade runner in question could well have been the *Anneliese Essberger* or the *Karin*; both vessels set sail heading outbound across the Bay of Biscay, on 5 and 6 November 1942, respectively. However, the vessel spotted by Ogilvy Watson was reported as being shot up. This leaves two other possibilities. One was the supply tanker *Spichern*, formally known as the *Krossfonn*, which sailed from France on 9 November; it had been attacked by RAF Coastal Command aircraft and, owing to damage received, had to put into the Spanish port of El Ferrol. The other was the *Elsa Essberger*, which sailed on 7 November from France and was also attacked, returning damaged soon afterwards. *Unbeaten* never made the rendezvous at Bishop Rock. What occurred after 6 November is open for debate to this day. Enquiries about the events surrounding the loss of *Unbeaten* have never satisfactorily been concluded. The author has researched the final days of the submarine in some detail. Although it is clear that *Unbeaten* was lost between her last transmission and the rendezvous, the author will be devil's advocate and present the evidence as it was found. The reader can come to their own conclusions as to the cause of the loss of HMS/M *Unbeaten*, taking into account the substantiated facts presented before them.

There is an airfield west of Barnstaple in Devon which was once the home of the Lundy and Atlantic Coast Airlines and a flying school. When World War II started, the airfield was requisitioned for the war effort. Farmland surrounding the airfield was purchased to increase the size of the area and an aerodrome constructed. This land, 5 miles west of Barnstaple, would be known as RAF Chivenor from 25 October 1940. No. 1417 Flight had trained crews in the use of Leigh Light-equipped Wellington GR.VIII aircraft at Chivenor. As we know, the unit was renumbered 172 Squadron Coastal Command in April 1942 and became operational on 3 June of that year. Wellington bombers were not the only military aircraft at Chivenor; the base also played host to Whitley bombers and four squadrons of RCAF (Royal Canadian Air Force) Beaufighters. Strangely enough back in 20 November 1941 another type of aircraft arrived rather unexpectedly, landing at the airfield which would become RAF Chivenor.

A Luftwaffe JU 88a had become lost over the Irish Sea and landed on the airfield thinking it was its base in Morlaix in France. Needless to say, the pilot and crew had a shock when they discovered where they were and that it was the end of the war for them. Back to 1942 and RAF Chivenor had been operational for two years and seventeen days when, on 10 November, Flight Officer D.E. Dixon and his five-man crew boarded their Mk. VIII Wellington 'D' Serial No HF828. It was around 17:45 when the aircraft lumbered down the runway and lurched into the air. Dixon and his crew were embarking on an anti-submarine patrol in the Bay of Biscay area. RAF Coastal Command 172 Squadron was part of 19 Group, which in turn was populated by a number of other Coastal Command Squadrons, including 172. The patrol areas of 19 Group were pretty large and covered an area to the west of Ireland and about halfway down into the Bay of Biscay, at which point 179 Squadron from Gibraltar would take over. The area also included part of the English Channel, roughly up to the Channel Islands.

The GR.VIII Wellington Bomber flown by Coastal Command was a formidable aircraft. Each aircraft was painted virtually all white underneath to disguise it when looking up into the sky. This was its camouflage colour and it worked well. The Wellington crew consisted of the pilot, second pilot, navigator and three other crew members who all took turns rotating through the positions of wireless operator, RADAR (ASV) operator, and air gunner. Commonly, patrols would last between eight and nine hours, depending on the aircraft's PLE (Prudent Limit of Endurance). Three hours and twenty-three minutes had passed since 'D' departed from Chivenor, the RADAR (ASV) operator spotted a target on the Special Equipment (owing to the secrecy surrounding the ASV it was referred to in Coastal Command operation records as SE). The target was in a position approximately 160NM south-west of Brest in France. The weather was fair and the contact was now only six miles away from the Wellington. F/O Dixon turned his aircraft on the reciprocal bearing while simultaneously dropping the height of the aircraft. The LE (Leigh Light) turret was lowered into its position from beneath the aircraft and the massively powerful light was turned on at half a mile from its intended target.

POW! There she was, illuminated in all her German glory – a Type IXC U-boat, the 76.8m *U66.* The German *Unterseeboot* was commanded by Kapitänleutnant Friedrich Markworth. *U66* had sailed in company with *U176* only the day before from the occupied French port of Lorient, on what was to be for *U66* her seventh war patrol. The two U-boats were tasked to attack the Allied invasion fleet of North Africa, vessels of which were supporting the British-American invasion codenamed *Operation Torch*. Back on-board the RAF Wellington, Dixon assessed the enemy submarine as being on a course of 340° and at a speed of 12-14 knots. On this, the first run, 'D' passed just ahead of the U-boat at a height of just 100ft. Dixon now knew where his target was. He turned the Wellington and picked up the target again on SE. The LE was switched at half a mile to light up the target. Just as 'D' reached the U-boat, four depth charges were dropped from beneath the attacking British aircraft. As the Torpex-filled charges glided down from 100ft they separated from each other and straddled the submarine's bow from her port quarter to her starboard bow. Consecutively, massive shock waves and vast torrents of water would have erupted around the startled U-boat as the depth charges arrived at the required depth of detonation. The Wellington's first run had given Markworth enough time to order his men to man the 37mm and 20mm anti-aircraft guns situated on the 'Winter Gardens' – this was the name of the guard rail-encircled platforms on which the guns were mounted, located at the stern of the boat's conning tower. The rear gunner on board the Wellington fired approximately 100 rounds towards the U-boat. As he was firing down he observed cannon shells being fired up from the enemy submarine and bursting above his own aircraft. After the second run the Wellington crew observed the submarine steer a half-circle to port and remain on the surface. The explosions of the depth charges had resulted in *U66* being lifted up by 1 to 1.5 meters causing some damage. Dixon and his crew stayed in visual contact with the U-boat until 23:20. The Wellington was now nearing its PLE and Dixon was forced, reluctantly, to set a course to base, seemingly leaving the suitably roughed-up submarine on the surface. At the same time as Wellington 'D' took off from RAF Chivenor that Tuesday evening, another Wellington had also departed the North Devon airbase.

22

MISSING ON WAR SERVICE

Painted on the Wellington Bomber's Irish linen-covered, white distemper-coloured lightweight duralumin frame were two large black letters – 'WN'. This squadron identifier was clearly visible, spaced to the rear of the familiar red, white and blue RAF roundel. Forward of this legendary RAF symbol another letter was painted. This letter identified the actual aircraft, in this case 'F' for Freddy. It was late afternoon on 10 November when Flying Officer Gordon D.A. Lundon RAFVR (Royal Air Force Volunteer Reserve) climbed into the cockpit of the GR Mk. VIII Wellington Bomber, Serial No. ES986. The Squadron Operations Record Book shows that this was not Gordon Lundon's first operational sortie, or flight, from Chivenor, his first being an air-sea rescue flight on 1 November 1942. On that occasion, Lundon was flying the Wellington Mk. VIII 'Tango', searching for a particular downed aircrew that were later rescued. F/O Lundon's second recorded operation was on 7 November in Wellington 'C'. However, today, on his third operational sortie, Gordon Lundon was flying 'F' along with his regular five crewmen: F/O Alfred, F/O Bernett RCAF (Royal Canadian Air Force), P/O Prideaux RCAF, Sgt. McLeod RCAF and Sgt. Smith RCAF. This Tuesday afternoon, Lundon and his crew took off from the North Devon base at the same reported time as Wellington 'D'. The two heavily-laden bomber aircraft were tasked to independently carry out anti-submarine patrols in the Bay of Biscay area.

Insidiantibus insidiamur, or 'We ambush the ambusher', was the very appropriate Latin motto attributed to the RAF Coastal Command and 172 Squadron. Nearly all the aircraft flown by Coastal Command, be they Wellington Bombers, Whitleys or, later in the war, American Liberators, were camouflaged so when looking up from the ocean towards the sky they blended in. Initially, the Wellingtons were painted with a white distemper, which invariably washed off, so the aircraft's side fuselage was painted matt white and the underside in a gloss white. To allow the aircraft to blend in with the sea when seen from above, the upper fuselage was painted a very dark sea grey and dark slate grey.

During the early hours of 11 November, at 00:30, 'Freddy' received a message from base tasking the Wellington to divert towards the position of the previous night's attack on the U-boat *U66* executed by Wellington 'D'. As we know, the attack that last evening had taken place around three hours before, at 21:08, in position '46° 13N, 07° 40W'. Wellington 'D', flown by P/O Dixon, stayed in the vicinity until 23:20, at which time his aircraft reached her PLE and had to return to base. So Gordon Lundon and his crew in 'F' were tasked to take over and continue the prosecution of the enemy submarine. Unknown to 'Freddy', the submarine in question was in fact the now shaken *U66*. Kapitänleutnant Markworth was trying to return his damaged U-boat back to the port of Lorient from where she had sailed the day before. Owing to the airborne depth charge attack, the rudder of *U66* had been stuck hard to port, forcing the U-boat to circle aimlessly until steerage way was reconfigured by alternating the U-boat's two engines. Lundon and his navigator took into account the U-boat's last known course and speed – 040° at 15 knots – and worked out a course to intercept the enemy submarine. 'Freddy' was in a position approximately 180NM south-west of Lorient when, at 01:29, she set a course for the estimated position of the submarine.

The aircrew had been over the Bay of Biscay for over eight hours since leaving Chivenor. It was at 02:16 that Lundon's crew picked up a contact on the Special Equipment, bearing 20° to port. The target of interest was at a range of six miles. Remember: *'If U-boats are known to be about, an unidentified echo first detected at the appropriate range must always be assumed to be a U-boat until proved to the contrary.'* Lundon had flown his aircraft to within three miles of the contact when suddenly, severe interference was encountered by the SE. ASV was susceptible to clutter in the form of sea returns, which could interfere with the display. Lundon kept his aircraft on a course of 180° at about 200ft in the hope they may spot the submarine. The Leigh Light was lowered into position and at a range of only three-quarters of a mile it was switched on. The bright beam instantly highlighted the unmistakeable looming shape of a submarine dead ahead, caught like a rabbit in a headlight. The pilot's report says the submarine was fully surfaced and on a course of 374°, moving through the water at a speed of 12-15 knots. Four minutes later, at 02:20, the Wellington Bomber was in position '46° 50N 06° 51W' and Lundon made a steep dive to starboard and dropped his aircraft down to 75ft. The pilot was trying to drop the depth charges ahead of the submarine so that the hydrostatically activated weapons would detonate at the optimum depth of 25ft. At this depth the devastating shock waves would catch the submarine as she attempted to dive; that was the theory, anyway. Much academic study had been undertaken by the likes of Patrick Blackett, who has been mentioned in this book previously. Blackett and his team studied the use of air-dropped depth charges against submarines and devised strategies into improving the kill rate in an attempt to win the war against the U-boat. The pilot's report states that Leigh Light was used throughout the attack. This innovative piece of equipment was not the easiest thing to control and if turned on too early could disorientate the pilot and cause the aircraft to crash into the ocean.

Lundon's attempt to drop the depth charges in the perfect position did not prove successful. As he explained in the recorded details of the sortie: 'The full turn of the aircraft was not completed and the D.C.'s were released at 75 ft at the moment 'F' was approaching from starboard beam, heading about 20 yards ahead of the U-boat.' [146] A huge column of water was seen to envelope the stern of the target. It was estimated by the Wellington crew that two explosions had straddled the submarine, which then made a 90° turn to port and stopped in the water. The submarine remained stationary at right angles to its original course. Lundon and his crew made a further three runs over the target. The RCAF sergeant on the rear gun fired approximately 200 rounds during these three passes, aiming in the direction of the straddled submarine. Wellington 'F' stayed in the area for a further 33 minutes after the attack. Lundon's Wellington must have reached its limit of endurance because after these 33 minutes had elapsed the RAF crew set course for base. They left the area, not confirming in the report whether the submarine was still on the surface or not. Poor weather was not a factor in this attack as the conditions throughout were recorded in the pilot's report as being fair, although the weather did deteriorate as the aircraft headed back towards base. Wellington 'Freddy' landed at RAF Chivenor at 05:25 on 11 November 1942 – Armistice Day.

This attack by Gordon Lundon and his crew was the incident to which the loss of *Unbeaten* has since been attributed. It was confirmed by the Admiralty that the estimated position of *N93* was in the vicinity of this attack. There are many factors for and against the identity of the submarine in question being *Unbeaten*. The loss of the submarine has been touched upon before by several other authors but never in any great detail and always with the notion that it could have been *Unbeaten* that succumbed to the depth charges of the RAF Wellington from 172 Squadron. To allow the reader to make an informed opinion in their own mind about what may have happened to *Unbeaten*, the author has approached the subject from all angles.

On 11 November 1942, a successful attack was reported by Coastal Command on a northbound U-boat. In the details of the sortie, Gordon Lundon states that the submarine in question was indeed a U-boat. The most common German submarine type, which was only minimally comparable to *Unbeaten*, in these areas, at this time, was the Type VIIC. Other bigger types also transited the areas but less frequently. There is around a 10-metre difference in length between a Type VIIC U-boat, at approximately 67m, and a U-Class submarine like *Unbeaten*, at around 58m. Apart from the obvious difference in size between the British boat and the German submarine there was, however, one similarity. The Type VIIC also had a gun forward of the conning tower like a U-Class submarine. However, this is where the similarity ends. The big difference is not just in the comparative size of the two boats but also in the visibility of the winter garden or gun band stand aft of the U-boat's conning tower; *Unbeaten* did not have one. As 'F' reported that she had attacked from the starboard side, would the crew have seen the obvious band stand? Or the lack of one?

Another factor which casts a shadow over the plausibility of the submarine being *Unbeaten*, notwithstanding the fact that *Unbeaten* had 'N93' painted in 14ft-tall white letters on each side of her conning tower, is the fact that the target was reported as moving through the water at a speed of 12-15 knots. This speed in more indicative of a U-boat than a U-Class submarine whose top surfaced speed was only 11.5 knots on a good day. The procedure for a British submarine which is being attacked by friendly aircraft is to release a 'floating smoke and flame'. No signal from the submarine was reported by Wellington 'F' during the 33 minutes she was in the area with the submarine stopped on the surface. The author has studied photographs of the U-Class submarine HMS/M *Umbra* caught in a Leigh Light beam during trials. These revealing declassified photographs attached to documents held at the National Archives show that the submarine's conning tower, including all its features, is clearly visible from the aircraft when illuminated.

There are many other circumstances which could ultimately lead to the loss of a submarine. The list of possibilities is not exhaustive because anything can happen at sea and often does. The loss of ballast control, sea valve failure, periscope seal failure, torpedo door failure, crash diving and not shutting the hatch quickly enough, or even a rouge torpedo can all be fatal. Not to mention the possibility that another submarine might have fired on *Unbeaten* or that she could have hit a mine. In stark comparison, the U-Class submarine HMS *Unique*, under the command of Lt. R.E. Boddington, was carrying out a patrol of the Bay of Biscay when she was reported overdue and presumed lost. *Unique* disappeared on 10 October 1942, almost exactly a month earlier than the loss of *Unbeaten*. She had been reported off Land's End on the 9th and then vanished. Some say the cause of her loss was a drifting mine but this has never been confirmed.

Although all circumstantial, the evidence alluding to the fact that the submarine was not *Unbeaten* could be viewed as compelling. However, in contradiction there are also several factors pointing to the possibility that the submarine attacked on 11 November was indeed *Unbeaten*. The submarine in question was in the approximate position where *Unbeaten* was thought to have been as she transited towards her rendezvous at Bishop Rock. She was said to be transiting in a safe zone or bombing restriction zone, i.e. a large moving box around her position. Was the RAF aware of this restricted bombing zone? It is also likely that in not wishing to give away her location by being detected by German High Frequency Direction Finding equipment, *Unbeaten's* crew may have turned off her Type 291W RDF, which simultaneously turned off the IFF that would squawk an indicator to friendly aircraft as to the identity of the submarine; once turned off the IFF was made redundant.

What happened to the submarine once the aircraft had left the area? Did she sink? Did the men have to abandon the submarine and enter the icy water with little hope of survival or rescue? We shall probably never know. The only witnesses to the submarine attack by Wellington 'Freddy' were the RAF aircrew themselves. However, their story was not to be a happy one. The wife of Donald Ogilvy Watson wrote in a letter to the author, 'I am glad I never met any of the crew of that Wellington bomber. Time and age soften and I no longer want their guts for garters!!' [147] Little did any of the relatives of *Unbeaten's* crew know but Flying Officer Lundon and his five-man crew all perished less than five months after *Unbeaten's* sinking.

It was 3 March 1943 and the celebrated German U-boat *U333* had set sail on its sixth war patrol. Unusually, her ace Captain was not on board for this patrol. Kapitänleutnant Peter Erich Cremer was famous in U-boat circles and equally infamous as far as the British Admiralty was concerned; he was a very competent submarine Captain and on par with the likes of Kretschmer and Prein in the German U-boat ace celebrity stakes. However, Cremer was still recovering from injuries sustained in an attack during a previous patrol back in October 1942. He was now riding a desk, working under Dönitz himself. Cremer longed, however, to rejoin his beloved Type VIIC boat *U333* and he followed the submarine's movements with paternal interest. In charge for the sixth patrol undertaken by *U333* and Cremer's crew was the capable Oberleutnant zur See Werner Schwaff.

At 18:35 the next evening F/O Gordon Lundon, along with the same crew who flew in the possible *Unbeaten* attack, took off from RAF Chivenor. Two weeks earlier Lundon and his crew had successfully attacked and sunk *U268*. The now blooded and confident RAF crew were destined for another anti-submarine patrol in the now familiar areas of the Bay of Biscay but this time Lundon was in command of a Wellington Mk. XII: 'B for Bertie'. At 21:31, in the German U-boat grid square of BF 5879, the crew manning the conning tower of *U333* were suddenly blinded by an incredibly bright light. Lundon had caught *U333* on the surface; he instantly lit her up with the Wellington's Leigh Light. 'The machine just jumped out of the darkness.' [148] However, the German U-boat crew instantly retaliated against the attacking British aircraft. The U-boat gunners manned the twin 20mm cannons aft on the *wintergarten* and fired towards the source of the light.

Their aim proved successful. The 20mm incendiary ammunition hit the Wellington's left wing as Lundon was making a well-practised approach prior to a depth charge attack. The front wing fuel tanks of a Wellington Mk. XII held 150 gallons each of fuel. By the time 'B for Bertie' crabbed over the submarine's conning tower her diving speed with the Leigh Light lowered was around 230mph. She was so low you could almost touch her. The whole aircraft was incandescent and burning up violently. However, Gordon Lundon did manage to reach the push button operating the bomb/depth charge release control, located to his left-hand side when seated in the cockpit. Luckily, the bomb aimer had selected the depth charges and the master switch was on. Four depth charges tumbled out of the belly of 'B'; only seconds after their release Gordon Lundon and his crew slammed into the ocean. There were no survivors. Gordon Lundon would be posthumously awarded the Distinguished Flying Cross (DFC) for his actions that night.

Back on *U333* the first depth charge hit the submarine below the conning tower and bounced overboard, causing minimal damage. It was presumed that the other three depth charges had fallen harmlessly astern of the U-boat. However, a fair while after the attack, several of the U-boat's crew heard a rhythmic rolling noise repeating in time with the swell of the ocean. On inspection and to the crew's horror they discovered an unexploded depth charge wedged into the stern casing. It was broken open but still posed a very real threat. The depth charge was disarmed by the removal of its fuse. All the remnants of the British device were given to the German weapons experts for analysis when *U333* got back alongside. Peter Cremer would eventually rejoin his boat and remain on board until mid-1944. However, Cremer did leave *U333* just prior to the U-boats last patrol, on which she would be sunk west of the Isles of Scilly on 31 July 1944 by HMS *Starling* and HMS *Loch Killin*. The attack by 'B' was one of the catalysts in Dönitz's issuing of the infamous '*Standiger Kriegsbefehl*', or 'Standing War Order 483' – the fight-back order. This order was issued on 1 May 1943 and did what it said on the tin. U-boats were to hit back by fighting it out with attacking aircraft. *U333's* experience showed U-boat crews that this type of defensive action could have a positive effect against Allied aircraft.

An RAF Board of Inquiry (or Court of Inquiry, as it was known) was instituted by Coastal Command and carried out in the months following of the loss of *Unbeaten*. The now ex-Commanding Officer of *Unbroken*, Alastair Mars, was working for the Admiralty at Northway's when the Board of Inquiry report regarding *Unbeaten* came over his desk. Mars said in his book *British Submarines at War 1939-1945*: 'The Board of Enquiry had cannily come to no definite conclusion but it was the general view at Northway's that *Unbeaten* had been sunk by our own aircraft.' [149] The author has spent a considerable amount of time searching for this Board of Inquiry report but to no avail. However, a letter was received from The Air Historical Branch (RAF), Ministry of Defence in response to a request for information from the author:

Dear Mr Smith

We have received your e-mail of 5 December requesting the Board of Inquiry report, or information as to its whereabouts, concerning the possible sinking of HMS/M Unbeaten on 11 November 1942.

We do not hold any Board of Inquiry (or Court of Inquiry as it was then known) report into this possible incident. As you may be aware, a Court of Inquiry was an internal fact-finding investigation undertaken by the Services for their own use. Its main purpose was to establish the facts concerning an accident or incident as quickly as possible and to make recommendations aimed at preventing a reoccurrence. The importance of these documents was heavily reduced, their subject matter was no longer pertinent and the majority were destroyed as a result. Regrettably therefore, few such papers are still extant. It is not unusual that official documents are destroyed; under the terms of the Public Records Act all government departments are required to review their records selecting those thought suitable for preservation. Records not selected are destroyed and it is estimated that approximately only 5% of government records are preserved. Further, I should also point out that, until recently, the Ministry of Defence did not, for legal reasons, place copies of Boards of Inquiry in the public domain, eg deposit them in the National Archives as historic documents worthy of preservation. Those which have made their way there have been deposited by another government department.

You may wish to know that 172 Squadron did report a sinking for that day; which will be recorded in their Operations Record Book held in the

National Archives. The area in which the attack took place will be included. I am sorry that I am unable to assist you further.

This almost brings the story of *Unbeaten* and her brave crew to an end. Some may be interested to know what became of several of the characters named in this book. After leaving *Unbeaten*, Teddy Woodward went on to work as an Instructor in the Attack trainer, teaching future submarine Captains during their Perisher course. After the war, Teddy worked on a nuclear submarine freighter project, looking into the feasibility of submarines carrying freight under the ice. Teddy met his second wife Barbara in Majorca, and a few years later they both moved to Barbara's native country of Australia. Teddy could often be found in the Naval and Military Club telling stories of his time in submarines. It was said by the then Deputy Premier of Australia, Graham Ingerson MP, who wrote an obituary for Teddy Woodward in 1997: 'His stories would always begin with, "I was in a little bar in Beirut…"' [150]

One of *Unbeaten's* Stokers, Ronald Stokes, also left *Unbeaten* prior to her last operation. Ronald went on to work with Teddy Woodward at HMS *Dolphin* and remembers his old Captain fondly. Along with his war service in *Unbeaten*, the now seasoned submariner Jack Casemore, also went on to serve on-board His Majesties' Submarines *Sealion*, *Surf, P556, H34, Unruly* and the *Vigorous* before eventually leaving the Royal Navy in January 1946. Jack had one final lucky escape. Ironically, after leaving both *Forfar* and *Unbeaten* just prior to their sinking's Jack found himself serving on-board HMS/M *P556*. This submarine was originally an S-1 Class boat named *S-29* which had been transferred to the Royal Navy from the United States Navy in 1942, for use in anti-submarine training. In an email sent to the author, Jack Casemores' daughter said 'they were in dock at Gosport when a fellow sailor asked to swap weekend leave with dad, which they did, but unfortunately for the other chap a mistake made on board during dad's absence, caused an explosion and the other chap together with others was sadly killed' [151] [sic]. In his later years Jack Casemore became the president of the South Kent Submariners Association, a position which he relished. Sadly during the writing of this book Jack Casemore passed away aged 91. This book is dedicated to the memory of this 'Swashbuckling Sailor'.

Norman Drury became an ASDIC instructor and remained in this job for the rest of the war. Lt. C.W. St. Clair-Lambert, DSC was the man who, along with Jock Forbes, dragged the German U-boat survivor over the fore planes after *Unbeaten's* sinking of *U374*. He later went on to command his own submarine, HMS/M *P615*. However, Lt. St. Clair-Lambert and all his crew perished when their submarine was sunk by *U123* on 18 April 1943. The man rescued from the aftermath of the sinking of *U374*, Johannes Ploch, was transferred to Great Britain for interrogation. The last record of Ploch is that he arrived in the British interrogation centre Camp 020 on 14 August 1942. Ploch was then transferred into the hands of MI19a on 28 October 1943. After much research and a lucky break, the author has discovered that today there is a man with the same name and of the same age living in the same small birth town of Ploch in Germany. However, the author has respected the fact that Johannes Ploch may not wish to be found. The Special Commando Lt. Richard F. Broome of the Folboat Section became a Captain and was part of No. 2 Commando 5 troop. Richard Frank Broome was killed in action at the age of 27 on 13 September 1943 at Salerno Italy, during '*Operation Avalanche*'.

Lt. B.C.G. Place VC left *Unbeaten* while the submarine was in refit at Chatham. In the Navy List update of October 1942, Godfrey Place is listed as having been selected for miscellaneous duties on 13 August 1942. In reality Godfrey Place had been head-hunted by Captain David C. Ingram, who was the Commanding Officer of HMS *Varbel*, formerly the Kyles Hydropathic Hotel, at Port Bannatyne Scotland. This requisitioned hotel was the location for the testing and training for Britain's secret X-Craft and home of the 12th Submarine Flotilla. Godfrey Place was a volunteer for midget submarines and was said to have been the only RN officer of all the early X-Craft volunteers who were mainly drawn from the RNVR. Place went on to command the second experimental X-Craft X4. Godfrey Place ultimately cemented his position in World War II history by being in command of X7 during an attack on the German battleship *Tirpitz*. For his leadership and bravery Lt. B.C.G. Place was awarded the Victoria Cross.

A large number of the crew of *Unbeaten* received awards for their actions during the many arduous Malta patrols. Several crew members received commendations and were mentioned in dispatches. Some of the crew were supposed to be awarded their medals while *Unbeaten* was still in Great Britain before they sailed for what would be their last operation. However, owing to the relentless bombing of Malta, the written recommendations for awards were destroyed. The file which denotes the recommendations for awards H&A 391/43 states: 'The original recommendations were destroyed by enemy action in Malta, and it was not realised that they had not been forwarded until enquiry was made by F.O(S). The copies were only received by the Admiralty on 4th April 1943.' [152] Consequently, a long period passed before family members of the lost men eventually went to posthumously receive their loved-ones' awards. The daughter of Petty Officer Stoker Geoffrey H.A. Wright DSM vividly remembers: 'We went to Buckingham Palace to receive my dad's DSM. My mother had lost her voice with the emotion and shock. King George took my hand and said, "You must always remember your father as a very brave man." No six-year-old forgets an experience like that.' [153]

The wife of a submarine Captain or Commanding Officer in any other service was always seen as a matriarchal figure among the families of crews or regiments. Despite her own tremendous personal loss, the wife of Donald Ogilvy Watson did write to several of the bereaved families of *Unbeaten's* crewmen. The family of seventeen year old Herbert Bayne received a handwritten letter from Donald's grieving wife. Lt. Ogilvy Watson's wife said in a letter to the author in 2012: 'I worked out the average age of the crew and it was so young, about 22 years if I remember correctly. I had a list as I wanted to write to each of the next of kin, but sadly lost or destroyed it and I would be interested what happened to them. I always remember one young sailor who only had "a friend". It seems so sad.' [154]

The alleged final resting place of *Unbeaten* is around 111NM from land and is estimated to be in the position '46° 50N, 06° 51W'. This was where she was last seen by the crew of Wellington 'F'. This location is just on the 100 fathom line, where the depth of sea water is approximately 183 metres. However just west of this line the depth plummets to 3,000 meters plus. The seabed in this area is soft mud, which would make finding *Unbeaten* very hard. There is every possibility however, that one day HMS/M *Unbeaten* will be discovered. Our exploration of the world's oceans is expanding and advances in technology increasingly allow deeper, clearer underwater research. It could be predicted with some conviction that *Unbeaten* will join the long list of missing World War II submarines which have now been found and that the reasons surrounding her untimely loss will be conclusively proven. The discoveries in recent times of the British submarines *Olympus*, *Vandal, P32* and *Perseus* support this prediction. When she is found, this book will still be extant and a fitting epitaph dedicated to those brave sons, husbands, brothers, fathers and lovers who served on board His Majesty's Submarine *Unbeaten*.

'He was home on leave again for my 5th Birthday and I remember waving goodbye to him from Streatham Station ... we ran along by the side of the train and I dropped the threepenny bit he had given me ... it rolled down onto the tracks and my mum would not climb down and get it !! That was the last time we saw him waving from the window with a big smile on his face and my mum in tears.' [155]

Jan Brenton, née Wright
Daughter of Petty Officer Stoker Geoff Wright

HMS/M UNBEATEN ROLL OF HONOUR

OFFICERS

OGILVY WATSON, Donald, Lt., Commanding Officer
CANNON, Patrick W., Lt., First Lieutenant
BROUGHAM, James J., Sub-Lieutenant
TWEEDY, Timothy C., Sub-Lieutenant

COXSWAINS

NORRIS, Raymond D., Chief Petty Officer, P/J 107443 Coxswain
FORBES, George D., Ty/Act/Leading Seaman, D/JX 161397 2nd Coxswain

ENGINEERS

LAURANCE, John S., Act/Chief Engine Room Artificer, C/MX 50281
WRIGHT, Geoffrey H.A., Stoker Petty Officer, C/KX 79996
STOCKWELL, John E.F., Ty/Act/Leading Stoker, RFR, C/SS 124546
STANLEY, Patrick J., Ty/Act/Leading Stoker, P/KX 92269
ANDERSON, Robert J., Stoker 1st Class, P/KX 121857
BAKER, Arthur E., Stoker 2nd Class, D/KX 135394
OLIVER, Denis L.B., Stoker 1st Class, P/KX 111942
BRUCE, James, Stoker 1st Class, C/KX 95426
LEAF, Sydney J., Engine Room Artificer 4th Class, C/MX 54031
TIFFIN, Lawrence, Engine Room Artificer 4th Class, C/MX 77484

TELEGRAPHISTS

BLEWETT, Edward J., Act/Petty Officer Telegraphist, P/J 109813
PIPER, Albert E., Leading Telegraphist, D/JX 133417
FURR, Frederick W., Telegraphist, C/JX 142498
HADDON, Francis T., Telegraphist, C/SSX 33383

SEAMEN

YOUNG, Herbert H., Petty Officer, P/JX 140386
APPLEBY, Charles H., Ty/Petty Officer, RFR, C/J 108060
MITTON, Leonard H., Act/Leading Signalman, P/JX 158163
BERRY, Leonard E.W., Able Seaman, C/SSX 28738

GERRARD, Louis, Able Seaman, P/SSX 17186
MALCOLM, James, Able Seaman, RNVR, P/ESD/X 1719
METHERELL, Gordon H., Able Seaman, P/JX 155742
MORGAN, William D., Able Seaman, P/SSX 29238
MORLEY, Gilbert, Able Seaman, RNVR, C/HD/X 63
SMITH, Clifford G., Able Seaman, C/SSX 26279
THOMPSON, Frank, Able Seaman, C/JX 168124
TWEEDY, Desmond, Able Seaman, C/SSX 19106
GALE, Edward, Act/Able Seaman, D/JX 176933
BRUIN, William, Ordinary Seaman, P/JX 326177
BAYNE, Herbert H., Ordinary Seaman, P/JX 224176
CLARK, Edwin A., Ordinary Seaman, P/JX 353544

'There is no headstone among the flowers for those who perish at sea'

Rear Admiral P. Wilcocks

Acknowledgements

The author would sincerely like to thank the following people for their contributions towards this book. Without your help and patience the researching and writing would not have been possible. It is because of you that the crew of *Unbeaten* are remembered. Thank you all.

Admiral Sir James Perowne, KBE *Flag Officer Submarines 1996*
Mrs Ogilvy Watson, Wife of Lt. Donald E. Ogilvy Watson *Unbeaten CO*
Douglas Ogilvy Watson, Grandson of Lt. Donald E. Ogilvy Watson
Margaret Donothey née Piper, Daughter of LS (Tel) Albert E. Piper, *Unbeaten crew*
Jan Brenton née Wright, Daughter of PO (Stoker) Geoffrey H. Wright, *Unbeaten crew*
Ronald Stokes Leading (Stoker), *Unbeaten crew*
David Stokes, Son of Ronald Stokes
Derek Bayne, Brother of Ordinary Seaman Herbert Bayne, *Unbeaten crew*
Jack Casemore, Leading Seaman, *Unbeaten crew*
Sandra Casemore, *Daughter of Jack Casemore*
Dr Charles Lott, *Nephew of Barbara Woodward Wife of Teddy Woodward*
Mrs Desiree Roderick, MBE, Wife of Lt. Richard. F. Broome: *Special Boat Section*
P.C.D. Norman, Papers of Lt. E.D. Norman *Upright CO*
John Lambert, Naval Illustrator
Philip Lazell, Son of Sergeant William John Lazell *Malta Photographs*
Platon Alexiades, Naval Researcher
Tony Drury, Naval Researcher
Jeff Dykes, Naval Researcher
Museum of RADAR and Communications
Peter Schofield, Naval Researcher
Vic Evason, *South Kent Branch Submariners Association*
Debbie Corner, Keeper of Photographs *Royal Navy Submarine Museum*
Alexandra Geary, Keeper of Artefacts *Royal Navy Submarine Museum*
George Malcolmson, Archivist *Royal Navy Submarine Museum*
Horst Bredow, Founder & MD *German U-Boat Museum*

Peter Monte, Archivist *German U-Boat Museum*
Heather Johnson, *Royal Navy Museum Library*
Sabine Skae, Collections Manager, *The Dock Museum Barrow*
Nick Miller, Senior Engineer, (Naval Architect) *BAE Systems-Submarine Solutions*
Peter Rogers, *Commando Veterans Association*
José Maffeo, *Argentinian Research*
Richard Carr, *Paxman History Pages*
Leigh Bishop, Technical Diver HMS/M *Vandal*
Howie Blanks & Adam Trimingham, *The Argus, Brighton*
Baz Craker, *Royal Navy Submarine School*
John Dickson, *Proof Reading*
Oliver Marquardt, *Cover Artwork*
Julian Mannering, Seaforth Publishing *'Periscope view'*
RAF Air Historical Branch
The National Archives
The Imperial War Museum

Referenced Sources

Epigraph

Bryant B, Submarine Command p125

Chapter 1: What a Wonderful Feat of Arms

1. *IWM 13766 Norman Drury Interview Sound Recording*
2. *Winston Churchill, The Second World War Vol 1, Cassell, 1948 p320*
3. *Richard Compton-Hall, Submarines at War 1939-1945, Periscope Publishing, 2004 p16*
4. *Winston Churchill, The Second World War Vol 1, Cassell, 1948 p385*

Chapter 2: His Wonders in the Deep

5. *BAE Systems, Ledger of Launch Particulars, Vickers Armstrong, 1939*
6. *I bid*
7. *I bid*
8. *Email to the author from Jan Wright daughter of Geoff Wright Unbeaten Crew*
9. *I bid*
10. *I bid*
11. *Port Logs*
12. *I bid*

Chapter 4: First View of the Rock

13. *IWM 13766 Norman Drury Interview Sound Recording*
14. *IWM 12946 Private Papers of J.R. Casemore*
15. *I bid*
16. *The Peoples History of the Second World War Jan-Dec 1941 page 58*
17. *I.bid*
18. *IWM 13766 op. cit.*
19. *I bid*

Chapter 5: Faith, Hope and Charity

20.Peter Elliot, The Cross and the Ensign, A Naval History of Malta, Granada Publishing, London, 1982 p118
21.IWM 99/75/11 Private Papers of E.D. Norman
22.Peter Elliot, The Cross and the Ensign op. cit. p123
23.IWM 99/75/11 op. cit.
24.IWM 99/75/11 op. cit.
25.IWM 99/75/11 op. cit.

Chapter 6: Gun Action

26.A. Cecil Hampshire, The Nautical Magazine p73 Q Ships of World War II
27.IWM 12946 Private Papers of J.R. Casemore
28.TNA ADM 236/42 Submarine War Patrol Reports HMS/M Unbeaten

Chapter 7: Ash Cans & Tin Fish

29.TNA CAB 66/16/32: Weekly Résumé (No. 90)
30.IWM 12946 Private Papers of J.R. Casemore
31.I bid
32.Jean. Hood Submarine, an Anthology of First-hand Accounts of the War Under the Sea, 1939-45, Conway, 2007 p140
33.Email to the author from David Stokes son of Ronald Stokes Unbeaten Crew
34.Jak.P. Mallmann Showell Wolf packs at War, Ian Allan publishing , 2002
35.IWM 13766 Norman Drury Interview Sound Recording
36.I bid
37.TNA ADM 236/43 Submarine War Patrol Reports HMS/M Unbeaten
38.IWM 12946 Private Papers of J.R. Casemore
39.TNA ADM 236/43 op. cit.
40.I bid
41.I bid
42.Statement by First Lord of the Admiralty in Response to a Parliamentary Debate Question 1901 Vol 89
43.TNA ADM 236/43 op. cit
44.TNA ADM 236/43 op. cit

45.TNA ADM 236/43 op. cit
46.IWM 13766 Norman Drury Interview Sound Recording

Chapter 8: We Shall Come Through

47.Extract from Prime Minister Speech 8th May 1941
48.IWM 12946 Private Papers of J.R. Casemore
49.I bid
50.IWM 13766 Norman Drury Interview Sound Recording
51.TNA ADM 236/43 Submarine War Patrol Reports HMS/M Unbeaten
52.TNA ADM 236/43 I bid
53.TNA ADM 236/43 I bid
54.TNA ADM 236/43 I bid
55.TNA ADM 236/43 I bid

Chapter 9: The Devil's Device

56.Edwyn Gray, The Devil's Device, The story of the invention of the torpedo, Seeley, Service & Co, 1975 p9
57.Letters written by Admiral John Arbuthnot Fisher 1904
58.Edwyn Gray, op cit p233
59.IWM 13766 Norman Drury Interview Sound Recording
60.Sydney Hart Submarine Upholder p 37
61.Sydney Hart op. cit. p 41

Chapter 10: HMS Talbot

62.George Simpson Periscope View Seaforth Publishing, Barnsley, 2010. p150
63.I bid
64.I bid
65.I bid
66.TNA ADM 236/43 Submarine War Patrol Reports HMS/M Unbeaten
67.I bid
68.TNA ADM 236/43 op. cit.
69.TNA CAB 66/18/41: Weekly Résumé (No. 106)
70.TNA ADM 236/43 op. cit.
71.Rex Woods Special Commando, William Kimber, 1985 p39

Chapter 11: Let Nothing Pass

72.Richard Compton-Hall Cutting the Lifeline, article in The Elite Vol 8,Orbis Publishing, 1986 p173

73.TNA ADM 236/43 Submarine War Patrol Reports HMS/M Unbeaten

74.Jim Allaway, Hero of the Upholder, Airlife Publishing, Shrewsbury, 1991 p126

75.TNA ADM 236/43 op. cit.

Chapter 12: Special Commando

76.George Simpson Periscope View Seaforth Publishing, Barnsley, 2010. p167

77.I bid

78.I bid

79.I bid

80.Papers of Commander Harold Wilkinson Goulding

81.I bid

82.I bid

83.George Simpson op. cit. p110

84.TNA ADM 236/43 Submarine War Patrol Reports HMS/M Unbeaten

85.I bid

Chapter 13: Awaken a Sleeping Giant

86.TNA 236/43 Submarine War Patrol Reports HMS/M Unbeaten

87.I bid

88.IWM 12946 Private Papers of J.R. Casemore

89.TNA 236/43 op. cit.

90.Admiral Isoroku Yamamoto

Chapter 14: Shoot the Sun

91.Ben Bryant Submarine Command p125

92.IWM 12946 Private Papers of J.R. Casemore

93.TNA C.B. 4051(44) U374 Interrogation of Sole Survivor

94.IWM 013298 A.D. Piper Interview Sound recording

95.I.bid

96.I.bid

97.IWM 12946 op. cit

98.IWM 13766 Norman Drury Interview Sound recording

99.IWM 013298 op. cit.
100. IWM 12946. op. cit
101. TNA 236/43 Submarine War Patrol Reports HMS/M Unbeaten
102. IWM 12946 op. cit
103. IWM 013298 op. cit

Chapter 15: Iron Coffin

104. IWM 13766 Norman Drury Interview Sound Recording
105. IWM 12946 Private Papers of J.R. Casemore
106. George Simpson Periscope View Seaforth Publishing, Barnsley, 2010. p88
107. IWM 13766 op. cit.
108. I bid
109. George Simpson op. cit. p190
110. C.B. 4052 (44) U374 Interrogation of Sole Survivor
111. TNA HW 18/310
112. C.B. 4052 (44) op. cit.
113. TNA HW 18/310 op. cit.

Chapter 16: Pier Head Jump

114. TNA ADM 236/43 Submarine War Patrol Reports HMS/M Unbeaten
115. I bid
116. I bid

Chapter 17: Gugliemotti

117. TNA ADM 236/43 Submarine War Patrol Reports HMS/M Unbeaten
118. I bid
119. TNA 1/14323
120. TNA ADM 236/43 op. cit.

Chapter 18: A Dapper Little Man

121. IWM 12946 Private Papers of J.R. Casemore
122. I bid
123. George Simpson Periscope View Seaforth Publishing, Barnsley, 2010. p297
124. IWM 13766 Norman Drury Interview Sound Recording

125. I bid
126. I bid
127. I bid

Chapter 19: Once is Enough in Anyone's Lifetime

128. Alastair Mars, Unbroken, The Story of a Submarine, Pen & Sword, Barnsley, 2006 p35
129. http://www.guardian.co.uk/uk/2003/nov/15/military.arts1
130. I bid
131. Port Logs
132. IWM 13766 Norman Drury Interview Sound Recording
133. AIR 27/1105 No 172 Squadron: Operations Record Book
134. I bid

Chapter 20: The Horizontal Champ

135. H.H. Bayne Unbeaten Crew letter to parents
136. O.L.Ratsey ASWE History 1896-1946
137. H.H Bayne letter to parent's op. cit.
138. I bid
139. Letter to the author from Mrs Ogilvy Watson
140. I bid
141. I bid

Chapter 21: Operation Bluestone Complete

142. ADM 199/1886 Operation Bluestone orders
143. I bid
144. I bid
145. I bid

Chapter 22: Missing on War Service

146. AIR 27/1105 No 172 Squadron: Operations Record Book
147. Letter to the author from Mrs Ogilvy Watson
148. Peter Cremer, U333, p159
149. Alastair Mars, British Submarines at War 1939-1945, William Kimber, London, 1971 p181
150. Extract from Australian House of Assembly Obituary of Teddy Woodward

151. Email to the author from Sandra Casemore daughter of Jack Casemore
152. ADM 1/14323 Honours and awards: HM Submarine Unbeaten
153. Email to the author from Jan Wright daughter of Geoff Wright Unbeaten Crew
154. Letter to the author from Mrs Ogilvy Watson op. cit.
155. Email to the author from Jan Wright op. cit.

Source References

The National Archives

ADM 236/43 Admiralty: Offices of Captains of Submarine Flotillas: Submarine War Patrol Reports, Second World War. HMS/M Unbeaten

ADM 236/48 Admiralty: Offices of Captains of Submarine Flotillas: Submarine War Patrol Reports, Second World War HMS/M Upholder

ADM 236/37 Admiralty: Offices of Captains of Submarine Flotillas: Submarine War Patrol Reports, Second World War. HMS/M Truant

ADM 236/44 Admiralty: Offices of Captains of Submarine Flotillas: Submarine War Patrol Reports, Second World War. HMS/M Union

ADM 236/42 Admiralty: Offices of Captains of Submarine Flotillas: Submarine War Patrol Reports, Second World War HMS/M Una

ADM 173/17109 Admiralty, and Ministry of Defence, Navy Department: Submarine Logs 1941 Aug. HMS/M Unbeaten

ADM 173/17699 Admiralty, and Ministry of Defence, Navy Department: Submarine Logs 1942 Jan. HMS/M Unbeaten

ADM 186/244 Armed Forces (General), Official publications, Weapons, Navy

ADM 1/14323 Honours and awards: HM Submarine Unbeaten, Mediterranean war patrol report: awards

ADM 199/1886 Admiral Submarines: War operations and patrols in home waters. Operation Bluestone

ADM 199/1820 Admiral Submarines: patrol reports of HM Submarines United and Unbeaten

ADM 234/380 Submarines: Volume I - Operations in home, northern and Atlantic waters

ADM 223/214 Appendix 1 (Part 5): History of 30 Commando (later called 30 Assault Unit)

AIR 15/414 Landing of enemy aircraft at R.A.F. Station Chivenor, Devonshire

AIR 15/23 Identification of aircraft markings and characteristics of aircraft

AIR 15/48 Identification of friend and foe (I.F.F.) and air to surface vessels (A.S.V.) equipment: policy

AIR 15/58 Reports on U-boat sighting and attacks by aircraft

AIR 15/60 Radio Direction Finding and Air to Surface Vessels equipment: requirements

AIR 15/101 Introduction of A.S.V.

AIR 27/1105 No 172 Squadron: Operations Record Book 1942 Mar - 1943 Dec.

AIR 65/77 Photography of night low level attacks with the Sea Search Photographic Unit, Type D-1, also known as the Edgerton Flash Unit Report No: 44/10

C.B. 4051 (44) U374 Interrogation of Sole Survivor

C.B. 4051 History of U-boat Policy 1939-1945

HW 18/310: Extracts from reports containing information about the activity of German U-boats: UD1, U20, U86, U93, U98, U121, U126, U374, U401, U563, U576, U654 1941 Jul 01-1941 Jul 31

HW 1/90 Statement of losses due to sinking of Oceania and Neptunia

DEFE 2/798 Canoes and cockles: report of trials of Goatley 12-man folding boat

War Cabinet Weekly Résumés

CAB 66/23/16: Weekly Résumé (No. 134) of the Naval, Military and Air Situation from 0700 March 19th, to 0700 March 26th, 1942.

CAB 66/23/20: Weekly Résumé (No. 135) of the Naval, Military and Air Situation from 0700 March 26th, to 0700 April 2nd, 1942.

CAB 66/31/11: Weekly Résumé (No. 168) of the Naval, Military and Air Situation from 0700 November 12th, to 0700 November 19th, 1942.

CAB 66/17/19: Weekly Résumé (No. 95) of the Naval, Military and Air Situation from 12 noon June 19th, to 12 noon June 26th, 1941.

CAB 66/18/2: Weekly Résumé (No. 99) of the Naval, Military and Air Situation from 12 noon July 17th, to 12 noon July 24th, 1941.

CAB 66/18/41: Weekly Résumé (No. 106) of the Naval, Military and Air Situation from 0700 September 4th, to 0700 September 11th, 1941.

CAB 66/21/4: Weekly Résumé (No. 125) of the Naval, Military and Air Situation from 0700 January 15th, to 0700 January 22nd, 1942.

CAB 66/18/30: Weekly Résumé (No. 104) of the Naval, Military and Air Situation from 0700 August 21st, to 0700 August 28th, 1941.

CAB 66/14/8: Weekly Résumé (No. 67) of the Naval, Military and Air Situation from 12 noon December 5th to 12 noon December 12th, 1940.

CAB 66/16/32: Weekly Résumé (No. 90) of the Naval, Military and Air Situation from 12 noon May 15th, to 12 noon May 22nd, 1941.

CAB 66/26/33: Conscription of British subjects in Egypt. Memorandum, by the Secretary of State for Foreign Affairs and the Secretary of State for War.

CAB 66/17/2 Naval, Military and Air Situation. Circulated with the approval of the Chiefs of Staff. 1941 June

CAB 66/16/32: Naval, Military and Air Situation. Circulated with the approval of the Chiefs of Staff. 1941 May

CAB 66/16/10: Naval, Military and Air Situation. Circulated with the approval of the Chiefs of Staff. 1941 April

Imperial War Museum

IWM 13766 N. Drury Interview Sound Recording

IWM 013298 A. D. Piper Interview Sound Recording

IWM 008788 J.H. Greswell Interview Sound Recording

IWM 12946 Private Papers of J.R. Casemore
IWM 99/75/11 Private Papers of E.D. Norman

Private Letter/Email Sources

Letters from Mrs Ogilvy Watson
Emails from Mr Douglas Ogilvy Watson
Emails from Mrs Jan Brenton née Wright
Letters and Emails from Mrs Margaret Donothey née Piper
Letters and Emails from Mr Derek Bayne
Emails from Mr David and Mr Ronald Stokes

Other Sources

BAE Systems, Ledger of Launch Particulars, Vickers Armstrong, 1939
Royal Navy Museum Library, Port Logs

Bibliography

Acworth B, *Life in a Submarine,* Raphael Tuck & Sons Ltd, London, 1941.

Air Ministry, *Air Publication 1578c Pilot Notes For Wellington*, HMSO, London, 1944.

Allaway, J, *Hero of the Upholder*, Airlife Publishing, Shrewsbury, 1991.

Bacon H.S, *Britains Glorious Navy*, Odhams Press, London 1943.

Brice M, *Axis Blockade Runners of World War II*, Batsford Ltd, London, 1981.

Bryant B, *Submarine Command*, William Kimber, London, 1958.

Carruthers B, *The Official U-boat Commanders Handbook*, Coda Books, Warwickshire, 2011.

Carruthers B, *The U-boat War in the Atlantic Volume 1 1939-1941*, Coda Books, Warwickshire, 2011.

Churchill W.S. , *The Second World War Vol 1* Cassell, London, 1948.

Clayton, T, *Sea Wolves*, Little, Brown, London, 2011.

Compton-Hall, R, *Submarines at War 1939-1945*, Periscope Publishing, Penzance, 2004.

Crane J, *Submarine*, BBC Publishing, London, 1984.

Cremer, P, *U333*, Triad Grafton, London, 1986.

Drummond, J, *H.M. UBoat*, W.H. Allen, London, 1958.

Elliot, P, *The Cross and the Ensign, A Naval History of Malta*, Granada Publishing, London, 1982.

Evans, A, *Beneath the Waves, History of H.M. Submarine Losses, 1904-71,* William Kimber, London, 1986.

Foot M.R.D, *SOE 1940-1946*, BBC Publishing, London, 1984.

Franks, N, *Conflict over the Bay*, William Kimber, London, 1986.

Franks, N, *Dark Skys Deep Water*, Grub Street, London, 1997.

Frayn Turner, J, *Periscope Patrol, The Story of Malta Submarines*, Airlife Publishing, Shrewsbury, 1997.

Garrett, R, *Scharnhorst and Gneisenau, The elusive sisters*, David & Charles, Newton Abbot, 1978.

Gray, E, *The Devil's Device, The story of the invention of the torpedo*, Seeley, Service & Co, London, 1975.

Gunton, M, *Dive Dive Dive, Submarines at War*, Constable & Robinson, London, 2003.

Hackman W, *Seek & Strike*, HMSO Books, London, 1984.

Hart, S, *Discharged Dead*, Odhams, London, 1959.

Hart, S, *Submarine Upholder*, Amberly Publishing, Stroud, 2008.

Henery C, *Depth Charge*, Pen & Sword, Barnsley, 2005.

Hinsley F.H, Stripp A, *Code Breakers*, Oxford University Press, Oxford 1993.

Hoare O, *Camp 020*, Public Records Office, Surry, 2000.

Hood, J, *Submarine, an Anthology of Firsthand Accounts of the War Under the Sea, 1939-45*, Conway, London, 2007.

Horton, M, *Max Horton and the Western Approaches*, Hodder & Stoughton, London, 1954.

Jones G.P, *Submarines Versus U-Boats*, William Kimber, London, 1986.

Kahn D, *Seizing the Enigma*, Barnes & Noble, New York, 1998.

Lenton,H.T, *German Submarines* 1 & 2, Macdonald, London, 1965.

Lipscomb, F, *The British Submarine*, Conway Maritime Press, Greenwich, 1975.

Lyman R, *Operation Suicide*, Quercus, London, 2012.

Mallmann Showell J, *Wolfpacks at War*, Ian Allan Publishing, Surry, 2002.

Mars, A, *Court Martial*, Frederick Muller Ltd, London, 1954.

Mars, A, *British Submarines at War 1939-1945,* William Kimber, London, 1971.

Mars, A, *Unbroken, The Story of a Submarine*, Pen & Sword, Barnsley, 2006.

Masters, D, *Up Periscope*, Eyre & Spottiswoode, London, 1942.

McCartney, I, *British Submarines 1939-45*, Osprey Publishing, Oxford, 2006.

Mibblebrook M, *Convoy*, Penguin Books, Middleesex, 1978.

Padfield, P, *Submarine Conflict 1939-1945, War Beneath the Sea*, John Murry, London, 1995.

Paterson, L, *Black Flag, The Surrender of Germany's U-boat Forces 1945*, Seaforth Publishing, Barnsley, 2009.

Rankin N, *Ian Felmings Commandos*, Faber & Faber, London 2011.

Rees Q, *The Cockleshell Canoes*, Amberley, Stroud, 2008.

Richards B, *Secret Flotillas Volume 1*, Frank Cass, London 2004.

Ritchie L, (Bartimeus) *The Epic of Malta*, Odhams Press Ltd, London, 1945.

Rohwer J, *Allied Submarine Attacks of World War Two European Theatre of Operations 1939-1945*, Green Hill Books, London, 1997.

Rohwer J, *Axis Submarines Successes 1939-1945*, Patrick Stephens, London, 1983.

Roskill S, *The Navy at War 1939-1945*, Collins, London, 1960.

Simpson, G, *Periscope view*, Seaforth Publishing, Barnsley, 2010.

Van der Vat D, *The Atlantic Campaign, The Great Struggle at Sea 1939-1945,* Hodder & Stoughton, London, 1988.

Von der Porton E.P, *The German Navy in World War Two*, Pan Books, London, 1972.

Walters, D, *The History of the U-Class Submarine*, Pen & Sword, Barnsley, 2004.

Werner H.A, *Iron Coffins*, Arthur Barker, London, 1969.

White, J, *U-Boat Tankers 1941-1945, Submarine Suppliers to Atlantic Wolf packs*, Airlife Publishing, Shrewsbury, 1998.

Williamson D.G.,*The Siege of Malta 1940-42*, Pen & Sword, Barnsley, 2007.

Wilmot C, *The Struggle for Europe*, Richard Clay & Co, Suffolk, 1952.

Wingate, J, *The Fighting Tenth*, Periscope Publishing, Penzance, 2003.

Winton J, *ULTRA at Sea*, Leo Cooper, London, 1998.

Winton, J, *The Submarines*, Constable & Robinson, London, 1999.

Woods R, *Special Commando*, William Kimber, London, 1985.

Young J, *Ships of the Royal Navy*, Patrick Stephens Ltd, Cambridge, 1975.

Index